T0305243

Product and Systems Development

Product and Systems Development

A Value Approach

Stanley I. Weiss

WILEY

Published by John Wiley & Sons, Inc., Hoboken, New Jersey.
Published simultaneously in Canada.

For general information on our other products and services or for technical support, please contact our
Customer Care Department within the United States at (800) 762-2974, outside the United States at
(317) 572-3993 or fax (317) 572-4002.

Wiley also publishes its books in a variety of electronic formats. Some content that appears in print may
not be available in electronic formats. For more information about Wiley products, visit our web site at
www.wiley.com.

Library of Congress Cataloging-in-Publication Data:

Weiss, Stanley I.
    Product and systems development: a value approach / Stanley I. Weiss.
        pages cm
    Includes bibliographical references.
    ISBN 978-1-118-33154-5 (cloth)
1. New products–Planning.   I. Title.
    TS170.W45 2013
    658.5′038–dc23

                                                          2012043884

10 9 8 7 6 5 4 3 2 1

Contents

Preface

In this book we identify and describe processes, practices, and tools that generate success in programs dedicated to the development of products and systems. We emphasize the succession of value-contributing practices and tools that form a framework for development success with the goal of satisfying not only customers and users but also the countless stakeholders, whose values derive from many disparate environments and some of whom can hold the key to fulfillment or defeat of a developer's vision.

Many organizations apply at least elements of the practices described in the text, and we start the journey by citing some of the best practices derived from successful projects and organizations. A few of these are worth noting, with the specific emphases that have marked their achievements. IDEO, the innovation and design firm that is the remarkable creative force behind so many new designs for innovators such as Apple and Disney, is almost fanatic about needs and values determination as a prerequisite to designing and prototyping. It also emphasizes team approaches, including continuing interaction with customers and users, as did the original "skunkworks" of Lockheed and now Lockheed Martin, which produced such remarkable aircraft as the U-2 and the SR-71. The Mercury Engine Division of the Brunswick Corporation integrates the use of such tools as quality function deployment matrices when establishing requirements and specifications as well as in other decision processes. The Consulting Group starts most evaluations of client company problems with a value stream analysis, and Long Beach Hospital in California is embracing numerous lean practices. For many U.S. and European defense contractors, systems engineering plans are part of the contractual activity required. Many others representatives of the various approaches to development are covered in this book.

My introduction to systems thinking occurred during my tenure in project management at the Lockheed Corporation. There, after only marginal success with the *Discoverer* satellite reconnaissance program, U.S. Air Force managers with a background in the successful ballistic missile program advised us to look at that use for space systems, with a resulting improvement from 50% flight success to 80% success in just 18 months. Thus, when I became the program manager for Hexagon, the next-generation eye in the sky, systems engineering emphasis drove an exceptionally successful project that, in retrospect, filled many of the blanks we now call lean systems engineering.

Another indicator of recognition is that numerous professional societies have built memberships of individuals and organizations dedicated to multiple elements of this framework. The terminologies sometimes vary, but the focus for each leads to the key aspects that we address in the book. A few are INCOSE (the International Council on Systems Engineering, PMI (the Program Management Institute), and the systems divisions of the IEEE (the Institute of Electrical and Electronic Engineers) and other principal engineering societies, as well as consortia and societies devoted to such topics as value engineering, agile technology, the lean advancement initiative, and its offshoot, the educational network, along with numerous international conferences, with sessions covering nearly every topic of every chapter. It is my hope that, semantics aside, the reader will find a methodology here that frames and solves the challenges of the development process.

INTRODUCTION

Quintessential goals of engineering and, in many cases, investment are rooted in product and system development. In the text we recognize that although product and system development must focus on the creation and delivery of excellence, it puts emphasis on the delivery of value—to customers, users, and key stakeholders. It also highlights the responsibility of a developer to the ultimate customers and users by considering each stakeholder who can influence the character of the product or system, its operations, its cost, and its eventual utility. This pairing of thoughts provides the *recurring* themes in this book that affect decisions regarding success, return on investment, and in some cases even the decision as to whether or not to proceed. Since the projects of interest are generally complex and multidisciplinary systems, holistic thinking is intrinsic to this approach.

A unique character of this volume is that of providing linkages throughout the value stream, incorporating the processes necessary for realizing value from initial vision and market analysis through to delivery, operations, and maintenance. The many tools facilitating the development process, and their implementation, are defined through numerous examples from various domains. Another aspect, often neglected, is the need for productivity in the process. Although this cannot preempt creativity, there are certain guidelines and experiences that can provide a framework for efficiencies and the limitation of waste. The term *lean* is used to focus on this aspect.

The text is based on lectures making up courses on product and system development and information systems taught by the author at Stanford, the

Massachusetts Institute of Technology, and the University of California at Davis. Furthermore, appendices augmented by material authored by experts in those fields deal with subjects that expand on advanced methods noted in the text. Additionally, Chapter 19 contains case examples illustrating the tools described throughout the chapters. The focus of this book, then, is the application of the concepts noted to the complex products and systems intrinsic to modern industry and governments, with specific references ranging from aerospace to medical equipment. It should be understood, however, that this approach does not preempt the adaptation of either tools or processes to individual development environments established by schedules, complexity, or organization.

Progressing through those activities that provide value to the development process, most fall into five main categories: planning, design development, assurance, delivery, and operations, each overlaid by project management. Within the text, those elements encompassed by planning include the identification of stakeholders, together with their values and needs, all leading to quantifiable requirements. Design development includes functional analysis and definition of interfaces to permit the creation of concepts and architectures. Assurance requires an understanding of failure modes and risks so as to provide for fault tolerance and the necessary verification and validation. Delivery and operations complete the development value stream and inevitably provide feedback to the preceding steps. Overarching are development management activities that provide organization, including the use of teams, budget, and work allocations, based on both technical parameters and cost estimating, together with the incorporation of productivity practices.

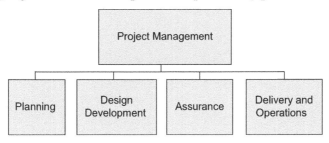

The development process involves critical considerations in many activities; it is the purpose of this book to define and explore these. Some are practices, some are tools; all involve decisions.

STANLEY I. WEISS

Acknowledgments

I am grateful to two remarkable and insightful reviewers of the early manuscript who challenged me to reread, rewrite, and reorder many parts of the book. Professor Juan Alonso, of Stanford University, and Dr. Lilac Muller, VP Research and Innovation, Clarisonics, both contributed critical, constructive comments and insights and made valuable suggestions for the linkages among the many topics covered in this book. I also owe special recognition to Professor Earll Murman, Emeritus, at MIT, who gave me my first opportunity to enter academia and mentored me as I learned the ropes that allowed me to accumulate the experiences and motivation integral to writing this volume.

I am also grateful to Bo Oppenheim and Tyson Browning, professors at Loyola Marymount and Texas Christian Universities, respectively, to Professor Alonso once again, and to Professor emeritus Heinz Stoewer, at the Technical University of Delft, for their signal contributions in writing the appendixes. Special materials were also provided by Edward Alyanak, of Mercury Marine, who supplied that company's methods and applications of quality function deployment that might otherwise not have been available. Credits and thanks are, of course, due to the many people and sources identified with figures and illustrations for their permission to use multiple figures from their own teaching and projects. They include Charles Boppe of Draper Labs, Barry Boehm of USC, Debbie Nightingale of MIT, Vadim Khaym of Lockheed Martin, and Kevin Forsberg and Hal Mooz of the Center for Systems Engineering.

I am particularly indebted to five talented Stanford graduate students whose work makes up the case studies in Chapter 19. Danny Lau and Cecilia Larrosa examined the means for dynamically dealing with an unmanned aircraft's state of health; Adeel Arif and Raghavar Krishnamurthy provided a proposal to upgrade the individual ID development for Indian citizens; and Jumie Yuventi showed how software can apply the principles normally attributed to hardware with his program for solar system incorporation to construction projects.

Additionally, without the several hundred of my students at MIT, UC Davis, and Stanford, who prompted development and organization of the material in this volume, there would be no body of knowledge here, nor such detailed examples gathered from their work. I don't want to forget as well the many outstanding experts in the fields who make product and system development the multidiscipline adventure it is. The majority of these experts are noted in the text in connection with examples and illustrative figures and in the reference sources cited throughout the book. I also want to thank Dave Mason of INCOSE, whose early criticism of the preface pushed me to many revisions of the entire text.

Further, I want to recognize the important support of the staff at John Wiley: George Telecki, Associate Publisher, Kari Capone, editorial staff, and Angioline Loredo, production editor. Many thanks are also due to Faraz Sharique Ali of Thomson Digital. All showed patience and expertise in enabling the development of this volume.

Finally, this book has notable family inputs. Catherine (Kitty) Weiss, my critic, editor, illustrator, secretary, advocate, and motivator wife was essential to the completion of this volume. My daughter Ann's contribution assisting with the detailed task of editing gave me confidence that there were not too many literary misdeeds. In addition, daughter Marion Weiss was responsible for the handsome cover design after initial review by her sister Audrey Don.

STANLEY I. WEISS

1

Preview of Best Practices

A good place to begin the journey through a process of development is to get an early glimpse of what most practitioners dealing with complex products consider "best" practices. Although these might not be precisely in the order of implementation, they will orient discussions of successful principles and practices. A number of these best practices are highlighted here, with the text providing amplification as to what will govern evolution of the development processes that follow.

Product and System Development Best Practices

Before identifying and discussing those practices dedicated to delivery of value, there is a body of activities in the life cycle of development that may be represented as best practices. Although not listed precisely in the order covered in the book, they do offer guideposts for understanding the framework for successful product and system development.

   1. *Value analysis.* The first practice cited lies in the generation of value analysis. Since the term is often seen as ambiguous, we spend some pages on the definitions used in this book, as well as how various industries, government, and other organizations affected interpret and express them. Value analysis of a project stems from the culture of the organization or the history of the stakeholder who is making judgments. It is intrinsic to understanding and generating the needs of customers and other stakeholders for a product or system, as well as providing the basis for deriving the requirements that will become the design development drivers.

   2. *Systems engineering and design approach.* Systems or holistic thinking must be at the heart of any design development activity. It provides a framework

Product and Systems Development: A Value Approach, First Edition. Stanley I. Weiss.
© 2013 John Wiley & Sons, Inc. Published 2013 by John Wiley & Sons, Inc.

for addressing all activities in planning and ensuring that project goals are met. These cover translating stakeholder values to their prioritized requirements, establishing baseline designs, and carrying via an architecture and suitable evaluation of options the derivable failure and risk analyses. Thus, by verifying the quality of the product or system and all interfaces, the customer and user expectations will be validated so that the desired end value can be delivered. This approach is initiated in Chapters 2 and 3.

3. *Front-end emphasis to ensure customer requirements.* Discussion in the early chapters emphasizes the fact that investment in the front end of a development cycle pays off in multiples of the time that might be wasted later in reconciling requirements, defining real return on investment, and the measures by which the outcomes can be assured. In keeping with these goals, generating the requirements that will direct development is not intended to preclude "out of the box" creativity, but to provide a framework for how a development project can proceed and to ensure common understanding among all the players as to goals, constraints, and the environment surrounding process and product utilization. It is also important to recognize the need to review requirements as one makes design decisions and eventually validates the expectations of customers and stakeholders.

4. *Involving all stakeholders early and often.* To ensure the inclusion of all factors, it is necessary to involve key stakeholders early and often. Certainly, customers and users are primary, but there are many players whose values and expectations can influence and affect the goals desired and the means by which these are achieved. The range of these "influencers" may cover top organization policy-makers, financiers, regulators, producers, maintainers, and others. As this set is defined in more detail, it will be evident how their values can be dealt with, including understanding the priorities that should be placed on these in the overall development of value for customer and user. This concept, initiated in Chapter 1 but intrinsic to all aspects of the development process, is addressed many times throughout the book.

5. *Integrated product and process development.* The use of integrated product and process teams is a valuable organizational arrangement, facilitated either by proximity of participants or by virtual means, the goal being rapid inter-communication. This grouping is often termed an integrated product team, designed to facilitate integrated product and process development. Chapter 13 is dedicated to this subject which is implicated in many stages of the process.

6. *Integrated hardware and software development.* Along with that con-sciousness of integration, particularly in today's multifaceted products and systems, is the necessity of linking hardware and software aspects from the very beginning. This means identifying and allocating the roles to be played by each in design, production, use, and sustainment, suggesting the use of integrated product teams in developing the bases for each of these activities. This practice is cited in Chapters 12 to 15.

7. *Designed-in capability to grow and adapt.* Another consideration, driven by the pace of technology and knowledge, is the requirement to think downstream in

defining, planning, and designing for the entire potential life cycle of a system or product. This must not only anticipate what happens in use and maintenance, but also the need to grow and/or adapt to changes in need, environment of deployment, or even change of users. This recognizes as well that the array of stakeholders may not be the same over the development life cycle. Thus, the ability to foresee such considerations as regulation changes, competitive environment, need for upgrading, and so on, is another important subject. This pervasive element is often implicit in the text, but the specifics are examined in Chapter 14.

8. *Database linkage throughout the product development cycle.* One way to ensure common visibility for all participants is to commit to linked databases. Thus, there should be no need for producers, whether in-house or outsourced, to require translation or conversion of data in all forms. Although this seems a straightforward understanding, examples will show both how few projects and organizations have been able to meet this standard, as well as the implications of failing to do so. Parts of Chapters 10 and 17 are dedicated to this process.

9. *Minimization of documentation and handouts.* Along with the evidence of truly managing the process and the value stream is a recognition that no matter how simple or complex a product of development, there are common means to limit the complexity, as well as the life-cycle cost and schedule. This is one of the "lean" practices, leading to limiting waste throughout the process to the benefit of all stakeholders. This can also be seen as an extension of the foregoing practice, database linkage, and as an outcome of management and value stream mapping (Chapters 15 to 18).

10. *Use of off-the-shelf tools and common computer-aided design and manufacturing.* This stems from the two preceding practices, as it facilitates minimization of documentation and handovers wherever possible by virtue of common vocabulary and capabilities, as well as the reduction of "reinvention," which generates a waste of resources and time. See also the discussion of lean practices in Chapter 17.

11. *Optimizing the product development value stream.* All the practices cited above provide approaches to optimizing the value stream toward the efficient use of resources without stifling creativity. Such considerations as single-piece flow and "pull" are used to facilitate the flow of activities intrinsic to development. This concept is the object of Chapter 18.

RESOURCE AND NOTE

K. Clark and T. Fujimoto, *Development Performance*, Harvard University Press, Cambridge, MA, 1990.
  This book is a classic that describes a philosophy of creating value based on the auto and electronics industries. Although the book includes many references applicable to best practices, these are thought best cited at the ends of chapters explaining these practices.

REVIEW CHECKLIST

☐ Have you bookmarked this chapter for reference checks on your development projects and to add your own lessons learned?

2

Stakeholder Values

Delivering value as the end goal of product and system development signifies that the customer and user of a product or system will see it as generating worth. But there are also other stakeholders whose values and expectations should not be in conflict. Since value delivery is the goal for development, each step in the stream of activities toward that end must deliver value to succeeding steps in the process. For example, the marketing process must deliver value to the developer through a complete understanding of all stakeholders, their values, competitive systems, and any related information. In a succeeding step this would be used to generate requirements from salient values and needs. Satisfying these adds value to the creation of concepts and architectures with sufficient definition for producers to fulfill designs satisfactorily. This succession is illustrated in Figure 2.1. These efforts ensure delivering value to the customer and user and satisfying key stakeholders. Clearly, since a stakeholder is any party that can affect or be affected by a product or system, there should be value added for the stakeholders at each step in the development process.

Although there is a tendency to think of worth in terms of dollars, many other facets must be considered. For example, the soldier-user of a weapon does not evaluate cost in judging the weapon's worth to him or her. Similarly, an offensive color or other impact on senses can affect the worth of a perfectly functioning product. So what are the measures of value or worth? They are so dependent on the customer by user, as well as other stakeholders affected, that before committing substantial resources to a development, it is critical to understand completely the values that will be attributed to a product and the importance of these values as they become drivers of requirements and thus drivers of design.

Product and Systems Development: A Value Approach, First Edition. Stanley I. Weiss.
© 2013 John Wiley & Sons, Inc. Published 2013 by John Wiley & Sons, Inc.

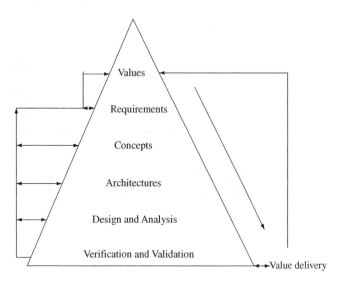

Figure 2.1 *All activities in the development value stream are related.*

2.1 VALUE AND STAKEHOLDER IDENTITIES

Value can be subjective, like color, or can be objective in monetary terms; therefore, having an algorithm that can be applied is questionable. But for those who like mathematical relationships, the following equation may be considered, although it is more notional than rigorous:

$$\text{product value} = \frac{N(1-R)}{C} f(t)$$

where N is the need, R the risk that the need won't be met, $f(t)$ the time dependency of the need, and C the total cost of ownership. Here, however, are several important definitions worth discussing:

value	=	worth
value systems	=	sets of values, codes, or principles
value proposition	=	basis for exchange
value stream	=	flow of tasks or information to yield value

Worth is equivalent to *value*, the latter often stemming from embedded value systems, as noted above. *Value proposition* is a term for the agreement of all involved as to the value of a given product, system, or project, with this agreement either contractual or understood and verifiable among all parties. The value proposition between buyer and seller is usually expressed in dollars or equivalent for value to be delivered in physical and performance terms. But, of course, buyer and seller are not the only interested parties, so values and agreements among other parties or stakeholders must also be examined.

A third important consideration is *value stream*, the stream or flow of activities necessary to create and deliver product or system value. It can represent the process of creation, design, production, and so on, as well as the ancillary work elements attending marketing, transportation, delivery, and operational maintenance. As we develop the processes themselves, it will be important to recognize those intrinsic to delivering value, those unnecessary but part of a system or environment in which the development takes place, and those that are pure waste to be eliminated, combined, or substituted for. Figure 2.1 maps a generic product development value stream that suggests a serial flow of activities. While the steps provide identification of the process, there will be iterations at almost every step to ensure that the end product or system meets all requirements and provides the basis for verification and validation. These considerations are covered when we discuss the elements reflected by the value stream.

2.2 THE STAKEHOLDER CONNECTION

In addition to having a firm grasp of value, it is necessary to understand the customer or potential customer and users thoroughly and to identify and give consideration to the other stakeholders. If one considers a specific product type to be developed, it is not difficult to rapidly identify purchaser and user. Now, how about other stakeholders? Taking a common usage product with relatively easy-to-define values desired by potential customers, there are still a large number of other entities with both the interests and capabilities to influence both the product design and its success. Consider an automobile. Aside from the driver and the buyer, the Environmental Protection Agency, highway patrols, fuel suppliers, maintenance groups, licensing agencies, safety and insurance organizations, and numerous regulatory factors must be part of the reckoning of who and what will drive the full set of requirements. These considerations can be projected to nearly any product when making decisions ranging from design issues to cost, marketing, and even whether or not to proceed with development.

One company, intent on broadening its product base of airplanes, considered entering the bus development business, particularly since at the time the fleets of Greyhound, Peter Pan, and other cross-country and municipal transportation vehicles were becoming ancient. But after identifying all the stakeholders and their "values" or needs, the decision was made that the venture involved too many stakeholders, including their uncertainties and interconnects, and was too complex for the company's expertise; wisely; the project was shelved. A clear lesson is that in dealing with systems, the satisfaction of all potential stakeholders, with their interfaces and interactions, is critical, and the latter increase exponentially with the number of stakeholders. Later it will become apparent that a proliferation of stakeholders and interfaces has a direct implication on cost and schedule.

The term *stakeholder* is particularly critical to an understanding of all sources of requirements that will drive development. Some representatives could be environmental and code regulators, financial lenders or investors, plus numerous others identified in part in Figure 2.2. Each of these has personal interests based on values

STAKEHOLDERS	VALUES	PRODUCT NEEDS	REQUIREMENTS
Customer			
User			
Sustainer			
Financers			
Regulators			
Public			
Insurers			
Producers			
Workforce			
Suppliers			
Marketers			

Figure 2.2 *System development is about creating value for customers and meeting the needs of stakeholders.*

from their own perspectives; illustrations will be presented to indicate the broad range of considerations that must be incorporated in setting guidelines or specifications (i.e., requirements governing developments). It should be noted that there are almost always more stakeholders than a first evaluation suggests and therefore that each of those initially defined should stimulate interviews, which will almost always identify others to be considered. For example, buyers will always be linked to users, then users to maintainers, to inventory management, to transportation, to accountants, and so on. Figure 2.2 shows a generic set, but there are subunits in the identities, each of which has associated value judgments. At the enterprise level, Figure 2.3 shows the linkage that might be seen from a chief executive's viewpoint.

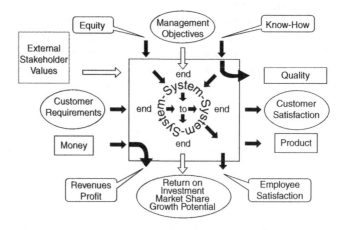

Figure 2.3 *Internal and external values for a commercial system.*

One company, for example, set its marketing and development team to evaluate a new consumer product with multiple manufacturing sites as a given. Eleven stakeholders were identified as the first set for consideration. Each of these were then interviewed, which yielded a total of 27 affected stakeholders who had to be assessed as to the priority of their values and needs, the stability of these over time, and which could actually be the drivers of the development design.

A first step, of course, is to ensure that the right product or system will be the end result. A vision of that result must be a driver, sometimes stimulated by market needs, unstated or thoroughly identified; customer requests for a proposal that might include specification; or by a mission or operations analysis yielding a concept of operations. Coupling this with considerations of financing, costs, profit margins, and cash flow can be used to develop what can be identified as the business case for the venture. Failure to do so leads to such disasters as the General Motors Aztec SUV, Ford's Edsel, or the initial Iridium communications satellite system.

Concept of Operations

Concept of operations (CONOPS) is a term applicable primarily to the defense and aerospace domains, although it is increasingly a part of the health management and software fields, particularly with procurements originating from U.S. federal agencies. CONOPS is a means of identifying how a product or system will be used in all operating environments, by whom, and with what interactions. It thus forms a significant basis for establishing requirements for a new system or procurement as defined by the potential user or operator and defines what characteristics will satisfy these stakeholders in its utilization. Although it is usually fixed documentation of needs and expectations, it is also subject to changes, either as a result of development issues or in rethought application of the end item.

It has been noted that each stakeholder's values govern views of product or system worth. But each may have different value priorities in influencing the requirements for design development. Figure 2.4 is from a case involving the development of an oil filter system for oil delivery and distribution use, with the body of stakeholders and their values identified. Notice that safety is the highest value for three stakeholders, cost for three others. But there are also potential conflicts among values: such as that between versatility and a desire for standardized parts or codes. The issue of value conflicts and their resolution is an important part of establishing requirements that will have as much stability as possible through the life cycle.

This example also highlights the role that values play in governing these development requirements and their priorities. The next step is understanding how one can proceed through development in such a way as to realize these values. Restated, value can be equated to worth in how it is measured and ranked in the judgment of each stakeholder. A design developer usually sees value in the acceptance by the customer and user and by their willingness to pay. They, in turn, see value in the product or system meeting their functional life-cycle cost, and even aesthetic needs and expectations. Each stakeholder starts from a value system generated by his or her background, circumstance, or environment. These are usually represented by sets of values, which

Stakeholders	Values
Manufacturer	Manufacturability, cost, rate of return on investment, similar platforms
Sales force	Value distinguishable
Shareholders	Rate of return
Design firm management	Transferable design, profitability, intellectual rights
Marketing firm management	Market share
Manufacturing company management	Compatibility with current lines, manufacturing cost, volume
Oil and gas customers	Safety, cost, reliability, versatility, filtration, capacity, maintenance cost
Inspectors/Insurers	Safety margin
Repair houses	Ease of repair
Aftermarket support	Compatibility, standardized parts
ASME groups	Adherence to ASME code
Safety organizations	Safety margin, corrosion protection

Figure 2.4 *Stakeholder values for an oil filter system. (Courtesy of Shell Oil.)*

may include codes, principles, and rules of their societies. It is often too easy to recognize that within an organization there are many stakeholders associated with development. These very influential players may be managers outside the specific project or may be supporting manufacturing, quality, procurement, and distribution actors. What they are willing to give in exchange for the product and its value, the basis for exchange, is called the *value proposition*. The development process flow, or *value stream*, which will be analyzed as it relates to efficient and effective development cycles, provides a means to evaluate development activities.

In summarizing the issues attending stakeholder identification and evaluation, there are key considerations to keep in mind. First, it is difficult for one person to identify all stakeholders in a new development unless the development was inherited directly from a previous success. But even then, the environment or other circumstances might have changed. For example, there may be new competition, methods of financing may not be the same, environmental regulations may have been updated, corporate goals may have been modified and insurance criteria reviewed, or the use of a product type may have changed significantly. Therefore, the best means of identifying stakeholders is to employ a broadly based team, with advantage of marketing and benchmarking taken beforehand. Then, too, a real understanding of these stakeholder values, needs, or expectations cannot be made certain without extensive interviews, which themselves may lead to the identification of other stakeholders. Two considerations become important immediately: first, prioritizing the stakeholder values that will drive requirements; and second, reconciling conflicts among these to give the best possible solution to requirements definition while continuing to satisfy customer and user needs. The purpose is to provide a consistent means of translating prioritized values into requirements which can then permit prioritizing development requirements and, a step further, provide a basis for design and operating specifications.

In summary, then, delivered value is the goal of development, and the goal of this book is to identify the practices and processes that make that possible. In subsequent chapters we continue to translate the best practices cited earlier into process steps that provide an environment for success.

RESOURCES AND NOTES

Lean Enterprise Value, E. Murman et al. (including the present author), Palgrave Press, Hampshire, UK, 2002.

This book addresses values from a definition and application standpoint, with emphasis on industry, particularly defense and aerospace.

Fundamentals of Systems Engineering, C. Khisty and S. Mohammadi, Prentice Hall, Upper Saddle River, NJ, 2001.

This work approaches value definition as it applies to the systems engineering process addressed in Chapter 3.

Value Driven Product Planning and Systems Engineering, H. Cook and L. Wissman, Springer-Verlag, New York, 2007.

This book approaches value in terms of the business case. Value equals worth in monetary terms.

REVIEW CHECKLIST

☐ Are you able to identify all stakeholders and their values?

☐ Have they been interviewed where possible?

☐ Have they identified other stakeholders not yet considered?

☐ If no interview is possible, can you use experts as substitutes?

☐ If there are conflicts among stakeholders, which, if any, might not compromise?

☐ Are there any that might be dropped?

☐ What impact is there from either conclusion?

3

Role of Systems Engineering

It is not happenstance that systems engineering tops the list of best practices. It is, in fact, consistent with its name, the practice that provides a systematic framework for the development process and invokes an orderly set of activities. These start with practices that generate the values serving as the basis for requirements and proceed in a logical fashion through steps that continually add value to the outcome. Thus, systems engineering is involved in initiating the development cycle and covers the processes of planning, designing, developing, validating, and controlling products and projects and their elements.

Figure 3.1 illustrates a notional set of practices in the system development process, showing value stream elements with value transfers occurring. For example, planning aspects that yield the basis for value analysis include the derivatives of successful market analysis, including benchmarking, customer and stakeholder interactions, and identification of their system and product values. It may also include such utility-related efforts as operations research and mission modeling to assist in the critical task of establishing requirements and priorities.

3.1 DEFINITION OF A SYSTEM

System definitions come in many flavors. A good basic definition is: A *system* is a collection of interrelated elements with functionality dependent on linking of the independent element functionalities. Thus, a car is a collection of structure,

Product and Systems Development: A Value Approach, First Edition. Stanley I. Weiss.
© 2013 John Wiley & Sons, Inc. Published 2013 by John Wiley & Sons, Inc.

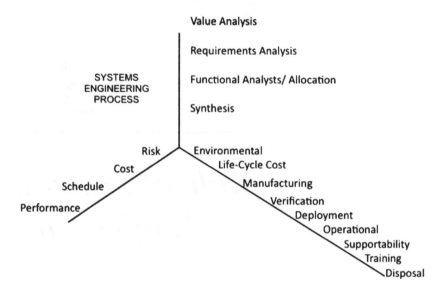

Figure 3.1 *Framework depicting systems engineering as the link between value analysis and measurable effectiveness.*

propulsion, drivetrain, passenger accommodation, suspension, and wheels, plus controls, all of which have unique functionality but none of which by itself is able to fulfill the transportation goal. This same collective concept applies to processes and organizations, both of which fit the definitions above. The latter is clearly understood by recognizing that accounting, manufacturing, engineering, and administrative departments, all have well-defined functions, but there is no outcome for the organization without all contributing to meeting the goals of the enterprise.

Figure 3.2 depicts arrangements for four different activity artifacts—all of which are systems. The product arrangement, called its architecture, is the topic of Chapter 9. The process flow depicts a system of activities necessary to produce a deliverable result. The organization, similar in hierarchical design to the product, illustrates the characterization in the preceding paragraph, while the enterprise, with its contributions from many contributing systems, has also become known as a *system of systems*, giving recognition to the scale of a system that involves a collection of task-oriented or dedicated individual systems that pool their resources to achieve an end functionality.

The interactive performance of armed forces (i.e., army, marine, and air force elements) is one often-cited military version. Relationships involving government, transportation, and industry components are others. Within each of these we may find elements that are themselves systems of systems, such as air, rail, and road traffic for transportation, and executive and regulatory, legislative, and judicial elements in government. Thus, complexity might be seen as a key distinguishing feature of a system of systems rather than the fundamental essence of system definition (Figure 3.3). Complexity is also introduced by changing interactions among elements

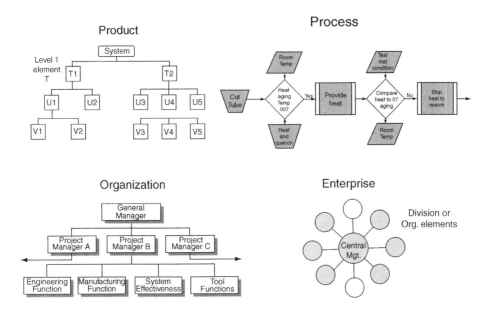

Figure 3.2 *Examples of systems with various hierarchical structures. (Composite from numerous publications.)*

with time. The means of dealing with this usually involves modeling and simulations, reflecting some commonalities with operations analysis. For example, any problem dealing with traffic flow is time variable, as are electrical power grid loading, and military communication.

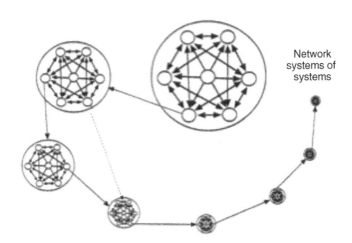

Figure 3.3 *System of systems. (Courtesy of C. Boppe, from an MIT course.)*

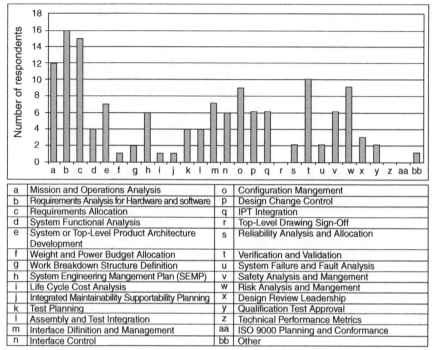

a	Mission and Operations Analysis	o	Configuration Mangement
b	Requirements Analysis for Hardware and software	p	Design Change Control
c	Requirements Allocation	q	IPT Integration
d	System Functional Analysis	r	Top-Level Drawing Sign-Off
e	System or Top-Level Product Architecture Development	s	Reliability Analysis and Allocation
f	Weight and Power Budget Allocation	t	Verification and Validation
g	Work Breakdown Structure Definition	u	System Failure and Fault Analysis
h	System Engineering Mangement Plan (SEMP)	v	Safety Analysis and Mangement
i	Life Cycle Cost Analysis	w	Risk Analysis and Mangement
j	Integrated Maintainability Supportability Planning	x	Design Review Leadership
k	Test Planning	y	Qualification Test Approval
l	Assembly and Test Integration	z	Technical Performance Metrics
m	Interface Difinition and Management	aa	ISO 9000 Planning and Conformance
n	Interface Control	bb	Other

Note : 25 total respondents - each identified 5 critical SE practices

Figure 3.4 *Systems engineering key practices. (Courtesy of LAI Research.)*

3.2 INDUSTRY VIEWS

It is also useful to understand the diverse views of systems engineering in industry. In such complex product developments as aerospace, autos, and electronic equipments, a survey of 30 organizations yielded some 27 activities defined as critical systems engineering tasks. Figure 3.4 shows the distribution frequencies, the most salient being in the realm of mission and requirements analysis and application, architecture design, configuration management, verification, validation, and risk analysis. If these are grouped into related categories, there is consensus on those aspects related to establishing requirements, architecture and design controls, reliability and verification–validation issues, and system integration management. Lacy's *logic dimension overview* (Figure 3.5) confirms and expands on the key characteristics associated with each step of value-adding activity carried through release of designs.

As indicated, systems engineering, while incorporated initially in ballistic missile development, is not a process confined to government programs, although many such contracts now require it. In fact, there has been increasing effort to introduce it at multiple levels of all complex industries, networks, medical equipment, hospital operations, and so on. A graphic showing the interaction of practices in the

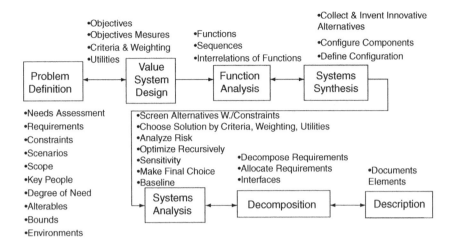

Figure 3.5 *Value activity flow diagram. [Courtesy of J. Lacy, from an INCOSE (International Council on Systems Engineering) presentation.]*

SYSTEM: A COLLECTION OF SUBELEMENTS FUNCTIONING
TOGETHER IN ASPECFIC ENVIRONMENT TO PROVIDE A USEFUL
PRODUCT OR SERVICE

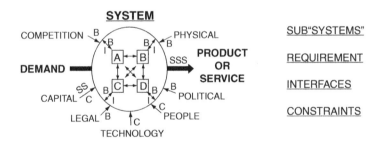

Figure 3.6 *Some concepts and definitions used by INCOSE. (Courtesy of INCOSE.)*

commercial world is shown in Figure 3.6. INCOSE, the International Council on Systems Engineering, has a well-defined working group dedicated to this integration. Some examples are provided later in the application of tools applied to such product developments as automated building-washing equipment and some of the more esoteric elements of the semiconductor industry as well as of aerospace and defense.

3.3 STAKEHOLDERS AND SYSTEMS

In summarizing the issues attending stakeholder identification and evaluation, there are key considerations to keep in mind. First, it is difficult for one person to identify all stakeholders in a new development unless it is inherited directly from a previous success. But even then, the environment or other circumstances might have changed. For example, there may be new competition, the methods of financing may not be the same, environmental regulations may have been updated, corporate goals may have been modified and insurance criteria reviewed, or the use of a product type may even have changed significantly. Therefore, the best means of identifying stakeholders is with a broadly based team with advantage taken of marketing and benchmarking beforehand. Then, too, a real understanding of these stakeholders values, needs, or expectations cannot be made certain without extensive interviews, which themselves may lead to identification of other stakeholders. Two considerations become immediately important: first, prioritizing the stakeholder values that will drive requirements; and second, reconciling conflicts among these to give the best possible solution to the requirements definition while still satisfying customer and user needs. The purpose is to provide a consistent means of translating prioritized values into requirements which can then permit prioritizing development requirements and, a step further, provide a basis for design and operating specifications.

3.4 SYSTEM VALUE STREAM

In citing the value stream for product development, it has been identified as a flow of activities that progressively delivers value to each successive phase of development. In the cycle of development, this can be seen as the flow from planning to requirements to design development to production to delivery to operations. The value stream might look like the central flow of activity illustrated in Figure 3.7, with the left side of the diagram reflecting constraints and the right side, outputs of the activity flow.

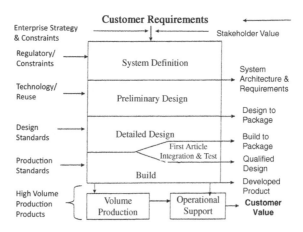

Figure 3.7 *Process to realize customer value.*

In fact, looking at all the elements that make up the chain from identification of stakeholders to delivery and operations, there are many value creation steps comprising these, with the value stream incorporating all of these in progressing through the development life cycle. There are, of course, nonlinear inputs and influences that may or may not contribute directly to value. One example would be the infusion of new value-amplifying technology, such as a change in design to introduce high-speed machining that reduces parts count, maintenance, and utility. Another would be the injection of new and unexpected funds that might make possible improvements on or the use of previously discarded design concepts, due to budget limitations. The linearity in the latter might derive from varying and even uncertain timing in either of the above. All of this potential for perturbing a perfectly linear flow indicates the need to check the influence at every step of new activity on the preceding steps and then reconcile any differences.

RESOURCES AND NOTES

Systems Engineering Handbook, INCOSE TP-2003-002-03, C. Haskins, Editor, International Council on Systems Engineering, San Diego, CA, 2006.

This primer on systems engineering is the basis for certification and is updated continually. It treats systems engineering principally as a front-end activity.

Systems Engineering and Analysis, 5th ed., B. Blanchard and W. Fabrycky, Prentice Hall, Upper Saddle River, NJ, 2010.

This updated version of the first integrated compilation of systems engineering processes is probably the most referred-to book in the literature. Fabrycky headed the first dedicated department at Virginia Tech.

Handbook of Systems Engineering and Management, A. Sage and W. Rouse, Editors, Wiley-Interscience, New York, 1999.

All aspects of systems engineering practices are authored by experts and integrated by the editors with introductory comments.

REVIEW CHECKLIST

- ☐ Which of the key practices of Figure 3.4 are incorporated in your development project?
- ☐ Are they not explicitly incorporated subsumed with others or knowledgeably omitted?
- ☐ Which are performed by the project?
- ☐ If not within the project, is the support activity integrated with the project in some fashion?

4

Stakeholder Value Drivers

The goal of our discussion on stakeholders and values is to lead to determining design-driving requirements. For example, in the world of commercial new product development, requirements may stem from the developer's desire to have a marketable product that meets a gap in consumer needs in time to preempt or beat competition. Or it might stem from bringing an invention into producible form for the marketplace. Even in requests for proposals from institutional customers which include performance specifications, requirements are not always stated completely.

One such example was in a competition for which the best technical and cost proposals had followed everything the customer requested. But not understood was an underlying desire to introduce and make provisions for wholly new technology and capabilities well beyond those stated. This was an example of incomplete knowledge of customers and stakeholders which became the basis for a critical loss. But, after losing, all possible stakeholders were interviewed to get a better understanding of the selection criteria, leading finally to development by the loser of a unique approach to the original request for proposal and, with thorough marketing and mock-ups, an ability to get the program recompeted and won. Lesson learned! It is critical to understand with certainty, and even help shape, customer and stakeholder values transformed into requirements. This front-end effort is always worth the investment in time and resources.

Product and Systems Development: A Value Approach, First Edition. Stanley I. Weiss.
© 2013 John Wiley & Sons, Inc. Published 2013 by John Wiley & Sons, Inc.

At a time of slackening in defense spending, an aerospace company decided to capitalize on its vehicle building background in the burgeoning commercial world. Although this was not for an identical application, the technical skills appeared to be applicable and potentially superior to those of the competition. Of course, the body of stakeholders was much different and broader than from those of previous experience, with a very wide variety of regulators and insurance issues. When these were all identified after many interviews, the value or needs set proved to be so extensive and daunting that it was decided not to go ahead with the program. The original set by the planning team had about a dozen stakeholders; the final grouping ended with nearly 30, and in excess of over 100 needs or values. These included, for example; insurance issues varying by location and customer, regulations ranging from delivery limits to varying environmental constraints, and the involvement of a totally new supply chain.

Another group of stakeholders often omitted are competitors or potential competitors, including those developing a new technology that could supersede that of the original developer before the latter could solidify the market. A good example was the Iridium program, devised by Motorola to begin mobile wireless communications, requiring substantial investment by the users as well as high usage cost. The combination of equipment size and cost of operations plus competitive systems with advanced and less expensive technology precluded a profitable venture. Technically, however, the multisatellite system had many virtues, and a buyer—for a fraction of Motorola's investment—now has a functioning business. Note that cost–benefits may vary with time—another element in the establishment of a business case.

4.1 VALUE ANALYSIS IN A STRATEGIC FRAMEWORK

The flow of values to requirements, which begins to define the flow of activities that govern the development process, is illustrated in Figure 4.1. The emphasis is that everything flows from the value/requirement input, coupled with the strategy of the parent organization. Thus, whereas contracts, customer volume, and beating the competition are the usual goals for developers, there are occasions when market share, even achieved unprofitably, may be the initial target, involving different values by management. Thus, profit may not be a goal initially, so that special characteristics of a product or service, inducing immediate customer acceptance at a low price, will permit entry into a new market and eventual crossover to profitability.

4.2 THE QFD STAKEHOLDER VALUES MATRIX PROCESS

One means of providing a visual relationship of stakeholders is a matrix identifying these stakeholders, together with their values, facilitating prioritization, defining commonalities and conflicts, and serving as a basis for translating key values to the technical requirements that will govern the design and operational

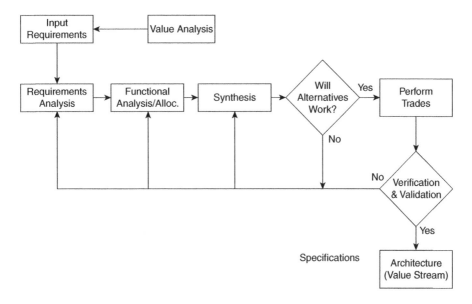

Figure 4.1   Initiating system development flow.

requirements. This matrix is derived from *quality function deployment* (QFD), a structured approach for developing requirements from user needs. It traces from three Japanese words meaning "quality or features," "function or mechanization," and "deployment or evaluation." Although the original use of this tool is in translating requirements to technical characteristics, it has been adapted here to provide an organizing means of connecting stakeholders to their values and, using a weighting scheme, to establish a basis for prioritizing. Looked at orthogonally, stakeholders are listed down one axis with values across the other axis of the matrix. The cells then identify a relationship between stakeholders and values and can be weighted numerically in terms of significance or importance. Figures 4.2 and 4.3 show the format. The set can, in the "roof" area, defining the House of Quality, cite commonalities and conflicts in the correlation matrix. As might be inferred, the set size is determined on the left (vertical) axis by the number of stakeholders; the values are limited only by the number attributable to each stakeholder. (In one use, for example, the matrix was 27 × 100.) As noted above, this array also gives a basis for using a weighting approach to determine ranking or importance in establishment of the next phase of requirements evaluation. Differing ranking schemes have been used at the discretion of the evaluators: common sets are 1–10 and 3,6,9, in increasing order of strength. But the significance is to give some numerical basis for summing the scores for each value and taking the most significant to a next step in which the values become associated with requirements and then technical attributes of the system or product to be developed. A set for a cryogen replacement project is shown in Figure 4.4.

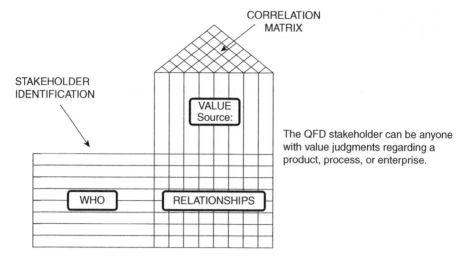

Figure 4.2   *Summary steps to value stream mapping. (Courtesy of S.I. Weiss, chapter 4 in* SMAD *(Space Mission Analysis and Design),* 3rd Edition. Wertz and Larson.)*

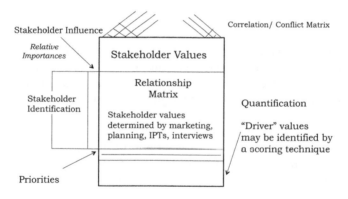

Figure 4.3   *QFD stakeholder values matrix.*

As noted several times later in the book, when a weighting approach is used in evaluating attributes or criteria, it must be recognized that these are somewhat subjectively assigned. Thus, judgments based on entries with only minor differences should be reviewed carefully and sensitivity analysis applied.

4.3 QFD PROCESS SUMMARY

- *Identify all stakeholders.* This is the real start of development. Structuring the list in groups may improve evaluation of importance and comparisons. Place

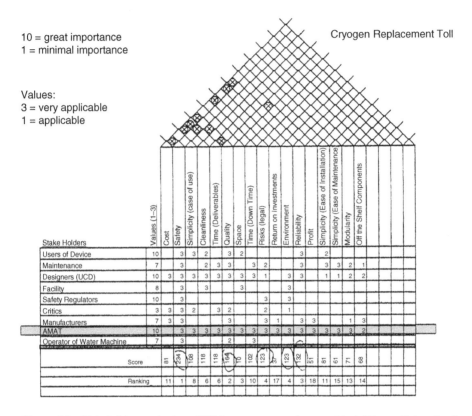

Figure 4.4 Stakeholders and values QFD for a cryogen replacement tool. (From a University of California–Davis project for Applied Materials.)

the set of stakeholders on the left side of the relationship matrix (i.e., the rows of the matrix).

- *Develop the principal values of the stakeholders.* This is a research and interview job. Place these at the top of the relationship matrix (i.e., the columns of the matrix).
- *Fill in the strong/moderate/weak symbols or numerical scoring in the matrix elements.* The question to be asked is: How important is a particular value to a particular stakeholder?
- *Compute relative scores for value priorities.* Identify those that must be met for program or enterprise success.
- *Fill in the correlation matrix by identifying the values that conflict.* These links will require special attention to avoid future program problems.
- *Address value conflict and misalignment issues.*
- *Translate driver values to a value–requirements relationship using QFD.*

Resolving Stakeholder Conflicts

The QFD roof is intended to identify the conflicts among stakeholders and their values. Some that can affect the project downstream must be resolved immediately. Some may be such as to permit resolution over time as the progress of development clarifies presumed conflicts. Others may exist from stakeholders with little real interest or capability to affect progress and thus might, for goodwill, be kept informed but not be included in reconciling the differences. However, with the first group, it is critical to get agreements early, with a value proposition acceptable, if not totally satisfying, to all. Thus, compromises that do not impinge on the performance outcome of product or system are the common answer, and these include modification of the expectations of the customer; it is the job of the developer to negotiate and supply the rationale. No, it is not always possible to hit the bull's-eye, but it is important to hit the target with as little deviation as possible from the original goals. For example, one finds this in nearly all major highway construction projects, where routing of roads due to objections to rights-of-way causes curves to be induced. Situation and use times for runways at airports are another example. On the product side, installation of insulation much heavier than desired, based on regulatory stakeholders' impositions, is another rather common example.

So the succession of QFDs shown in Figure 4.5 becomes a means for a design team to establish not only primary customer requirements, but also those of other stakeholders and the necessity to reconcile any conflicts among these. Thus, the QFD for stakeholder values is followed in requirements development and beyond by, for example, substituting "values" for "stakeholders" and "requirements" for "values" in the sequence in Figure 4.5.

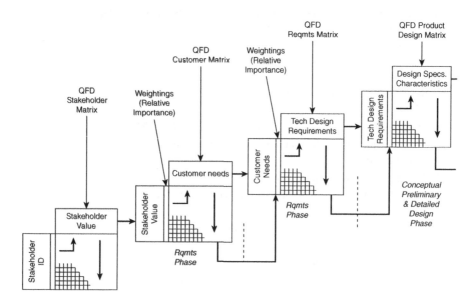

Figure 4.5 *QFD matrix relationships.*

This matrix QFD approach has had many variants and uses and has been adapted to listings of organizations and functions interfaced with activities, responsibilities, or other content parameters as both a means of maintaining a record for reference or of prioritizing these parameters for decision making. Appendix I includes a few examples, including a means of prioritizing research.

RESOURCES AND NOTES

Total Quality Development: A Step-by-Step Guide to World Class Concurrent Engineering,
   D. Clausing, ASME Press, New York, 1998.
   Clausing was one of the major advocates for the multiple uses of QFD and integrating this in conjunction with concurrent engineering and Taguchi quality engineering; includes several step-by-step descriptions.
References noted for Chapter 1 also have useful applications.
Some Web-based or software tools: QFD Capture, Qualica, QFD Online, DOORS.

REVIEW CHECKLIST

- ☐ In selecting values and needs that will drive requirements, what potential biases lie in scoring?
- ☐ Which might be considered mandatory or serve as constraints regardless of scoring?
- ☐ What conflicts have become evident?
- ☐ Are they reconcilable? How?
- ☐ Have value priorities been established via QFD?

5

Value-Driven
Requirements Development

Returning to the progression of QFD relationships, it is logical to move from stakeholder values to technical requirements. This continuing progression (as illustrated in Section 4.2) is intended to lead to a matrix providing quantifiable technical requirements. Unfortunately, in the translation, some requirements are identified only subjectively; to be a basis for design, subjectivity equals ambiguity, yielding multiple interpretations, including those that differ between developer and stakeholders, let alone customers or market expectations. So the need for quantifying as much as possible is critical for a common understanding of design goals and parameters as well as the ability to verify a product characteristic at any time in the development. The latter understanding is often overlooked until time to perform a test or inspection. This consideration must be included in the generation of requirements and must include the relevant metrics.

5.1 ESTABLISHING THE PARAMETERS

It is useful to relook at the QFD structure as it was applied originally (see Clausing, *Total Quality Development*). This House of Quality is shown classically as in Figure 5.1. Referring back to Chapter 4 and the application to value analysis, the template is identical, although the purpose here is the relationship of requirements to technical parameters and specifications. The progressive translations identified

---

Product and Systems Development: A Value Approach, First Edition. Stanley I. Weiss.
© 2013 John Wiley & Sons, Inc. Published 2013 by John Wiley & Sons, Inc.

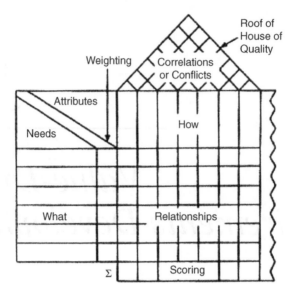

Figure 5.1   *Classic House of Quality. (From Clausing,* Total Quality Development.*)*

in Figure 4.5 can be seen as directing the developer to this application. Of course, it is not unusual to find terminology differences, so while the progression illustrated in Figure 5.2 (and in some cases, elsewhere) uses slightly different notation than that followed in this book, accommodations for adapting the processes and vocabulary described herein will be examined from time to time.

Then, looking at the flow of activities in the value stream of development, the role of requirements can be seen as a critical contributor and entry to the many other

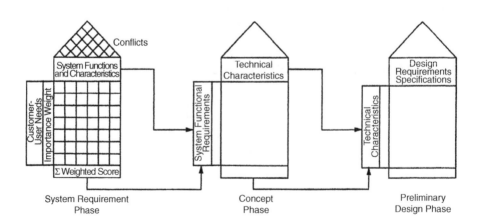

Figure 5.2   *Classic progression of QFDs.*

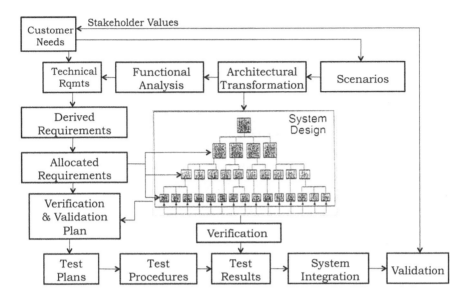

Figure 5.3 *Requirements: a system perspective. (Adapted and modified from various instructional materials.)*

phases of the project. This systems perspective is shown in Figure 5.3. A feature of this diagram is illustrating how much the downstream flow of development activity is driven by the requirements development process. The basis for converging on requirements is simply recognition that the success of a product or system depends inevitably on understanding the real characteristics that will generate value to all stakeholders. When assessing why products succeed, this understanding has been found to be a major contributor deserving further discussion when following the value stream of development activities.

There are also a number of unanticipated issues that surface in establishing performance requirements. Considerations of access for repair and replacement are often forgotten. One such experience lay with the location of a camera in the preliminary design of a new reconnaissance aircraft. That design would have required major structural removals for servicing. Another example lay with the difficulty in replacing a car battery held in place by two separate attachments. One part involved was manufactured in the United States, the other in Canada. In this case, the first, the battery frame, used American standards, whereas the hold-down clamp, manufactured in Canada, used metric standards. The difference in tools necessary was not evident until repairs were required.

Some requirements that form the bases for selecting and trading designs are programmatic, such as predesignation of schedules and resources. These are also derivable from a stakeholder's values. For example, cost targets and delivery dates are often expressed as values or constraints and have a great impact on technical decisions.

5.2 TRANSLATING VALUES TO REQUIREMENTS

It is useful to look at some examples that translate market research and "corporate" goals to stakeholder values and then to requirements and design drivers. The pressure-washing device of Figure 5.4 used a truck-mounted boom to reach elevated surfaces. Prioritization of requirements employed the QFDs from the stakeholder value analysis; safety was foremost, followed by ease of use as well as financial and insurance issues. Close behind, implementation was critical in order to yield operational productivity over that of the totally manual, "workers up in a cherry picker," means used previously. The design that evolved was an interesting test of the development process.

The next example, from a supersonic business jet study, is derived from QFD analyses (Figure 5.5) of stakeholder values and requirements. There are many issues here that bring home the need for quantitative requirements that can truly be used to provide a basis for design. However, although the list is impressive, it is very subjective and is lacking in quantitative values. While safety may not drive the highest scores, it is increasingly a constraint driver wherever humans are directly involved or indirectly affected. A good example is with nuclear power plants or

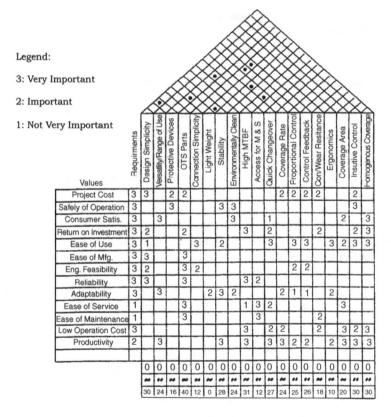

Legend:

3: Very Important

2: Important

1: Not Very Important

Values	Requirements	Design Simplicity	Versatility/Range of Use	Protective Devices	OTS Parts	Connection Simplicity	Light Weight	Stability	Environmentally Clean	High MTBF	Access for M & S	Quick Changeover	Coverage Rate	Proportional Control	Control Feedback	Con/Wear Resistance	Ergonomics	Coverage Area	Insutive Control	Homogenous Coverage
Project Cost	3	3		2	2								2	2	2	2		2		
Safety of Operation	3		3					3	3								3			
Consumer Satis.	3	3							3		1							2		3
Return on Investment	3	2			2					3		2				2			2	3
Ease of Use	3	1				3	2					3	3	3		3	2	3		3
Ease of Mfg.	3	3			3															
Eng. Feasibility	3	2			3	2								2	2					
Reliability	3	3			3					3	2									
Adaptability	3		3				2	3	2				2	1	1		2			
Ease of Service	1				3					1	3	2					3			
Ease of Maintenance	1				3						3					2				
Low Operation Cost	3									3		2	2			2		3	2	3
Productivity	2	3					3			3		3	3	2	2		2	3	3	3
	0	0	0	0	0	0	0	0	0	0	0	0	0	0	0	0	0	0	0	0
		30	24	16	40	12	0	28	24	31	12	27	24	25	26	18	10	20	30	30

Figure 5.4 *Values–requirements QFD matrix for a telerobotic washer and painter system. (From a University of California–Davis project for Murray Clark Painting and Construction Company.)*

Stakeholders	Values	Requirements
Customers	Low initial cost, low operating cost, performance reliability, meets specifications	Nonexotic materials Use of existing technologies Range Takeoff distance Payload; high-efficiency propulsion system
Users	Operational ease, safety, low cost, ease of maintenance and integration	Controllable and stable Can be integrated into current infrastructure Cockpit Payload Low ground turnaround time Modular constraints
Financers	Return on investments, cost certainty, business ease	Simple design Minimal research on new technologies Quick tie to market Customer demand Low acquisition cost
Regulators	Meet legal and environmental standards, FAA standards	Low sonic boom Minimal ozone (NO_x and SO_x) Noise emission at takeoff and landing Complies with federal aviation regulations
Public	Safety, noise, and pollution concerns	Sonic boom overpressures Ozone layer effects Noise pollution Reliable components
Insurers	Low risk	Reliablecomponents Proven and well-tested technologies
Suppliers	Profit, continuity	Modularity Large orders
Workforce	Job security, minimum outsourcing	Customer demand Detailed market analysis
Marketers	Coolness factor, novelty, state of the art, reliability, safety, performance	Sleek design Use of reliable systems and products Performance Payload Cost
Producers	Ease of production, cost certainty, profit, use of existing facilities	Simplicity No exotic construction methods or materials
Unions	Job continuity, benefits, minimal outsourcing	Customer demand

Figure 5.5 *Stakeholder values and qualitative requirements for a supersonic businesses study. (Courtesy of Stanford University.)*

pipelines or transportation systems. Clearly, there must be a next stage in which requirements or a specification definition is established, or definitive design and analysis cannot be assured as satisfying criteria.

5.3 CHANGING REQUIREMENTS

A key facet of requirements management is an understanding that response to changes should be an initial consideration, together with a recognition that the transfer or translation of these changes inevitably flows down to a variety of suppliers (the supply chain). The newer or more complex the product or system, as well as the longer the schedule, the more inevitable are changes. With the rapid pace of technology, for any development schedule longer than a year or so, there are often technology changes that overtake the initial basis for requirements. The message here is that since one can expect changes, the value stream must allow for repeated examination of requirements as a feedback for both developers and stakeholders, to recognize the need to either modify expectations, the requirements themselves, or the means of validating them upon delivery.

In addition, since it is necessary to direct the requirements to flow down all the elements of a project or product, a consideration of changes to a potentially large group of suppliers is critical, especially where there are possibilities of technical or manufacturing difficulties. And as progress is made through the development value stream, cost implications are significant, as shown in Figure 5.6 in the adaptation of

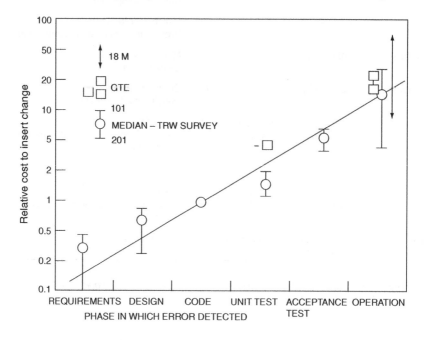

Figure 5.6 Cost impact of requirement changes. (Courtesy of IBM.)

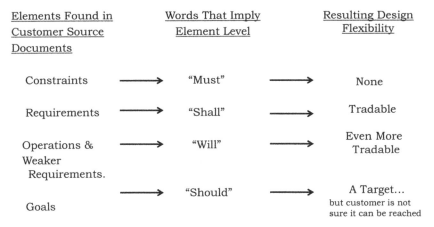

Elements Found in Customer Source Documents		Words That Imply Element Level		Resulting Design Flexibility
Constraints	⟶	"Must"	⟶	None
Requirements	⟶	"Shall"	⟶	Tradable
Operations & Weaker Requirements.	⟶	"Will"	⟶	Even More Tradable
Goals	⟶	"Should"	⟶	A Target... but customer is not sure it can be reached

Note: Customer needs typically found in a source document have different levels of significance. *Constraints* are more stringent than *requirements* and *requirements* are more stringent than *goals.* If the customer does not specify the needs classification, it might be inferred by the context in which it is described or by the verb that accompanies it...see above.

Figure 5.7 *Words used in defining customer needs typically have special meanings. (Courtesy of C. Boppe, MIT Systems Engineering course.)*

the IBM study. The logarithmic scale emphasizes how important, particularly as to requirements, it is to fix errors early. But more of this later when looking into project and development management.

In stating requirements and translating these into specifications, language does matter. In one sense, the difference between *shall* and *will* may seem highly legal, but may specify a basis for negotiation and contracts. The term *should*, for example, is a statement of objectives, which may be traded against other parameters. One example might be a "requirement" that a new vehicle should achieve a particular mpg (miles per gallon) value. To reach this goal, some weight reductions that potentially limit crash resistance may cause a modest lowering of the mpg target. The list of terms in Figure 5.7 can be instructive at contract negotiation time. A related terminology issue is ambiguity. What does a particular term mean, and in what context? What, for example, does *maximize* mean? Increase as far as possible? Whose judgment? It depends on who is using the word. And what about user friendly? Which user? How friendly?

5.4 QUANTIFYING REQUIREMENTS

Just what are quantifying requirements? Figure 5.8 gives examples of the means by which one can quantify requirements. For example, in looking at a missile

Measurable Attribute	System			
	Communication Satellite	Rapid Transit	Aircraft	Tank
Quality	Noises or BER	Ride comfort	Flight stability P/L volume Loading capacity	Accuracy (ft) Lethality (ft) Detection range
Quantity	Number of channels of capacity	Number of passengers	Gross take-off weight P/L weight	Number of rounds carried Number of guns and sensors
Availability	Geographical coverage area (sq. mi.)	Geographical area served (sq. mi.)	Range, cruise, speed	Range (mph)
Timeliness	Channel availibility on demand (sec)	Time to travel between major points (min)	Maintenance and expendables Reloading time between flights Sortie recycle time	Speed (mph)
Coverage	99.99% (CCIR regulation)	Time between trains	MTBF, MTTR, periodic maintenance, recycle time	Battle readiness

Figure 5.8   *Measurable attributes examples. Criteria are either limits or desirables. (Courtesy of B. G. Morais.)*

system, it is possible to establish the CEP or impact circle size, range in kilometers, response time for launch, and other measures. Even more important, it is possible to verify these as the basis for determining if the outcome or product itself has lived up to the values desired. Recalling the bus project of Chapter 4, the list of values or needs of the stakeholders identified the difficulties in achieving these. One such was the requirement "acceptable to the public," a severe test of human reactions.

It is important now to see how some subjectively developed requirements can be translated into quantifiable values or parameters that will be a basis for design. Are there identifiable metrics in terms of geometry or mass (i.e., design characteristics)? Also, can the ability to verify the product characteristics at any time in the development process be established? This step is critical before proceeding to the more enjoyable aspects of creating designs.

In the end, requirements management consists of integrating the requirements derived from all sources: customers, other stakeholders, specifications, standards, enterprise issues, and other constraints. These must then be analyzed for ambiguities, conflicts, and bases for validation and verification, including quantifiable objectives. Finally, controlled evolution must be provided for throughout the life cycle. This means a willingness to reexamine and potentially renegotiate requirements as changes affect the development value stream (Figure 5.9).

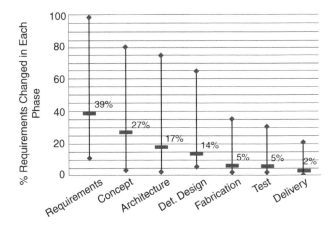

Figure 5.9   *Requirement changes during various design phase.*

5.5   REQUIREMENTS PROCESS SUMMARY

Before proceeding to the next node in the development value stream, leading from requirements to functional analysis, this chapter can be summarized as follows:

- Identify and prioritize customer and user objectives and values and requirements for the mission to be accomplished. Identify stakeholders, their values, and their influence on requirements.
- Identify internal and external constraints.
- Translate customer, user, and stakeholder expectations into technical attributes. Quality function deployment applications are useful tools.
- Establish technical requirements in a quantitative fashion and provide for decomposition or allocation to elements of the product or system. Provide metrics for requirements that will be the basis for verification and testing.

We continue to stress that the tools and processes in this book are intended to provide a framework for development and that adapting them to a project and an organization should be anticipated. An example from the Mercury Marine Engine Division of the Brunswick Corporation is instructive. This developer and supplier of outboard and inboard motors has embraced "lean six sigma" practices, which incorporate the use of quality function deployment. Figures 5.10 to 5.12 show the application to the crankcase cover of one of their more complex units.

Use VOC_QFD_SIPOC Template (Excel Worksheet)

Process

1. Identity Customer Requirements (enter in column C) and Type of Requirement [Basic, Expected, Exciting] (enter in column B)

2. Prioritize Customer Requirements on CTC workbook by entering letter of preferred requirement

3. Brainstorm Design Requirements to meet Customer Requirements (enter in row 14)

4. Each Customer Requirement is compared to each Design Requirement and the strength of each relationship is determined

   Correlation Strength (strong [9], moderate [3], weak [1])

5. After the Correlation Strengths are entered, the Requirement Weight and Relative Weight will be automatically calculated to show the prioritized design requirements

6. Complete Design Correlations by entering + or − into the roof matrix to show conflicting design requirements (+ means the design requirements conflict)

7. Identify Target Values for the Design Requirements by entering in Upper Spec Limits and Lower Spec Limits

Figure 5.10   *QFD/House of Quality worksheet. (Courtesy of E. J. Alyanak, Brunswick Corporation, Mercury Marine Engine Division.)*

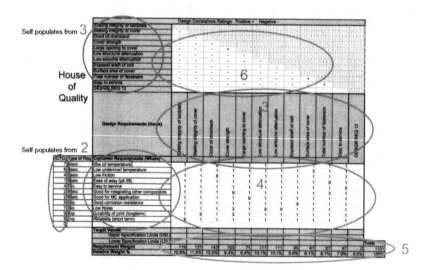

Figure 5.11   *QFD/House of Quality crankcase cover example. (Courtesy of E. J. Alyanak, Brunswick Corporation, Mercury Marine Engine Division.)*

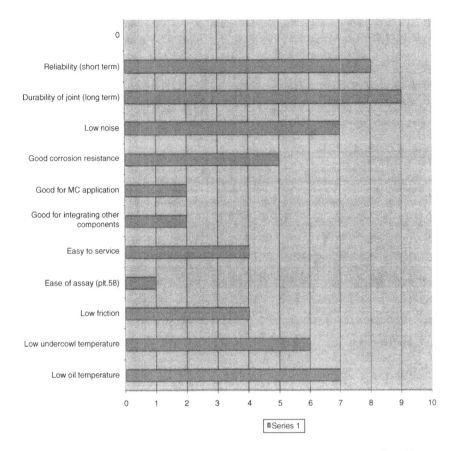

Figure 5.12 QFD/House of Quality crankcase cover example: critical-to-customer chart. (Courtesy of E. J. Alyanak, Brunswick Corporation, Mercury Marine Engine Division.)

RESOURCES AND NOTES

Space Mission Analysis and Design, 3rd ed., J. Wertz and W. Larson, Editors, Microcosm Press, Kluwer Academic, Norwell, MA, 1999.

Chapter 4, by the present author, is the application of the requirements process to a specific project.

Product Design and Development, 5th ed., K. Ulrich and R. Eppinger, High Peak Press, Meridian, ID, 2010.

Some unique considerations in trading requirements are described, with the use of QFD in establishing product specifications.

Product Design: Techniques in Reverse Engineering and New Product Development, K. Otto and K. Wood, Prentice Hall, Upper Saddle River, NJ, 2000.

This is an excellent treatise on converting information and benchmarking knowledge bases into product requirements and functions. Introduces activity diagrams and can be an introduction to functional analysis.

Note that the systems engineering–related books cited previously also contain approaches and methods dealing with requirements development.

Some Web-based or software tools: see Chapter 4 plus Pathmaker.

REVIEW CHECKLIST

☐ What requirements are the design drivers?

☐ Which requirements are actually constraints?

☐ Has QFD scoring been reviewed for marginal differences that might exclude important requirements?

☐ Where there are conflicts, how will reconciling them affect the design drivers?

☐ Can requirements be verified at every step of the value stream of development?

6

Functional Analysis

Requirements define what is needed in a design. How those requirements are implemented resides in functions or actions. In identifying the functions that operationalize requirements and then establish the means (or optional means) that can perform those functions, a foundation is initiated for concept definition. The options also establish a basis for evaluating choices for concept selection that will provide a baseline for successive development steps toward production and delivery. This step also permits interactions with customers and others to maintain a common understanding not only of the outcome but also of the ability to evaluate and identify the impact of changes.

6.1 FUNCTIONAL FLOWS

Another way of specifying *function* is presented in Blanchard and Fabrycky's *Systems Engineering and Analysis*. Here a function is defined as a discrete action required to achieve a need or requirement. The flow of these activities can be shown as a functional flow diagram (Figure 6.1). As noted earlier, there may be several variations as to how these functions may be implemented. In addition, just as it is important to see how requirements flow down or decompose through the elements of a design, so do functions, as illustrated in Figure 6.2.

To contrast functions and requirements: Functions are task oriented, stated as verbs, and define means for implementing requirements. A function represents any action necessary to change a system state to accomplish performance objectives. Requirements are what a function must accomplish, as stated in performance characteristics.

Product and Systems Development: A Value Approach, First Edition. Stanley I. Weiss.
© 2013 John Wiley & Sons, Inc. Published 2013 by John Wiley & Sons, Inc.

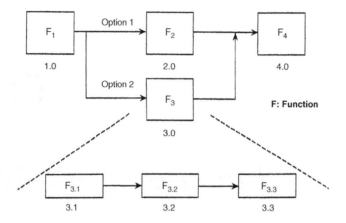

Figure 6.1 *Sequential functional flow diagram example. (Courtesy of Blanchard and Fabrycky, Systems Engineering and Analysis.)*

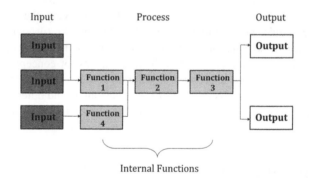

Figure 6.2 *Multiple input/multiple output function flow diagram. (Courtesy of Blanchard and Fabrycky, Systems Engineering and Analysis.)*

It should be recognized that since functional flow diagrams indicate the sequential relationship of functions, they are also the basis for performance time lines.

It is important to note that functions are actions that are accomplished by products or systems and their elements, the latter being an outgrowth of decomposition. So if descriptors pass the grammar test, once establishing the functions and their relationships or flow, it should be possible to identify the entities that can implement or make the functions happen. A rocket launch could, for example, be initiated by "erect launch system," then "ignite propulsion." Note that neither has established the design of the mechanizing products, but identifying the options for these can, with descriptive blocks and relevant interfaces, guide the character of design concepts that could satisfy these functions and permit trades to find those best able to achieve the results desired.

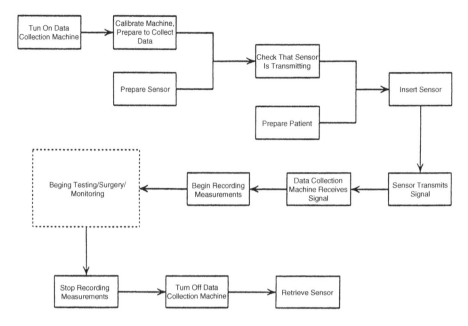

Figure 6.3 Translating functional diagram for blood pressure sensor monitoring during surgery. (Courtesy of Sarah Atwater, Stanford University Project.)

In the case of a medical instrument, the blood pressure monitor shown in Figure 6.3, the sequence of functions that establishes its use will facilitate defining the entities that can perform those functions and consequently lead to the design concepts derived.

Another project example is the Amphibicycle, a vehicle required to travel on a variety of surfaces and in water as a sort of pedaled Hummer. The functional flow shown in Figure 6.4 expresses both actions and options induced by the environments specified by the requirements. Note that where optional conditions exist in the flow, an inverted square is shown. This type of notation may be organization specific.

Since functions, like the requirements that drive them, can be decomposed to identify subordinate but necessary activities, understanding the process is useful in determining what governs the design of the elements making up a product or system. In the case of an unpiloted vehicle, Figure 6.5 identifies top-level actions of key elements of the system to produce the performance required. But the decomposition shown does a much more definitive job in identifying activities that will govern entities making up the design.

6.2 FUNCTIONAL BLOCK DIAGRAMS

To repeat, functional flow diagrams show what a product must do to satisfy requirements. Functional block diagrams provide schematics for the entities that can perform the functions as well as identifying key interfaces among these

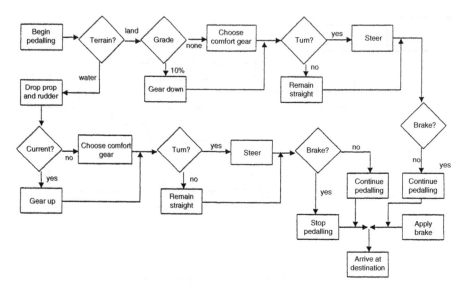

Figure 6.4 *Functional flow for the Amphibicycle, a human-powered land vehicle. (Courtesy of Michael Brooks, University of California at Davis project.)*

elements. This information is the grist for developing concepts and their descriptive architectures. The method also provides documentation, sometimes introduced after a design architecture has been fixed, to give analysts an understanding of a system or product. As a facilitator of the system or product design process, the functional block diagram, or schematic, represents a grouping of functional performers. It can also describe optional functional approaches as well as decomposition into lower-level segments. It should incorporate all interfaces as well as data flows that represent functions internal and external to the system. Interfaces are therefore critical to

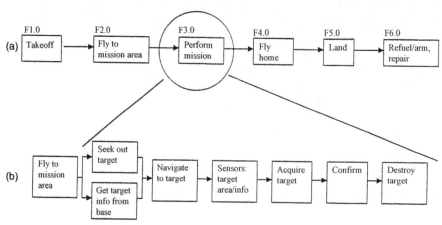

Figure 6.5 *(a) A notional top-level functional flow diagram for an unmanned version of the F-35 fighter. (b) Multi-level functional flow aircraft performance of mission. (Courtesy of Stanford University.)*

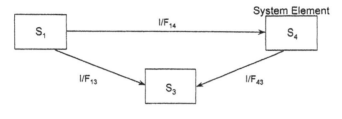

I/F: Interface

Figure 6.6 Top-level functional interface diagram for a multisatellite project. (From Blanchard and Fabrycky, Systems Engineering and Analysis.)

describing the system fully. Thus, all the functional system elements are linked in what might be referred to as a system schematic, providing a basis for decision making among options as well as a guide to concept development. This is illustrated at the top level in Figure 6.6, with the example of a multisatellite research project shown in Figure 6.7 also identifying interfaces and character.

In summary, the functional analysis process involves functional flows that indicate the sequential relationship of all functions that must be accomplished by the system. This also provides a basis for time lines of activity and data and information flow. The resulting functional block diagrams provide the system schematic upon which concepts may be based. As shown in Figure 6.8, the block diagram establishing the implementers of these functions carries the functional analysis toward its end goal of providing a basis for establishing and evaluating design concepts.

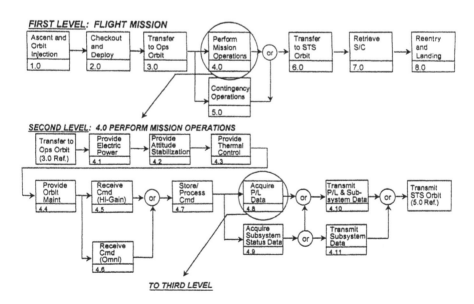

Figure 6.7 Block diagram interfaces for a spacecraft deployment mission.

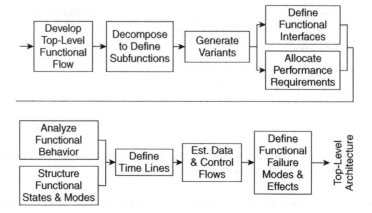

Figure 6.8 *Functional analysis process. (Adapted from Blanchard and Fabrycky,* Systems Engineering and Analysis.*)*

RESOURCES AND NOTES

Systems Engineering Handbook, C. Haskins, Editor, INCOSE TP-2003-002-03, International Council on Systems Engineering, San Diego, CA, 2006.

Handbook of Systems Engineering and Management, A. Sage and W. Rouse, Editors, Wiley-Interscience, New York, 1999.

Systems Engineering and Analysis, 5th ed., B. Blanchard and W. Fabrycky, Prentice Hall, Upper Saddle River, NJ, 2010.

Space Mission Analysis and Design, 3rd ed., J. Wertz and W. Larson, Editors, Microcosm Press, Kluwer Academic, Norwell, MA, 1999, Chap. 4.

All of the sources above cover requirements development, an *intrinsic* aspect of systems engineering.

Some Web-based or software tools: SmartDraw, Visio, Hobby Projects, Barrett.

REVIEW CHECKLIST

☐ In establishing the functional flow of activities satisfying the requirements, have all optional paths been considered?

☐ Have all information transfers been included?

☐ Are iteration loops included?

☐ Is decomposition sufficient to define all key elements of the product or system?

☐ Has a functional block diagram been used to identify interfaces for products services and information?

☐ Do these include internal as well as external (to the product or system) interfaces?

☐ Does the functional analysis limit or open up options for concept development?

☐ Are there any performance requirements that can't be translated into functions?

7

Interface Definition and Management

It has been noted that a critical aspect of system definition is the development of relationships among functions and their implementers through interactions, or interfaces. If these are formally fixed before development, they will themselves represent constraints as requirements. The interaction of a product or system with its environment or with other external relationships defines external interfaces, while the relationships among elements within the product or system defines their internal interfaces. These relationships may be physical, as with mating or joined parts; functional, involving signal or data transfer; or environmental. But, however established, they always require identification, documentation, and control. By way of illustration, the former might be envisioned in an interaction of an item in a corrosive atmosphere, with corrosion as a potential outcome to be addressed in developing a design or concept of operations. In the latter case, a switch internal to an electric circuit has a physical interface with the supply or signal transfer. If, however, the switch could be activated by a manual or wireless signal, they could be seen as external interfaces.

This recognition of interfaces that are a part of any complex product or system extends to considerations such as stakeholder involvements and conflicts and all relating entities. In product and system development, the interfaces normally considered involve physical contacts, often forgetting, until prototyping or mockups, signals and information interactions and, more important, human-to-system interactions. In addition, there is a tendency to consider interfaces as static or constant in time. This is not true, of course, in many time-dependent environments as well as in field service work-arounds.

Product and Systems Development: A Value Approach, First Edition. Stanley I. Weiss.
© 2013 John Wiley & Sons, Inc. Published 2013 by John Wiley & Sons, Inc.

Boundaries between areas or objects of interest

- Physical
  - Fitting or mating elements
  - Human or robotic interaction
  - Interconnects
- Functional
  - Fluid interactions
  - Signals, information
- Environmental
  - Atmospheric states and influence
  - Other externals: societal, regulatory, etc.

Figure 7.1   *Various sources of interface categorization.*

7.1   INTERFACE COMPLEXITY

Figure 7.1 lists categories of the many sources defining and influencing interfaces; the number of these interfaces will, in fact, imply the complexity of the system. Thus, systems that have made long-distance telecommunications possible involve highly complex and interactive systems or networks, as illustrated in Figure 7.2. This system of systems has a combination of physical and wireless or information interfaces that must perform smoothly for successful performance of the network. Each of the nodes in this network is itself a complex system with its own multiplicity of internal interfaces. In reality, each of these might be developed by a different contractor, so that the integrator of the whole must provide and ensure thorough definitions of the interfaces.

There are many systems that, given their place in society, have innumerable interfaces that govern acceptance and sustainment of the products involved. One of these is the automobile, depending on an extensive interaction with both the inside world of the car maker and the outside world of suppliers, distributors, customers, service organizations, and so on. Others include systems found in the military, where so many interfaces include not only equipment and its users, but also such elements as internal and external command and control affecting the performance and character of that equipment. Figure 7.3 characterizes the inputs and outputs of a control and communication system for a navy submarine, illustrating that wherever there are transfers of signals, information, or mechanical or electric movement, there are interfaces fundamental to the operation of the system. These may be internal or external, the latter particularly part of systems in which command and control and information sharing exist. This combination of operational interfaces, including administrative and evaluative elements such as servicing, are interactions that must be considered in new developments entering a wide range of environments. Interestingly, it is possible to see in many of these connections direct linkages to stakeholders.

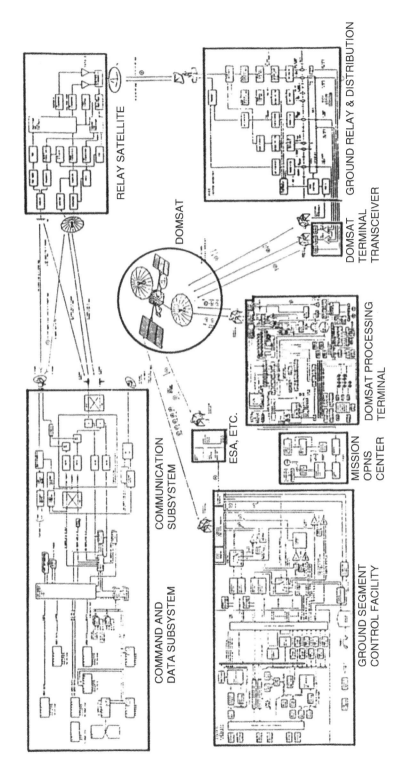

RELAY SATELLITE

GROUND RELAY & DISTRIBUTION

DOMSAT

DOMSAT
TERMINAL
TRANSCEIVER

DOMSAT PROCESSING
TERMINAL

COMMUNICATION
SUBSYSTEM

ESA, ETC.

MISSION
OPNS
CENTER

COMMAND AND
DATA SUBSYSTEM

GROUND SEGMENT
CONTROL FACILITY

Figure 7.2 Interfaces for a wireless communication system. Note the combination of complex elements. *(Courtesy of NASA.)*

49

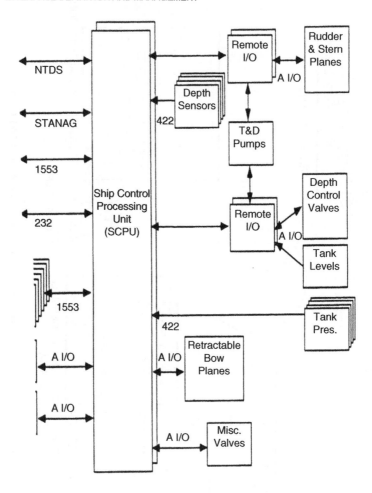

Figure 7.3 *Seawolf swim-by-wire ship control. Every control and communication system is built on interfaces. (From a Draper Laboratory study for the U.S. Navy.)*

7.2 THE *N*-SQUARED MATRIX

It is useful to display relationships or interfaces in a readily understandable visual image. The *N*-squared (N^2) matrix is a convenient means of doing this, with cells reflecting interfaces and, in more sophisticated use, the character of these. Thus, each axis contains all the elements involved, and the diagonals reflect zero interaction, being cells reflecting common identification. The process of interface assessment and management makes powerful use of this format, with guidelines as follows:

- The $N \times N$ matrix used to organize interfaces is pictured in Figure 7.4 as a template.

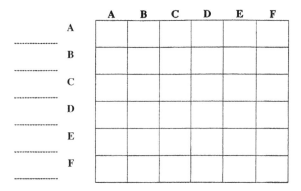

Figure 7.4   *Template for interface information matrix.*

- Individual entities or functions can be placed so as to label the matrix axes or along the diagonal. Figure 7.5 shows cell elements as functions, with their interfaces identifying the relationship between cells.
- Critical functions or entities with many inputs and outputs are easily identified by cell-to-cell frequency and notation.

<u>System interfaces</u> can be presented in an organized fashion using an N^2 diagram in which the relationship of an item on the diagonal to all other items (functions, data, hardware) is identified on the horizontal to the other cells projected vertically (up or down). When each cell includes descriptions of the interactions, it is sometimes called an interrelationship or interaction matrix.

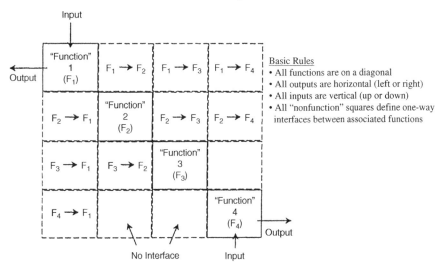

Figure 7.5   *Rules for N^2 matrix organization for functions. (Adapted from Lockheed Systems Engineering Handbook, circa 1990.)*

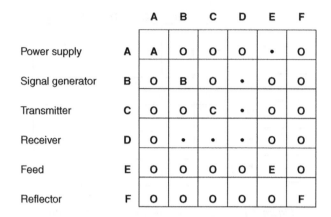

		A	B	C	D	E	F
Power supply	A	A	O	O	O	•	O
Signal generator	B	O	B	O	•	O	O
Transmitter	C	O	O	C	•	O	O
Receiver	D	O	•	•	•	O	O
Feed	E	O	O	O	O	E	O
Reflector	F	O	O	O	O	O	F

Figure 7.6 *Matrix for transmitter interfaces. (Courtesy of NASA.)*

- Interface elements (signals, data, hardware, functions) flow clockwise: inputs vertically and outputs horizontally.
- This graphical method can be used to facilitate any organizational relationship, including work and communication allocations.

The simplified transmitter $N \times N$ matrix in Figure 7.6 shows where there are interfaces by using a O simply to designate their existence. But a next step is to identify the character of the relationships and possible impact as shown in the National Aeronautic and Space Administration (NASA) project that links the power supply to its internal elements (Figure 7.7). So while the $N \times N$ matrix is indeed

	LDI	FI	RBI	BILATERAL CONVERTER	DC/DC CONVERTER	BSCCM DC/DC CONVERTER	SW1, SW2	LVBC
LDI	X	LDI resets the FI	LDI sends On/Off commands	LDI regulates Information flow	xx	LDI sends On/Off commands	LDI controls switches	LDI sets charger regulation current
FI	FI provides 3 telemetry signals	X	FI provides signal to RBI	xx	xx			
RBI	RBI provides 3 telemetry signals	xx	X					
BILATERAL CONVERTER	B.C. sends voltage, current signals	xx		X	xx		xx	xx
DC/DC CONVERTER	xx	xx	DC/DC provides power	DC/DC provides power signal	X	DC/DC provides main input power	xx	xx
BSCCM DC/DC CONVERTER	BSCCM provides telemetry signal	BSCCM provides power			xx	X		
SW1, SW2	Switches central power flow to battery via LDI			xx	xx		X	xx
LVBC		xx		LVBC sends On/Off commands	xx		xx	X

Figure 7.7 *NASA internal interface matrix. (Courtesy of NASA.)*

static, the cells can indicate the character of interfaces such as time relationships and discontinuous interactions. These can then signal a need either to evaluate the impact of these interfaces over time or to identify where simulation and modeling will be necessary to truly evaluate them. These interfaces are also a trigger for locations and types of possible failure modes.

N^2 Applications

The N^2 diagram has also served to identify information transfer interactions among functional discipline organizations. One case studied involved approximately a dozen technical discipline groups, each having assumptions of what their roles were in a design development activity. This included what information they were to generate and to whom it was to be sent and when. The $N \times N$ matrix was a 12×12 matrix, with the cells intended to identify interaction. The result showed that there were a number of cells evidencing no information transfer when one of the parties depended on its availability, as well as several that transferred data to groups that had no need for it. This survey produced the basis for corrective action and a matrix used to establish schedules for all transfers–management use of a tool devised for functional interactions and physical interfaces. We see other outgrowths of the matrix in the translation of the N^2 matrix into design structure matrices, noted in this chapter and elaborated on in Appendix I. This example is also chronicled in the book by Murman *et al.*, *Lean Enterprise Value.*

7.3 INTERFACE CONTROL

Interface control consists of establishing common understanding of interfaces for all project participants. The N^2 diagram provides a quick visualization. But with multiple participants, particularly with a number of non-in-house players, there is need for a contract among all parties affected. So for very complex products, an interface control document (ICD) details interface aspects that can be agreed to formally. These include the identification of interfaces and the responsibilities of the individual parties to the agreement. This document is often attached to or included in procurement papers and plays a significant role in the evaluation of changes. It also serves as a basis for relooking at requirements or constraints and, of course, is critical to reviews at all stages of development as well as in verification and test steps.

A summary set of guidelines follows:

- Identify interfaces through drawings, N^2 matrices, specifications, and/or text.
- Establish the character of the interfaces (i.e., mechanical, electrical, signal, etc.).
- Establish responsibility for each aspect of an interface and get signed agreements from all parties.
- Fix this agreement as the basis for change evaluation and control for both technical and contract performance.
- Review all changes for impact on, or of, interfaces.

RESOURCES AND NOTES

The Systems Approach, S. Ramo and R. St.Clair, KNI, Inc., Anaheim, CA, 1998.

Ramo is considered to be the father of modern systems engineering, and the character and philosophy covered broadly here emphasizes interfaces and interactions as keys to understanding complexity.

Design Structure Matrix Methods and Applications, S. Eppinger and T. Browning, MIT Press, Cambridge, MA, 2012.

Although design structure matrices are a special case of interfaces or interactions, their relationships are covered in introducing means of operating on them for management purposes, discussed especially in Chapter 15 and Appendix I.

Lean Enterprise Value, E. Murman et al., Palgrave Press, Hampshire, UK, 2002.

Mentioned several times as a chapter reference, this book includes the noted study initiated by Tyson Browning in his Master's degree thesis. Browning is also cited above and in Appendix I.

Many systems engineering handbooks also address interfaces, with initial focus on those between functions.

Some Web-based or software tools: Chapter 6 tools can be useful for graphics applicable to interfaces; also, N^2 matrices and interface control documents.

REVIEW CHECKLIST

☐ Have physical, functional, and information interfaces been covered?

☐ Do these include communication, data, and environmental?

☐ Is the N^2 matrix used to both identify and characterize interfaces?

☐ Is the method carried forward to define interfaces within a concept or architecture?

☐ Where there is interaction among organizations responsible for interfacing or interacting elements, have interface control documents been established with signature agreement?

8

Concept Selection and Trades

How does one develop a concept from scratch once the requirements and their functional realizations are reasonably defined? One means is to have a development team with creative folks brainstorming ideas, identifying the options that are seen to meet requirements, and satisfying the functions and interfaces established. A starting point might be benchmarking what has been done in the past or is potentially competitive, with a similarity or relationship to the objective, either inside the development organization or elsewhere. Of course, if the product or system is completely unrelated to identifiable comparisons, there must be true innovative and inventive effort.

8.1 CONCEPT OPTIONS

A concept is a relatively unstructured realization of a design. When multiple concept options are created or defined from existing designs, these can be subject to trades in order to yield a "best" choice or choices. These then become the baselines upon which product and system architectures, detail design, and activities that will deliver value can be based. Of course, concepts can incorporate many subelements that may not need development if previously developed entities can be applied. Among these are propulsion units that might incorporate existing controls, software, or parts such as valves. Others might be suspensions using existing damping devices, sensors with available detectors, seating, switches, and so on. Regardless, system concept

Product and Systems Development: A Value Approach, First Edition. Stanley I. Weiss.
© 2013 John Wiley & Sons, Inc. Published 2013 by John Wiley & Sons, Inc.

alternatives must be driven by requirements, functions, and interfaces before a true baseline can be established.

A concept may range from a general idea of an end system or product to one that can be taken to rough prototyping or mock-up. It is usually the first time that a visual or functioning representation is provided, and it should include key external and major interfaces. Most important, it should not be seen as defining only one solution, but should present all feasible options that have enough information to permit trades among them to narrow choices or to choose a single design with which to proceed.

A number of concept design approaches have been developed beyond enthusiastic brainstorming. That unstructured process is exceedingly common, but to have a measure of success, even this must include all stakeholders affected. In that form, combining innovative collaborative team thinking with structure, a method called *design thinking* has been incorporated into Stanford University's "D School" (Design Institute) program. It emphasizes creativity through collaboration, with innovation and prototyping fueling each other. On the other hand, TRIZ (the theory of inventive problem solving), axiomatic design, and legacy/morphology are structured approaches fashionable in different industries. TRIZ seeks to relate development of current solutions to methods and practices in unrelated fields. Axiomatic design is a systematic function-driven approach at the detail level but may suffer in application to large, complex products. Legacy/morphology is the modification or upgrading of existing designs, but may be extended by deriving concepts from dissimilar but related applications.

Increasingly, simulation tools are becoming available to aid and optimize the making of concept choices. The measures of effectiveness that have been addressed when incorporated into computer-driven tools provide means for multidiscipline optimization, described more fully in Appendix IV. Concepts may also be driven by corporate strategies such as new market capture, driving out competition, evidencing new technology, and in early development, maximum use of existing systems or capabilities. In some cases, use of a platform-based approach for a family of new products may be the driver. One such is the use of a common body frame or suspension for a family of automobile models. From a corporate standpoint, the key goal may simply be to retain core capabilities by an extension or modification of previous products. But at every stage of concept development it is important to determine if any change in the requirements for interface sets, or the functional analysis has been implied. This may induce a review that could generate modifications to simplify the concept development or induce negotiations to modify requirements.

The concept establishes many things beyond just a picture. As implied earlier, it provides the preparation for an architecture and a level of design that will permit production of articles that will finally deliver value to customers. Indeed, concept development looms large since it is here that conducting trades or decision processes must yield the best of choices, given available resources and knowledge. It is also, unfortunately, a place to make mistakes by preemptive choice or by attempting to shortcut processes, including the failure to look back to assure that requirements are

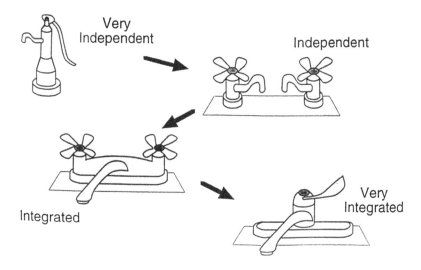

Figure 8.1 *Hot and cold water: example of functional integration concepts. (Courtesy of C. Boppe.)*

met. Some unhappy examples were the IBM PC Junior, which had inadequate and noncompetitive capabilities, and the Pontiac Aztec SUV, which had no customer appeal or satisfaction.

The concept stage is also a time to verify that the stakeholders are or will be satisfied. This can be done by having them be involved at this time in reviews of designs, mock-ups, or simulations. One example of failure to do this occurred in the early phase of a major government program addressed earlier, where all technical and cost requirements had been met, but the desire of the customer for extendable new technologies was never considered, a case of incomplete interaction leading to loss of a contract. Similarly, loosely defined functions might be satisfied in many ways, as shown in Figure 8.1, but merely providing hot and cold water to a sink rarely satisfies a homeowner's values. Yet presenting all concepts shown permits evaluations based on criteria that will drive a final selection.

8.2 CONCEPT CREATIVITY

Some may believe that the relatively structured process described stifles innovation. That would never be true, however, because it provides primarily a framework for clarifying goals and a means of achieving them. Besides, innovation has many stimuli (Figure 8.2). In addition, the largest number of new products are in fact, derivatives of existing designs or extensions of families of products. But how inventive must one be when conceiving of concepts? Figure 8.3 does not belittle creativity, but at this stage of development, most concepts can be related to history or defined strategy. For example, a platform approach permits the utilization of basic

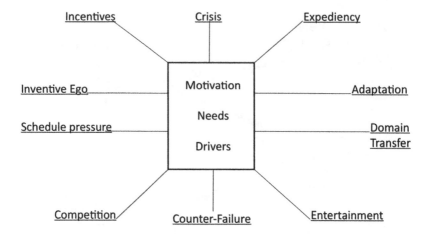

Figure 8.2 *Various drivers of innovation.*

modules in the development of new applications. In a sense, then, it is possible to set some ground rules for concept creation:

- Identify high-value requirements and their functional implementation that will be satisfied by concept options.
- Establish concept selection criteria, including risks, costs, constraints, and verifiability.
- Initiate trades, based on the rules above, to select options for architecture development.
- Review with stakeholders and verify their satisfaction as to meeting requirements.
- Recognize and resolve issues.
- Create mock-ups or simulations to assist visualization and trades or disclose problems.

Level	Degree of Inventiveness	Percent of Solutions	Source of Knowledge
1	Obvious solution	32	Personal knowledge
2	Minor improvement	45	Knowledge within a company
3	Major improvement	18	Knowledge within an industry
4	New concept	4	Knowledge outside an industry
5	Discovery	1	All that is knowable

Figure 8.3 *Concept innovation invention. How inventive must you be when conceiving concepts? (From a screening of over 200,000 patents by Genrich S. Altlshuller, the "Father of Triz.")*

Concept Heritage

There is a tendency to believe that the majority of new concepts are born as products of genius in garage-like settings or in sequestered locations if within a large company. While both have produced remarkable outcomes, the evidence of Figures 8.1 and 8.2 suggests that the bulk of new creations and services are derivable from a variety of existing or historical products and technologies. For example, even the airplane "invented" by the Wright brothers was based on a legacy of gliders and failed attempts at powering them with a variety of engines. Whittle's jet engine used knowledge from steam turbine domains. Today's automobiles are not strikingly different from those of 75 years ago, with the changes coming from improved manufacturing and materials. Transport aircraft scheduled for delivery over the next 10 years are not dramatically different from the jet airliners of the 1950s. That is not to demean the remarkable inventions that have made many of the foregoing possible: the semiconductor, the telephone, wireless communication, the discovery of aluminum as a suitable structural material, and so on. But the vast majority of new products, services, and even systems trade on legacies and derivatives, even those resulting from such motivations as wartime needs or other crises. The reader is encouraged to identify two or three "new" concepts from each of the innovation stimuli—they may be sponsors of a next-breakthrough concept.

At every stage of the development process, it is necessary to look back to determine if the previous stages are realized.

8.3 DECISION PROCESSES

The need for decision processes at this stage has already been cited as necessary to arrive at the most feasible concept or, perhaps, the few concepts that should be carried a while to determine if some specially desirable or needed technologies will become available. There are also occasions when cost or schedule issues might drive one toward other than first-choice options. This decision, or trades among options, is a next critical step. A number of methods can facilitate the choice.

A summary of trade analysis methods is shown in Figure 8.4. No matter what process is used, the key to making satisfactory choices is in establishing the specific criteria by which options can be evaluated. Figure 8.5 shows some examples of setting and evaluating quantitative criteria. What precautions should be noted for the process? Perhaps the first is avoidance of bias in assessing how well a concept characteristic meets the criteria. It is not uncommon to find that decisions are preconceived and evaluations organized to justify this. Companies such as Northrop Grumman have set team decision methods as a means to mitigate against such bias (see Figure 8.6). A second precaution is to avoid applying too many constraints in a team-based approach. A third is neglecting stakeholder inputs as part of the decision. But for all involved, the focus must be on critical parameters as criteria to arrive at acceptable versus overly perfected or exotic solutions. Sometimes the reasons that the "ideal" is not the best answer lie in such things as company or customer policies, limited resources, and limited time. So what can be done to provide a structured

- Who trades? What to trade? When to trade? How to trade?
- Can some trades be made at all levels?

    - Needs: utility issues
    - Requirements
        Functional: visibility in flow diagrams—time lines
        Physical: visibility in block schematics—interfaces
    - Architectural, concepts, subsystems
- Are the methods the same for each?
- What makes a trade possible?
    - Capability
    - Compatibility
    - Adaptability
    - Cost
    - Relative values
    - Quantative

- How do we trade elements that are dependent on other trades? Or cause conflicts?
    - Use one trade's options or choices as metrics for another.

- Are there guidelines for the trade process—metrics to make decisions?
    - Define what's to be traded.
    - Determine alternatives and/or reference.
    - Establish metrics.
    - Evaluate without bias.
    - Apply utility analyses where appropriate.
    - Don't eliminate close contenders without extending evaluation to further
        levels, but look carefully at those that score well but may have
        unacceptable risks.
    - Document.

Figure 8.4 *Trade analysis guiding questions.*

	System					
Measurable Attribute	Observation Satellite	Communication Satellite	Rapid Transit	Missile	Tank	Aircraft
Quality	Resolution (ft)	Noise of BER	Ride comfort	CEP (ft)	Accuracy (ft), lethality (ft), detection range	Flight stability, P/L volume, loading capacity
Quantity	Frames/day, sq.mi/day	Number of channels, capacity	Number of passengers	Number to achieve PK	Number of rounds carried, number of guns and sensors	Gross takeoff weight, P/L weight
Availability	Geographical coverage access area (sq. mi.)	Geographical coverage area (sq. mi.)	Geographical area served (sq. mi.)	Range (mi)	Range (mi)	Range, cruising speed
Timeliness	Revisit time command time process and delivery time (min)	Channel availability on demand (sec)	Time to travel between major points (min)	Launch response on demand (swc)	Speed (mph)	Maintenance, and expendables, reloading, time between fits, sortie recycle time
Coverage	Available for use on demand	99.99% (CCIR) regulation	Time between trains	Launch readiness	Battle readiness	MTBF, MTTR, periodic maintenance, recycle time

Figure 8.5 *Measurable attribute examples. Criteria are either limits or desirables. (Courtesy of B. G. Morais, Synergistic Applications, Inc.)*

Potential Benefits	Potential Problems
• Broad coverage of ideas	• Time wasted arguing or discussing trivial items
• Minimized risk of bias	
• Motivation increased by "ownership"	• Difficulty getting everyone to focus on important issues
• Greater knowledge base available	• Hidden agendas
	• Camel syndrome (A horse designed by a committee)

Figure 8.6 *Examples of benefits and problems concerned with team decision making. (Courtesy of Northrop Grumman.)*

means of quantifying evaluations? Have measures of effectiveness been used? Have sensitivities of the scoring process been considered? Can whatever tools are used be tailored to the character of the project?

There are a variety of structured decision processes. Those most used in industry have been described as "weight-and-rate" approaches, sometimes seen as "static" methods, as shown in Figure 8.7. There are also probabilistic methods, such as the use of decision trees, called "dynamic" by its proponents and illustrated in Figure 8.8. Other methodologies include using cost as an independent variable,

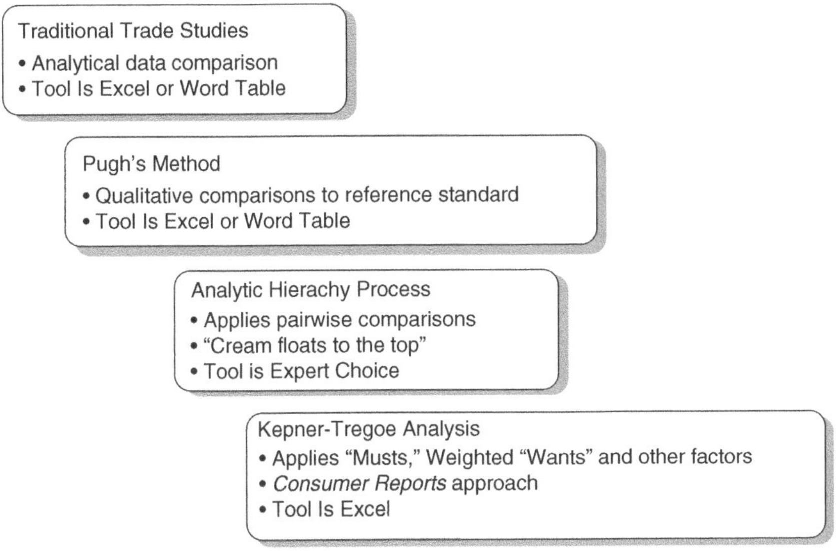

Traditional Trade Studies
• Analytical data comparison
• Tool Is Excel or Word Table

Pugh's Method
• Qualitative comparisons to reference standard
• Tool Is Excel or Word Table

Analytic Hierachy Process
• Applies pairwise comparisons
• "Cream floats to the top"
• Tool is Expert Choice

Kepner-Tregoe Analysis
• Applies "Musts," Weighted "Wants" and other factors
• *Consumer Reports* approach
• Tool Is Excel

Figure 8.7 *Examples of various static decision methods. (From the Stanford University Systems Engineering Certificate program.)*

Example: Two vendors A and B bid $10M and $8M respectively on a project to develop a gadget. If successful, the company using the gadget would gain $15M. Bidder A is 80% likely to be successful. Bidder B is 70% likely to be successful.

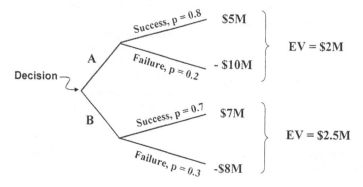

Figure 8.8   Decision tree analysis. (Courtesy of R. Howard, Stanford University.)

design to cost, analysis of alternatives, and multiattribute utility analysis (an optimization approach).

As noted earlier, the most important elements in a trade study are the evaluation criteria. Trades should include the widest possible number of solution options and recognize that winnowing down the group of possibilities is part of the decision process. Also, the criteria must not be overgeneralized. It is important to use measurable attributes by which one can make judgments. A summary look at the process includes the following steps:

- Formulate the selection criteria.
- Weight the criteria.
- Identify possible alternatives.
- Reflect on and refine criteria.
- Rate concept option characteristics with respect to criteria.
- Perform analysis, consider sensitivities, and potentially refine weights.
- Select a concept or concepts.

Recognizing the similarity to QFD prioritizing procedures; weighting is the weak part of the process. Weights must be based on their importance as established by requirements and constraints. But when scoring yields irrational results, the entire array of weightings must be challenged for bias or considerations overlooked. It is a process of reexamination. Also, since risk analysis is part of the decision process, it will warrant further discussion, along with the technical, schedule, and cost elements, to be examined in more depth later. Decision making is clearly a system activity with multidisciplinary issues.

Although, in general, structured techniques that permit the use of tabular methods (such as using Excel), are usually reliable, the often-used pro and con assessment may

		System				
Measurable Attribute	Observation Satellite	Communication Satellite	Rapid Transit	Missile	Tank	Aircraft
Quality	Resolution (ft)	Noise of BER	Ride comfort	CEP (ft)	Accuracy (ft), lethality (ft), detection range	Flight stability, P/L volume, loading capacity
Quantity	Frames/day, sq.mi/day	Number of channels, capacity	Number of passengers	Number to achieve PK	Number of rounds carried, number of guns and sensors	Gross takeoff weight, P/L weight
Availability	Geographical coverage access area (sq. mi.)	Geographical coverage area (sq. mi.)	Geographical area served (sq. mi.)	Range (mi)	Range (mi)	Range, cruising speed
Timeliness	Revisit time command time process and delivery time (min)	Channel availability on demand (sec)	Time to travel between major points (min)	Launch response on demand (swc)	Speed (mph)	Maintenance, and expendables, reloading, time between fits, sortie recycle time
Coverage	Available for use on demand	99.99% (CCIR) regulation	Time between trains	Launch readiness	Battle readiness	MTBF, MTTR, periodic maintenance, recycle time

Figure 8.9 *Examples of criteria used for designing various complex systems: Criteria are either limits or desirables. (Courtesy of B. G. Morais, Synergistic Applications, Inc.)*

sometimes serve as a screening technique. But it is far too subjective for true decision making. One straightforward weight and rate approach is the Kepner–Trego. It simply lists all the attributes or criteria, and each concept is scored against these parameters. This is a direct parallel to QFD scoring. To repeat, the criteria and their weightings are the weak points, so this requires critical evaluation of definition and sensitivities in the driver's influencing choices. Examples of measurable attributes that become definitive criteria are shown in Figure 8.9, which will be recognized as being the same as Figure 8.5. There, the emphasis was on quantification. Here the focus is on the translation of this for measurement. Other means of dealing with criteria decisions are measures of effectiveness, usually in the context of performance, as shown in Figure 8.10, and necessary for optimization considerations.

When there is a baseline or reference against which other concepts are evaluated, the Pugh matrix (Figure 8.11), is most often used. Here, scoring is done on a comparison basis: for example, "equal" in value or benefit; "plus" or superior; "minus" or inferior, with respect to the baseline. If this is amplified with each parameter considered on a weight-and-rate approach similar to the Kepner–Trego, it is called the *weighted Pugh* and is very widely used. The amphibicycle example of Figure 8.12 shows the applications for a number of possible options. Recalling the functional flow example, the concepts satisfying that operational description proved to be single-hull designs, with one or two front wheels and with the driver positioned either upright or recumbent. The criteria were drawn from the set of requirements derived previously, and a weighted Pugh analysis is performed, with both issues addressed and scored.

Another variant that compares different concepts in pairs and compares probabilities of meeting a criterion progressively is the analytical hierarchy process

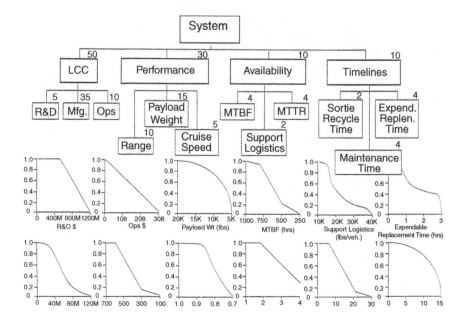

Figure 8.10 *Measures of effectiveness using decomposition and utility curves. (From Kockler et al.,* Systems Engineering Management Guide.*)*

(AHP). This method, advanced by Saaty in 1970, works with a hierarchy of criteria and thence choice options (Figure 8.13). Regardless, whenever there is scoring, just as with QFD, prioritizing sensitivity to the scoring techniques and weightings is mandatory.

Parameter	Weight	Concept 1		Reference	Concept 2	
P/L size	10	0		0	−	
Minimum processing time	9	+		0	+	
Performance margins	8	+		0	+	
High reliability	6	+		0	+	
High inclination	6	+		0	−	
Backup system	5	+		0	0	
Proven technique	5	+		0	+	
Operations costs	5	+		0	+	
Systems cost	4	0		0	0	
Design for maintainability	4	+		0	+	
Total +		+8	(+48)	0	+6	(+37)
Total −		−0	(−0)	0	−2	(−15)

Figure 8.11 *Weighted Pugh matrix example for a spacecraft. Comparisons have been made to a reference concept: superior, +; equal, 0; inferior, −. The matrix provides rapid evaluations for prioritizing choices and dominant characteristics. Limitations are mitigated by weightings for characteristics.*

Requirement	Weight	Upright (A)	Split Hull (B)	Single Hull Two Front Wheels (C)	Recumbent Double (D)
				Design Concept	
Water ability	5	4	5	4	5
12-mph water speed	3	2	4	4	3
20-ft water turning radius	2	5	3	4	3
Stability in water	4	1	3	3	5
Handle 1.5-ft swells	3	1	4	4	4
Maximize strength/weight ratio	4	3	4	3	4
Support 350-lb: 250-lb rider + cargo	4	3	4	5	3
Comfortable	3	3	4	4	3
Commuter-type vehicle	4	4	4	4	4
Liftable by humans	2	4	4	3	3
Home maintenance	2	4	4	4	4
Human powered	5	5	5	5	5
Maximize efficiency	5	3	5	5	5
Land ability: asphalt, grass, dirt, sand, mud	5	5	5	5	5
Optimize for smooth asphalt/concrete	4	3	4	4	4
25-mph land speed	3	2	4	4	4
10% uphill grade	3	3	3	3	3
10-ft land turning radius	3	4	3	4	3
Stability on land	3	2	4	5	3
Affordable ($1000) production	4	4	3	2	3
Totals		229	278	280	274

Figure 8.12 Weighted Pugh for the amphibicycle. (Courtesy of Michael Brooks; see Figure 6.4.)

- Scoring is more discrete than Pugh
- Pairwise comparison of concepts or features is key. Divides trades into a series of hierarchies (i.e, A:B, A:C, B:C)
- Can be linked to QFD-developed attributes and weightings
- Matrix of comparisons of all candidates is developed by summing weighted pair comparisons (using derived eigenvalues or normalized weightings)

Example summary matrix: (only one variant)

Concept	A	B	C	Weight	Score
A	1	A/B	A/C		
B	B/A	1	B/C		
C	C/A	C/B	1		

Scale for Pairwise Comparisons

Value	Definition	Explanation
1	Equal preference	Both factors contribute equally to the objective or criterion
3	Weak preference of one over another	Experience and judgment slightly favor one factor over another
5	Essential or strong preference	Experience and judgment strongly favor one factor over another
7	Very strong or demonstrated preference	A factor is favored very strongly over another; its dominance is demonstrated in practice
9	Absolute preference	The evidence favoring one factor over another is unquestionable
2, 4, 6, 8	Intermediate values	Used when compromise is needed

Figure 8.13 Analytic hierarchy process. (Courtesy of SpaceTech.)

Although selecting a single concept is the goal, there is often value in carrying more than one in order to insert criteria refinements or clarify uncertainties. One such might be the start of a particularly desirable technology which, as noted earlier, if available could favor one or another concept. With complex decisions, team-based approaches to decision making tend to limit bias. As with the Northrop Grumman example, the benefits are great but there are issues to be dealt with to avoid bottlenecks of conflict and indecision. There is need for training, strong leadership, and sometimes even facilitators. We discuss this in future discussions of integrated product and process development.

8.4 MULTIDISCIPLINE ANALYSIS AND OPTIMIZATION

While all of the above methods identify critical parameters as criteria, without expert evaluators, the interaction of these parameters, as governed by different disciplines, are often neglected since their inclusion may lead to complexity, mathematically and computationally. As was noted in defining measures of effectiveness (MOEs), though, optimizing one attribute may have negative effects on others. This is most obviously seen with cost as a parameter that may be increased beyond acceptance by optimizing design attributes.

MDAO is one means of finding the best compromise among parameters by including all the significant disciplines. Limited application has been made in design development of automobiles, ships, and various electronics, but the greatest use has been in aerospace, where interrelationships of variables is intrinsic to the design process. It is readily apparent, for instance, that decreasing drag, increasing speed, reducing weight, and constraining cost are all interrelated. Building and implementing the models that permit manipulating variables to optimize their combination is both desirable and feasible, so long as the number of variables and expectations are limited. The MOEs noted earlier provide a basis for building such models, either by direct iterative techniques or regression methods. Thus, the tools available do provide for certain very useful capabilities, particularly in concept/preliminary design. Since this is a process drawing on computational capabilities, there are now commercial packages available to provide utility to the average designer. Utilizing MDAO, however, does require judgment as to where it is most beneficial and this involves some understanding as to relevant approaches, methodology, and constraints. Appendix IV, an overview provided by Professor Juan Alonso, should establish a baseline for that understanding.

It is worth noting that many government contracts use the term *concept of operations* (CONOPS), which describes how concept solutions will be used to satisfy operational situations. It may derive from, or contribute to, requirements or be established based on concepts proposed, where it may be treated in trades much as a requirement. Most important, since concepts represent the first visible characterization of a development product, they provide a framework for establishing the architecture or decomposition that will define the structure and interfaces of all the elements making up the end item.

RESOURCES AND NOTES

Visualizing Project Management, K. Forsberg, H. Mooz, and H. Cotterman, Wiley, Hoboken, NJ, 2005.

These practitioners see concept definition as the real starting point for project development, serving as a baseline for management.

The Mechanical Design Process, 2nd ed., D. Ullman, McGraw-Hill, New York, 1997.

This work establishes a variety of methods, emphasizing evolution and translation of designs to other domains, using functions as a basis. Means of evaluating concepts with decision and scoring techniques are included.

Product Design and Development, 5th ed., K. Ulrich and S. Eppinger, High Peak Press, Meridian, ID, 2010.

These authors concentrate on smaller mechanical products but introduce both heuristics and matrix methodology for decision making.

Foundations of Decision Analysis, R. Howard and A. Albas, Prentice Hall, Upper Saddle River, NJ, 2009.

Probabilistic decision tree methods are explained in detail, with many examples.

The Engineering Design Process, A. Ertas and J. Jones, Wiley, New York, 1996.

This book provides a good description of probabilistic and optimization methods applied to design.

Some Web-based or software tools, mostly applicable to trades, provide templates for Kepner–Trego (KT Software) and Pugh Institute methods. AHP tools are also available from Axiomatic Design Solutions, for example, and L. Monson's "Reformed" Hacker. Of course, most are variants of Excel.

REVIEW CHECKLIST

- ☐ Have all concept options been explored?
- ☐ In evaluating these, where are biases possible?
- ☐ Are any of them motivated by relationships internal to the developing organization? External? Political? Enterprise strategies? Identify and clarify any and if possible incorporate in the decision process.
- ☐ What are the limitations in your decisions process for the current project?
- ☐ How could this be changed? With more multidisciplinary involvement? With finer-grained weighting and rating?
- ☐ Is it possible to combine attributes from among concept options?
- ☐ Has an attempt been made to optimize characteristics and concepts?

9

Architectures and "Architecting"

In making the trades that provide a choice of concept or concepts to carry forward, it is also possible to choose the most favorable parameters for establishing an architecture(s) for the product or system. This architecture is the organization of the elements making up the product or system that describes their relationships to the whole. It should incorporate sufficient levels of decomposition to identify the entities that provide the design with critical subsystems and components. The architecture leads in many directions toward a formulation of top-level design and subelements (Figure 9.1), including all the levels representing decomposition of the integrated end item. Thus, the system architecture is the structure, arrangement, or configuration of system elements and the relationships among these required to satisfy requirements and constraints, functions, performance, reliability, maintainability, and extensibility. It may be hierarchical, an arrangement of functions in a process, or identifying relationships in a network.

9.1 SELECTING AN ARCHITECTURE

Why an architecture?

- An architecture provides a visual identification of all the elements of a product or system: that is, an organization chart for the project.

Product and Systems Development: A Value Approach, First Edition. Stanley I. Weiss.
© 2013 John Wiley & Sons, Inc. Published 2013 by John Wiley & Sons, Inc.

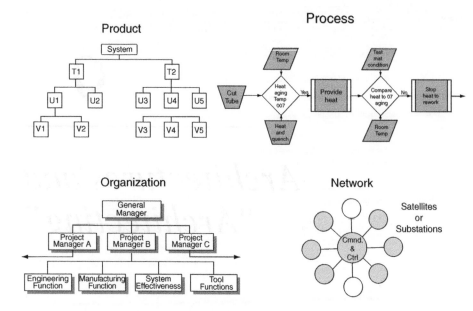

Figure 9.1   *Product and system architectures. (Courtesy of C. Boppe.)*

- An architecture provides a basis for decomposition to the lowest elements for both design and work (i.e., production and operations assignments), including a view of what must be integrated to yield the final product.
- An architecture is effective in establishing bills of materials.
- An architecture is useful in partitioning for outsourcing elements.
- An architecture is both a marketing tool and an artifact for record keeping.

On the other hand, it should be recognized that the subelements themselves have architectures and can be subject to trades among applicable options, including off-the-shelf subsystems and components. Beyond this, in a system of systems, the interaction of multiple systems must recognize interfaces at almost any level of their separate architectures. This set of relationships must also consider that the external interfaces between major entities can vary with time and affect internal architectures and their adaptabilities (Figure 9.2).

But what are architecture selection criteria? Many of the considerations used in concept selection apply, although with emphases that lead to the ability to decompose and allocate the criteria throughout a structure. Since an architectural representation is a relationship diagram, many aspects of these relationships must be considered. Examples include interaction of functions among and within segments, and the impact of reliability at one level on succeeding levels. In a similar fashion, the architectural tree provides a basis for allocating budgets to characteristics such as mass, software versus hardware, and the variety of parameters shown in Figure 9.3.

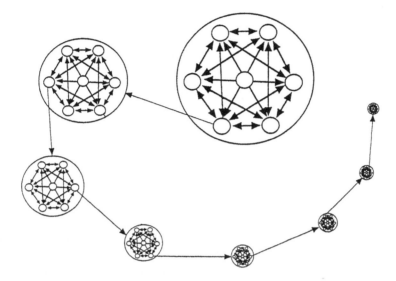

Figure 9.2 *Architectural elements of a system of systems. (Courtesy of C. Boppe, for an MIT course.)*

- Requirements

- Mass/weight

- Reliability

- Interfaces

- Integration–assembly sequence

- Test planning

- Cost

- Work and outsourcing

Figure 9.3 *Architecture flowdown application to developmental parameters and practices.*

9.2 ARCHITECTURAL DESIGN

The term *architecting* has been given to the design of elements and their relationships. In identifying architectural selection criteria, much as for concepts, the following apply:

- Is easy to upgrade and modify
- Is easy to maintain and archive
- Permits the use of commercial off-the-shelf items

- Combines entities to achieve criteria
- Provides a basis for work packages
- Facilitates verification/testing/failure analysis
- Is easy to integrate and manage
- Provides ease of communication among elements

Recounting the tools used to reach this point (Figure 9.4), each tool represents a means of ensuring the flow of values that will affect the design and how it may be produced. They also provide a basis for looking backward as necessary for inadvertent changes that affect development. Following are two examples that illustrate simple architectures. The first, a blood pressure monitoring system whose functions were illustrated in Chapter 6, shown here in Figure 9.5, while decomposed to the fourth level, could incorporate numerous trades at even lower levels. For example, where a power supply is noted, there may be many choices not only of type, but also of vendor or in-house design.

The next example, tier II+ (Figure 9.6), is a major system of systems, each shown here decomposable to three levels, with the unpiloted aircraft having many sensors and external interactions that illustrate a definable decomposition with potential options for trades. In general, the subelements of an architecture can be traded at any phase of development to cause modifications of the architecture, as indicated in Figure 9.7.

Architectures may not always be illustrated with a hierarchical cascade of levels. The spoke and axle arrangement (or star) in Figure 9.8 defined the major elements involved in a laser welding device (developed for the Livermore Laboratories), but decomposition is difficult in any graphic sense. So to truly identify the subelements and determine the character and architecture of manufacture, the more conventional configuration shown in Figure 9.9 was established. There are also architectures in information transfer configurations intrinsic to communications and sensor processor relationships. Recall that the laser welding first-level architecture was shown in star form, much as a computer or processor might be linked to multiple sensors or actuators. Other information transfer designs, usually for electrical and data systems, can be identified as linear or ring types or buses, as shown in Figure 9.10, often signifying bus topologies since they tie together the flow of inputs and outputs in information transfer architecture. One interesting aircraft case, that of the Boeing 777, cites its architectural diagram of signal paths as a ring with triplex redundancy and linear interlinkages of multiple systems that make up the information and processing system for the aircraft.

9.3 ARCHITECTURAL IMPERATIVES AND PRECAUTIONS

It is worth identifying some architectural characteristics and necessities:

- The number of levels or decomposition: depending on the complexity as well as the levels governing outsourcing or joint development and the interfaces involved

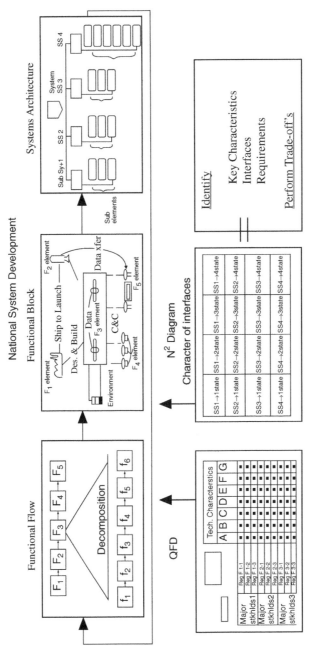

Figure 9.4 System architecting tools summary. (From Johan Denecke, Director of Worldwide Quality, Life Technologies.)

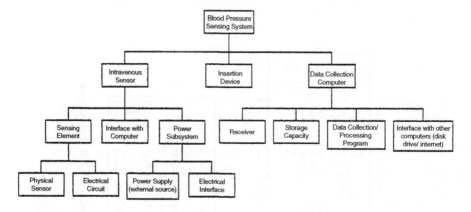

Figure 9.5 *Medical system architecture: blood pressure monitor. (Courtesy of Sarah Atwater; see Figure 6.3.)*

- Element (entity) options and trades: identifying at all levels those trades that will provide the best solution for critical parameters
- The flow-down of requirements plus technical, cost, and schedule budgets
- An identification of hardware and software elements as parts of an integrated whole that evidences an integration or assembly

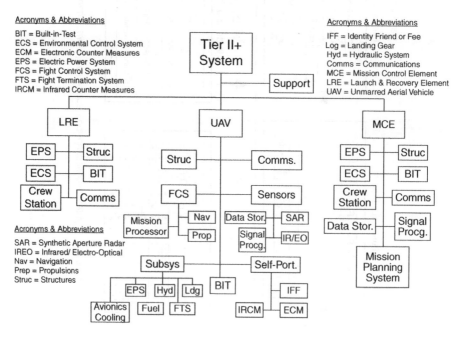

Figure 9.6 *Architectural block diagram: tier II+ system candidate. (Courtesy of General Atomics.)*

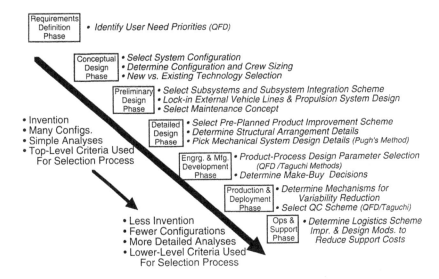

Figure 9.7 *Trade examples in each phase with transition effects. (Adapted from a presentation by Vadym Khaym, Lockheed Martin Corp.)*

- A means of translating the architecture into a work breakdown structure, including being able to designate those elements to be outsourced or otherwise supplied
- A portrayal of the system in sufficient detail to permit change management

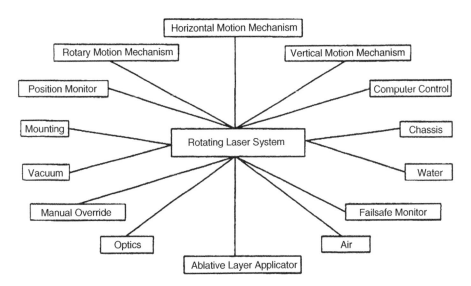

Figure 9.8 *First-level system architecture. (From a University of California–Davis project for the Lawrence Livermore Laboratory.)*

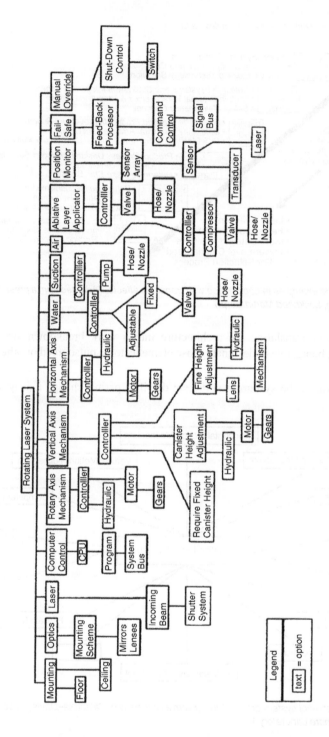

Figure 9.9 System architecture hierarchical (linear) representation. (From a University of California–Davis project for the Lawrence Livermore Laboratory,.)

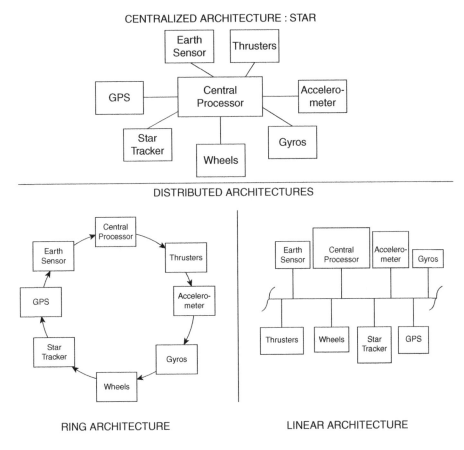

Figure 9.10 *Network architecture bus topologies.*

Although these do not discriminate between hardware and software, their combination is usually expressed separately in architectural descriptions. There are, indeed, some specific considerations for software, either as part of an integrated system or as a product in itself. Some guidelines for this technology include:

- Low coupling among modules is used to build up software capability.
- A high level of cohesion is present among the similarity of tasks within a module in all subfunctions.
- All communications within and between modules employ common databases and clear flow paths.

Then, comparing hardware and software architecture optimization (Figure 9.11), one can readily cite the optimization of resources dealing with physical characteristics, providing for growth and the flow-down of technical and programmatic budgets. For software, resource optimization might include use of modules

Hardware architecture

- Optimize resources for size, weight, and power.
- Provide adequate cooling and maintenance access and room for growth.

Software architecture

- Growth: provisions for increasing the size of existing software and the addition of new software components. Transportability to higher-speed hardware components is desirable.
- Software control/partitioning: operating system should accommodate POSIX online and on-demand integrated diagnostics, reconfiguration, degradation/error handling/exception handling.
- Effective data flow: data storage and retrieval
- Timing and throughput: to satisfy system real-time requirements
- Interface layering and protocol standards: for pilot/crew/maintenance personnel, operating system, display/graphics, networking/communications, sensors, security database management, and software support environment
- Embedded training: inclusion of functions/tasks so that aircrew training can be performed onboard aircraft.
- V & V testing: facilitate software function testing and hardware testing that can be performen by software.

Figure 9.11 *Hardware and software architecture optimization. (Adapted from Boehm,* Software Risk Management.*)*

previously developed and proven, provision for growth and for interface and change management, and an expectation that verification will be readily achievable.

Everhard Rechtin and Mark Maier assembled a number of heuristics, learned lessons, and logic for architectural development. Their book, *The Art of Systems Architecting*, is highly recommended, and we cite here five cryptic postulates drawn from their observations. Some simply reinforce the notes above; others add insightful logic in useful guidelines when designing, evaluating, and even modifying architectures derived in the processes identified to date.

- Relationships among elements is what gives systems their added value.
- The greatest leveraging of an architecture is at the interfaces.
- Success is defined by the beholder, not by the architect.
- Once an architecture is in place, sanity checks on requirements and assumptions must be made.
- Simplify, simplify, simplify!

RESOURCES AND NOTES

The Art of Systems Architecting, 2nd ed., E. Rechtin and M. Maier, CRC Press, Boca Raton, FL, 2000.

This book provides invaluable sets of heuristics, including those associated with software, augmenting those presented in the present book.

Architecting Software Intensive Systems, A. Lattanze, CRC Press, Boca Raton, FL, 2009.

> This unique book recognizes the difference and maturity between hardware- and software-intensive systems. It provides principles for building architectures for information technology systems, simulators, and embedded systems, with an eye toward eventual design.

Understanding Data Communications, G. Held, Wiley, New York, 1997.

> This work provides insights into the many network-related architectures and their interfaces.

The many systems engineering–related books generally treat only the hierarchical approach, but they do provide a wide variety of examples, including decomposition and the trades among sublevels.

Some Web-based or software tools: Microsoft Office (organization charts), Draw Soft, C.

REVIEW CHECKLIST

☐ Does the architecture have sufficient levels of decomposition to provide both material and IT identification as well as to become the basis for work breakdown and outsourcing assignments?

☐ Are still-to-be-considered options identified in some way (e.g., dotted lines)?

☐ Can interfaces be clear or at least inferred?

☐ Are connections between hardware and software clarified?

10

Failure Modes and Fault Tolerance

One virtue of the architecture has been noted as identifying elements and their relationships that could be nodes for potential failure. It is important now to address an understanding of the failure potential and what might be done to ensure value during the product or system life cycle. First, an understanding of terms is important. System and product failure are occurrences that involve loss of function or performance, total or intermittent, causing the product or system to fail catastrophically or in such a way as to permit continuing operation. Although the latter may be in a degraded mode, it is important that it be at least in a safe mode, that is, that it be capable of failing, so that personnel and equipment are secure. Of course, different agencies and organizations may classify failures using other terminology. Recalling the architectural model, the terms used to characterize failure types can apply at any or all levels, from a top-level system down to parts and components. Examples of fail-safe modes include the use of circuit breakers or equivalents, and failure of one engine in a multiengine aircraft.

10.1 CAUSES OF FAILURE

But what are causes of these failures? Figure 10.1 lists some that are worth discussing. Design mistakes, for example are, unhappily, still not that uncommon; there have been bridge and building collapses because all loads were not considered. In manufacturing, incorrect tolerances or mismatching of interface measurements

Product and Systems Development: A Value Approach, First Edition. Stanley I. Weiss.
© 2013 John Wiley & Sons, Inc. Published 2013 by John Wiley & Sons, Inc.

- Design

- Manufacturing/quality assurance

- Operational use

- Field changes

- Environments

- Test setups and processes

- Human error

Figure 10.1   *Causes of failures.*

may cause failures before harm to the end product might occur, but these are still costly in time and resources and cause rework and expensive design changes. Another design-caused problem is the failure to incorporate a capability for verification of product quality or operation before delivering or fielding it operationally. One example is inadequate access to parts or systems that could fail during test or transportation.

Operational use in the wrong environment, or designs inadequate for all potential usage environments, such as for air-cooled vehicle engines operating in a sandy desert without proper screening, are particularly disturbing. Another notable military example is that of a lack of protective armor for vehicles operating in territory where land mines proliferated. Similar issues include functioning in temperature ranges exceeding the designed-for values; the same can be applied to pressure and weather. Other out-of-specification operations can subject a product to loads beyond design allowables, whether structural, mechanical, or electrical/electronic.

Examples of these include electrical power distribution system failures during extended heat waves, causing brownouts, with loss of power to thousands of homes and businesses. Another was fuselage cracking found in the C141 air lifter due to consistent loading of over 30% beyond design limits. Other operationally induced failures can be related to changes or repairs made in field use for which "jerry-built" arrangements and equipment become either necessary or expedient. Wiring around failed circuits and duct-taping loose connections are too common.

Other sources of failures, either during testing or in operation, are faulty test setups that might cause overloads, excessive cycling, or even substitution of parts for expediency. Add the lack of suitable instrumentation, and the many opportunities for disaster are obvious. One such was the explosion of a NASA Ames wind tunnel due primarily to overloading the pressurized test section. Of course, in the latter example human error was involved, just as human error was involved in the Pennsylvania Three Mile Island and Russian Chernobyl nuclear power plant disasters. An interesting list of many failure examples from Otto and Wood's *Product Design* text is shown in Figure 10.2. In particular, note the term *overshooting*, which characterizes the Ames tunnel failure cited.

Every one of the guidelines is based on lessons learned from real failures. A brief reference to some of these is instructive and even fascinating. In the case of a few

Corrosion	Leaking	Scoring
Fracture	Ingress	Radiation damage
Material yield	Vibrations	Delamination
Electrical short	Whirl	Erosion
Open circuit	Sagging	Thermal shock
Buckling	Cracking	Thermal relaxation
Resonance	Stall	Bonding failure
Fatigue	Creep	Starved for lubrication
Deflections or deformations	Thermal expansion	Staining
Scizure	Oxidation	Inefficient
Burning	Ultraviolet deterioration	Fretting
Misalignment	Acoustic noise	Thermal fatigue
Stripping	Scratching and hardness	Sticking
Wear	Unstable	Intermittent system
Binding	Loose fittings	operation
Overshooting (control)	Unbalanced	Egress
Ringing	Embrittlement	Surge
Loose	Loosening	

Figure 10.2 *Failure examples. (Courtesy of Otto and Woods, Product Design.)*

things failing in isolation, the author recalls the major collapse, at a loading of 700 pounds, of the support structure for a winch designed to lift 2000 pounds. The support had a built-in safety factor of 2, but the loads that destroyed the installation arose from the behavior of the winch. It was driven hydraulically, so that with each stop and start, the operation of the pump induced shock loads never considered. Corrective action led to the use of an electric-powered replacement. Another failure to consider interfaces on a systems basis was the breaking of multiple circuits for freezers and air conditioning in a supermarket renovation. In this case the previous system was sustained, even with surges, well below 40 amperes of current load. The new installation operated close to but below this level (which is why no one paid attention), and the first heavy-duty cycle tripped the 40-ampere circuit breakers and shut the system down.

Understanding how to deal with failures or potential failures requires understanding the root causes of the events. Such basic causes seem necessary to know, but it is often much more convenient to fix a symptom rather than the root. For example, many systems exhibit a propensity for more than one type of failure. Often, the response is to fix the perceived basis for each failure as it may happen, although there could be the same underlying cause for multiple failures. An example might be a

Product	Failure or Problem	Cause	Lessons Learned
Elevator Monitoring Data Analysis System	Project Cancelled System SW Not Completed Within Time Constraint	•Project scope, complexity and requirements not available at start	• Good requirements prior to project commit
Lockheed AH-56 Cheyenne Helicopter	Program cancelled Technical problems and cost overruns	•Unrealistic conflicting requirements were accepted	•Validate requirements •Establish suitable acceptance criteria
Kodak Photographic Coating Eqpmt.	Unexpected Quality Loss-High Waste Levels	• Interface dynamics	• Design verification prior to implementation •Process standards
Aircraft Engine High Pressure Core	Excessive Operational Damage from Abnormal Clearances	•Hot shut-down induced thermal rotor bow during starts	• Operational use verification • Robust design
Fiber Optic Transmission System	273,000 Telephone Calls "Dropped" Due to Design Flaw	•System state behavior not fully understood • Testing insufficient	• Careful saving costs • Final validating testing for risk reduction

Figure 10.3 *Product failure root cause analysis. (Note that in this figure the names interposed on the left of the box should be eliminated. Also, the source, B.G. Morais, is cited in Figures 8.5 and 8.9.)*

marginally stressed electronic component in circuitry driving a number of systems, with the result that elements are likely to fail at different times. Another is the reuse of software that does not fail in normal operation, but fails at the extremes of the operating envelope. Figure 10.3 shows some significant examples of failures, together with their causes and impacts.

10.2 FAILURE MODES AND EFFECTS

As is evident from this discussion, failure modes and effects analysis (FMEA) is fundamental to good development and design practice. Although we've mentioned or implied some guidelines above, here are eight that may serve as a checklist, together with Figure 10.4, which describes a format governing analysis.

- FMEA is a systems job; few things fail in isolation or are unrelated in cause or effect to other elements.
- An architecture and schematics are particularly useful in evaluating failure potential and failure modes.
- Interfaces (physical, software, or signal) are prime locations for first looks and include connections of all types as well as elements several nodes farther into the system.
- The performance environment, during operations, maintenance, and even the predelivery test, is critical.
- Documentation is essential for both the analyses and history.

Function	Failure Mode	Failure Cause	Failure Detection	Failure Effect	Failure Compensation	Severity Class[a]
Product or component description	Description of all predictable failure modes	Description of the most probable causes associated with the postulated failure mode	Description of the method(s) by which occurrence of the failure mode is detected	Consequence of a failure mode on the operation or function of a system	Description of compensating provisions or actions that mitigate the effect of the failure (i.e., redundancy, relief devices, etc.)	Assigned to each failure mode to characterize the severity of the effect

[a]**Severity categories:**

- Category I (Catastrophic): may cause death or mission/system loss
- Category II (Critical): may cause severe injury, major property damage, or major system damage
- Category III (Marginal): may cause minor injury, minor property damage, or minor system damage that will result in delay or loss of availability or mission degradation
- Category IV (Minor): not serious enough to cause injury, property damage, or system damage, but will result in unscheduled maintenance or repair

Figure 10.4 *Failure modes and effects analysis. (From* Composite Integration.*)*

- Changes should be assessed in all facets noted above as well as for implied problems caused by accelerated schedules, personnel reallocations, and cost-saving shortcuts.
- Simulation and testing are valuable techniques for discovery.
- Use of averages for any metric is usually invalid since these do not necessarily consider ranges of the parameters that are averaged.

Schematics

The value of the use of schematics was demonstrated during the early period of satellite photographic reconnaissance. After achieving what then appeared to be a difficult-to-improve success rate of 50%, the Lockheed program was challenged by a U.S. Air Force official: "How come you do an excellent job of analyzing what happened with each failure but a miserable job in analyzing why and what could be done to prevent it?" The outcome was a demand to incorporate rigorous systems approaches, including detailed failure mode evaluation of interfaces and at least two nodes beyond each. This effort, including maintaining more critical interface control, was responsible for finding many hitherto unrecognized failure sources, with a resulting improvement to 80% success in about a year, with well over 90% in two years.

Another method of failure analysis is fault tree analysis, built on an architecture of elements, defining the probability of failure at each level. Although the hot water heater example of Figure 10.5 is a bit mundane, it shows two branches of a tree, while more sophisticated is the example of loss of control of an aircraft, illustrated in

- *Fault Tree Analysis (FTA)* is a systematic methodology for identifying a single specific event and determining all possible reasons that could cause that event to occur
  - identifies possible system reliability problems or design defects at design time
  - helps identify root causes of equipment failures and supports failure analysis and corrective action efforts
  - supplies a logical method for troubleshooting and elimination of causes for an observed failure

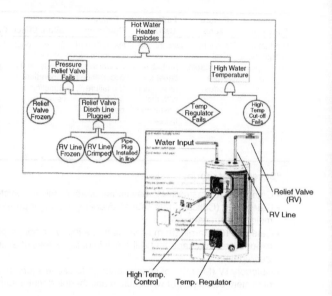

Figure 10.5 Fault tree analysis. (Courtesy of Vadim Kahym, Lockheed Martin Corp.)

Figure 10.6. Each element is shown with its probability of failure, and the cascading upward yields expected failure at the top integration level. But the real reason to focus on understanding failure modes is to provide us with the capability of incorporating in designs or processes the means either to avoid failures or to

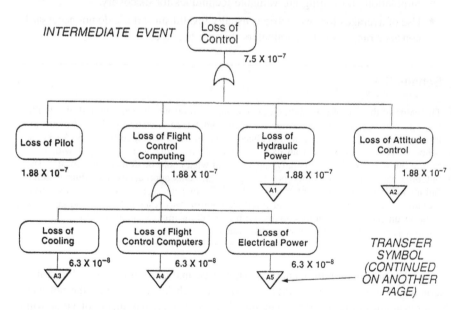

Figure 10.6 Fault tree analysis example: loss of aircraft control. (Courtesy of Vadim Kahym, Lockheed Martin Corp.)

compensate for them. The latter, given the term *fault tolerance*, can be defined as the availability or survivability of critical functions or parameters of a product or system after failure.

10.3 FAULT TOLERANCE

Much as FMEA was cited as a systems issue, it applies as well to fault tolerance. As we discussed, failing "safe," "operational," or "degraded" are the cases we wish to address in making systems fault tolerant. There is also another classification, which one might call "Phoenix," a case where you can fail, return to safety and a place for repair, and then return to operation. This is common for stationary systems as well as for household products and automotive vehicles. Some common, taken-for-granted fault tolerance implementations are emergency brakes, surge protectors, circuit breakers, multiengine aircraft, pacemakers, and the human body itself, with many duplicate physiological systems.

Fault-tolerant system requirements vary from not having any malfunction states, to being able to tolerate more than a single fault, a common NASA requirement where human beings are involved. There are also regulatory requirements from other agencies. The FAA issues airworthiness codes that must be met, such as performance after loss of power, flotation, controllability margins, and fire protection. Human–machine interfaces are covered by the Nuclear Regulatory Commission, with overrides and multiple control options specified. Mine safety is increasingly subject to similar regulations. Some of these are listed in Figure 10.7.

So what design concepts meet these requirements? Figure 10.8 lists many. Some are self-evident; others have rather standard practices for reliability enhancement via redundancy. Isolation may refer to isolating diodes, or bulkheads in fire-prone or

- Airworthiness codes
  - Performance after loss of power(s)
  - Engine rotor burst protection
  - Flotation requirements
  - Controllability margins
  - Fire protection
- Human–machine interaction
  - Overrides
  - Multiple control options
- Testing verification agenda
- Building codes

Figure 10.7 Regulatory fault tolerance requirements.

- Design integrity and quality
- Reliability enhancement
- Isolation
- Failure indications
- Operator procedures

- Design for verification and validation
- Damage tolerance
- Designed in failure paths
- Safety/error margins

Figure 10.8 Fail-safe design concepts.

pressurized compartments. Failure indications and operator procedures imply knowledge of where and what a failure may be. Called *coverage*, this requires the use of sensors and rapid data transfer. Designing for verification, the ability to test or inspect a system for its capability to withstand or contain failures is also critical and may require prototypes or qualification models with or without simulation. Designed-in failure paths occur in many places in society, including truck cutoffs on highways and flood control diversion of river flow. These can also be found in mechanical or structural items, where weak links may be used as mechanical fuses, or stop holes might be drilled in sheet metal to limit cracking anticipated from fatigue.

Most of these concepts rely on using highly reliable hardware or processes. These include high-reliability components such as special-grade parts incorporated in processing, testing, and handling equipment. Reliability and life-cycle testing are also methods; however, when we think of fault tolerance, we usually think of redundancy. This multiplication, or backup, of a primary system with, ideally, no common failure modes is relatively standard practice for all systems or practices seen as critical. Thus, all fault-tolerant systems are designed to be able to deal with at least single-point failures. This requires independence of redundancies, sometimes via dissimilar hardware and software, or at least the preserved potential failure path. All of these must, of course, be verifiable before fielding a unit.

10.4 REDUNDANCY CONCEPTS

The discussion above targeted reliability, the probability of performing successfully in *N* operations. Figure 10.9 is a combination of sublevel reliabilities used to achieve the reliability of a complex product or system. It is influenced by the complexity or number of parts, statistical history of performance, and the sample size that provides this. In sum, designing for reliability involves redundancy, the use of safety factors, and parts selection.

The varieties of redundancies employed have drawbacks as well as benefits. Single-string reliability, that is, reliability composed of a simple series of elements, incorporates diminishing reliability since the top-level figure is derived by multiplication of each unit's reliability. For example, $0.9 \times 0.9 \times 0.9$ for three items in series

- Simplex: single string

- Dual: two in parallel paths

- Triplex: three in parallel paths

- P fail (simplex) = P fail (component) = 1×10^{-3}

- R simplex = $1 - $ P fail (simplex) = 0.999

- P fail (dual) $-$ P2 fail (component) = 0.0012 = 1×10^{-6}

- R dual = 0.999999

- P fail (triplex) = P3 fail (component) = 0.0013 = 1×10^{-9}

- R dual = 0.999999999

- Components assumed to have a mean

- Time between failures of 1000 hours

Figure 10.9 *Parallel redundancy provides increased reliability.*

yields 0.729 for the complete ensemble. Thus, in evaluating designs, it is necessary to flow-down to each element in an architecture the reliabilities that by their combination will yield the desired reliability of the whole. The available reliability of an integrated system is thus determinable by bottoms-up progression.

When fault tolerance or response to predictive failure is discussed, the most common response is "redundancy," and as Figure 10.10 indicates, theoretically, the more the better. But, of course, as noted, this means more parts and complexity and the possibility of being more prone to single-point failures. It also means more weight, more testing, more cost. So what we try to achieve in designing for fault tolerance is how best to provide it for a given circumstance. Choosing the right approach may fall into one or more of several categories of redundancy in various modes.

- Having an element or function in a standby mode that can be initiated either automatically or by command.
- Voting among redundant circuits (usually, three), in which testing of each circuit permits a voting process. If one response disagrees with the other two, in most cases it indicates that the differing line is the failed unit.
- Probably the most beneficial use of redundancy is with cross strapping or providing each element in a line with the ability to connect to any other line in the event of failure of its circuit. This added complexity must be carried out carefully to avoid single-point failures at each connection. A schematic for the approach is shown in Figure 10.11.
- Use of redundancy with analog systems is problematic, although sometimes it is the only choice, because bandwidths for signals can distort comparison measurements.

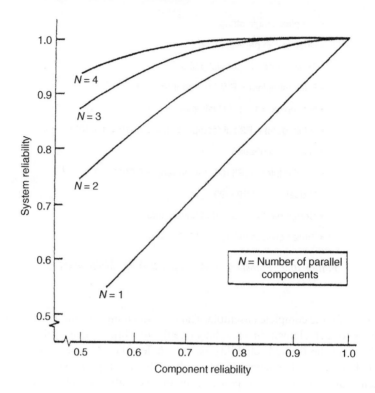

Figure 10.10 *Redundancy provides increased reliability. (From K.C. Kapur and L.R. Lamberson,* Reliability in Engineering Design.*)*

It is useful to observe the reasons for the use of fault-tolerant computers. These deal with complexity and failure potential. One example of massive fault tolerance planning lay with NASA's Space Shuttle. There, extremely high reliability require-ments were set because of human safety and vulnerability: unfortunately, not totally well implemented in the case of their two losses. Figure 10.12 describes the practices that were required, including the questionable use of analog voting by hydraulic

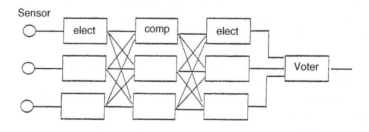

Figure 10.11 *Cross-strapping of channels to avoid single-point failures improves reliability. (Courtesy of the Draper Laboratory.)*

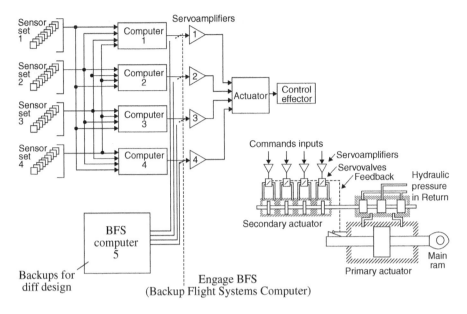

Figure 10.12 *The Space Shuttle's redundant set of computers drives force summing activities. (Courtesy of NASA.)*

actuators, although in a summing mode, to give less chance of false negatives. (Note, however, the last entry, expressing the lack of hazard planning in the failure to include external and environmental impacts on safety and performance—of later disastrous consequences.)

10.5 HUMAN FACTORS AND HAZARDS

While human safety is the initiator of many regulatory fault tolerance requirements, as shown in Figure 10.7, they lead to considerations that add both constraints and complexity that should be addressed at the beginning of the development process. Human safety is, of course, a principal driver in aircraft design, and the Boeing 777 is a significant example. It emphasizes triplex redundancy and vigorous cross-strapping with high independency of each of the more than 1000 nodes in aircraft information and control circuits.

In addition, the 777 Aircraft Information Management System (AIMS) gives the crew the capability of monitoring all nodes to evaluate any failure and its implications, in order to take corrective or fail-safe action as required. This capability in AIMS is evidence of fault coverage, the conditional probability that when a fault has occurred it can be detected, isolated, and recovered from before an unrecoverable event has been introduced into the system. So while redundancy is one avenue toward fault tolerance without coverage, it can be of questionable value. Note also that this leads to considerations of verification of performance and to software error detection (Chapter 12).

Another orientation to the subject is to consider "safeware," a systems approach including hardware and software covering the entire life cycle of a product or system. System safety engineering consists of emphasizing building in safety, in contrast to the use of add-ons that result from operational problems. Recalls of products and ensuing fixes are publicized examples. This perforce includes hazard analysis; although approachable using analytical techniques, it is a topic that benefits greatly from simulation. Additionally, there must be recognition of the importance of consistency of documentation, added to verification of logic and code through simulated operational testing. Of course, the importance of change analysis cannot be exaggerated, as are manufacturing and postdelivery feedback with a recognized safety information system. But overarching is the necessity for a cognizant management structure and process; above all, this is another realm emphasizing life cycle and cost of ownership.

Perhaps some further reference to hazards will be of value. The term *hazard* itself refers to existing or, more important, externally induced obstacles to performance or safety. Reduction or elimination often leads to special consideration of human interfaces, plus the ability to isolate or contain problems. The Three Mile Island nuclear power plant failure took place not because there weren't warnings and a shutoff capability, but because there were three different methods with three different operators—a human performance hazard. The same was true in the destruction of much of NASA's largest wind tunnel at the Ames Research Center. Here, the excess pressure generated in testing the newly modified system was signaled by instruments whose readings were ignored or thought to be in error by test engineers. Additionally, weld joints improperly made were not inspected thoroughly because of confidence in the contractor. Another vulnerable domain is that associated with medical devices and practices, where handling practices involving human interfaces and environments impose hazards. It should also be noted that hazard analysis, usually from external sources to a system, can be seen as a top-down process, while failure mode analysis is more commonly bottom up. Figure 10.13 addresses an array of considerations of hazard reduction and elimination.

Hazard Elimination	Hazard Reduction
• Substitution	• Controllable
• Simplification	parameters
• Decoupling	• Isolation
• Human interfaces	• Containment
• Material/environment	• Safe modes
integration	• Fail-safe design
	• Verification and testing

Figure 10.13 *System safety dealing with hazards, any existing or induced obstacles to performance or safety.*

- Technology delays
  - Backup technology
  - Incremental growth
- Schedule delays
  - Accelerated work
  - Work-arounds
  - Diminished performance
- Cost/finance "failure"
  - Diminished performance
  - Regeneration
  - Reduced quantities

Figure 10.14   *Some programmatic faults and potential fault tolerance.*

10.6 PROGRAMMATIC FAILURES AND FAULT TOLERANCE

There are also numerous programmatically induced faults and potential fault tolerance needs. Among these are technology delays requiring backup technology availability with a provision for incremental growth that permits gradual upgrading as technology becomes available. There are also schedule delays or accelerations requiring accelerated work and with this, the potential for diminished performance and mistakes by the workforce, of which there are plenty of examples. Careful attention and preplanning of work-arounds may be the only acceptable response. Failures or changes in financing can also lead to diminished performance, the removal of key and experienced personnel from a project, delays and difficulties as noted above, and more presumed cost savings without the careful analysis necessary to avoid problematic shortcuts (examples include delays on the Hubble Space Telescope, due to failure to test a critical optical parameter, the NASA Ames tunnel disaster, car deliveries and recalls, and construction failures). Many of these are shown in Figure 10.14.

Although there is a tendency to think of personnel and equipment safety, increasingly the role of software deserves special attention. Just as with hardware, unintended behavior beyond specific requirements or specified boundaries for operations can occur, as can the development of logic and software using incomplete requirements, especially in the face of schedule and cost pressures.

10.7 SUMMARY

In summary, the roster of fail-safe design practices and concepts is sizable and worthy of a checklist, as shown earlier in Figure 10.8. These apply across many domains, where to one extent or another the concepts of fault tolerance are being applied. Most salient are those in nuclear power, waste systems, and many areas of energy creation and distribution. Also, manufacturing systems in many industries, such as complex building construction and chemical and pharmaceutical plants, are examples. Transportation systems beyond aircraft and space are also vulnerable, as are other precision products, such as medical and manufacturing equipment. Finally, the human body itself, partially evolved with numerous redundancies, can utilize many of these fail-safe concepts in increasingly applicable organ and surgical replacements and interaction with remote facilities.

What, then, are the possible impacts of fault tolerance? Potential cost increases can occur from added or special parts and increased signal paths. Then additional spare parts are required, increased weight, added verification in test and inspection, as well as more postdelivery maintenance. All this must be balanced against cost savings due to increased reliability and less in-process maintenance. The contrast must be the basis for critical, often nonintuitive trades, a true cost–benefit analysis.

RESOURCES AND NOTES

Failure Mode and Effect Analysis: FMEA from Theory to Execution, 2nd ed., D. Stamatis, ASQ Quality Press, Milwaukie, WI, 2003.

FMEA is the structured basis for failure analysis, and this book provides a step-by-step process while emphasizing a team approach, with a useful application to electromechanical products.

Design Concepts for Engineers, 2nd ed., M. Horenstein, Prentice Hall, Upper Saddle River, NJ, 2002.

The author considers failure analysis to be a critical part of the design process and relates it to design decisions.

Safeware: System Safety and Computers, N. Leveson, Addison-Wesley, Reading, MA, 1995.

Although the focus in this work is on computers, the approach to failure analysis as it relates to safety is broadly applicable and is included for that reason.

Some Web-based or software tools: Markov diagrams, Monte Carlo and other simulations, Palisade software.

REVIEW CHECKLIST

- ☐ Do failure modes address all internal and external interfaces as well as the environment?
- ☐ How many nodes beyond each interface have been analyzed? At least two?
- ☐ How many levels of the architecture have been addressed?
- ☐ Have the "effects" aspects of the FMEA been examined thoroughly?
- ☐ Has the root cause of each potential failure been identified?
- ☐ What mitigation or prevention techniques have been used?
- ☐ Where redundancy is applied, can it be verified as truly functional under failure?
- ☐ Does this include adequate coverage for the user or automated response system?
- ☐ Are there ways to induce failures validly in simulations?
- ☐ Does the cost of fault tolerance exceed its benefits?
- ☐ In simulating or demonstrating failure modes, have all environments affecting results been considered?
- ☐ Are both pre- and postdelivery failures included in fault tolerance design?

11

Risk Analysis

Whatever is designed, built, and operated involves risks that are intrinsic to a consideration of failures, hazards, and programmatics. Risks are the chances that a system will fail or affect the safety of personnel or equipment, the inverse of reliability from a measurement standpoint; a reliability of 0.9 signifies a risk of 0.1, or 10%. Thus, *reliability* is the probability that things will go right; *risk* is the probability of unwanted occurrences. It is the basis for uncertainty analysis and management. One might say that progressing through the value stream of development, the goal is to decrease the risk of failures of whatever sort—and that is the goal of reliability and fault tolerance.

11.1 RISK PHILOSOPHIES

Since risk influences uncertainty in decision making, the risk philosophy of customers and stakeholders will be a driving influence (Figure 11.1). Every person or organization has a conscious or unconscious risk philosophy, usually culture-related: adventurous and risk willing, or conservative and risk averse. Decisions about how to treat risk are determined by these philosophies. Sometimes this means withdrawal from risky environments; sometimes it means looking at benefits worthy of significant risk taking. Regardless, many elements in the development of products or systems will be affected. The chart used earlier to show that decisions exist at every point along the value stream could have been labeled "risk" existing at all phases of the process as well.

Although understanding failure modes permits compensating for them via incorporating fault tolerance in designs, there is no means by which 100%

Product and Systems Development: A Value Approach, First Edition. Stanley I. Weiss.
© 2013 John Wiley & Sons, Inc. Published 2013 by John Wiley & Sons, Inc.

• Redundancy
• Part Quality
• Material Certification
• Supplier Certification
• People Certification
• Testing
• Testing Environment
• Test Formality
• Inspection
• Design Margins
• Part De-rating
• Audits
	• Walk-throughs
	• Physical Configuration
	  Audit (PCA)
	• Functional Configuration
	  Audit (FCA)
	• Process Control
	• Beta Test
	• Self Test
	• Qualification Margins
	• Consumable Margins
	• Micromanagement
	• Sparing

Figure 11.1 *Ways of implementing risk management. (From Mooz, Khayms, and Weiss, Stanford courses.)*

risk-free expectation can exist in processes, systems, operations, or human interfaces. Defining risk as the chance or probability that a system or activity will fail suggests that the potential consequences are critical. These range from loss of a product to injury or death—in short, the chances and consequences of an unwanted event occurring. Of course, if the sources of risks can be identified, there are means to anticipate, limit, or manage the occurrence, or at least the outcome. Risk management must be an organized, analytical process, first to identify and assess risk items, then to implement appropriate actions for preventing or mitigating them.

Risk is another of those probabilistic considerations that involve either a large sample size permitting statistical expectation, or judgment based on past experience of the same or like product or system elements. But it is also a realm in which highly subjective assessments are made. These tend to fall into such terminologies as "not likely," "low likelihood," "likely," "highly likely," and "almost certain." To use these estimates in any calculations, probability percentages are often ascribed to them, using the judgments of experienced personnel. Figure 11.2 shows reasonable values, and relationships to other common terms, such as "high," "medium," and "low." As one might expect, this approach leads to numbers or predictions with high standard deviations. Although devised for software development, the approach has equivalent relevance for hardware and hardware/software systems.

11.2 RISK MANAGEMENT

Much as in dealing with fault tolerance, the reduction of risk carries costs that must be traded against expected consequences, requiring the same sort of cost–benefit evaluation as with fault prevention. Accordingly, relative risks are significant parameters involved in decision trades. Risk management first requires the identification of risks, then the evaluation of consequences and opportunities for litigation.

Statement

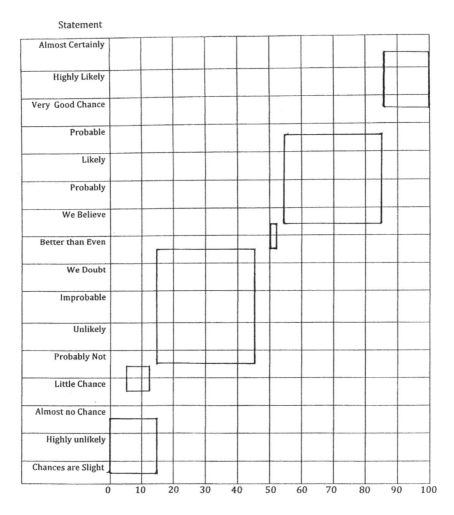

Figure 11.2 *Interpretation of uncertainty. (From Boehm,* Software Risk Management.*)*

But consideration must also be given to the accuracy of predictions and possible outcomes. Averages will rarely suffice in estimating probabilities, as will the failure to take interrelated elements of a system into consideration. Here decision trees have some value, with consequence probability factored by risk probability. The examples shown in Figures 11.3 and 11.4 are useful templates.

Programmatic risks are also often harbingers of project failures. External to technical causes, they include changing market character and trends, funding, political support, and technology availability. Internally, they might include person-nel skills and availability, tool inadequacy, supplier performance, and technology readiness. Figure 11.5 shows levels of technology readiness that are often used to demonstrate the basis for backup planning. The goal is to ensure the availability of

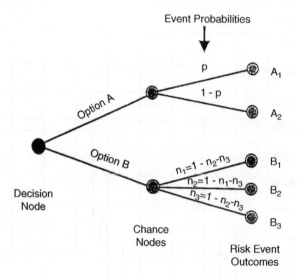

Figure 11.3 *Decision tree for risk events. (Adapted from Sage,* Systems Engineering.)

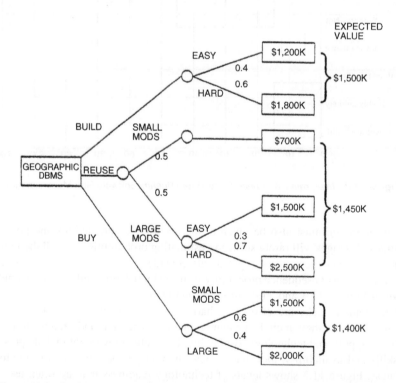

Figure 11.4 *Decision tree analysis example. (From Boehm,* Software Risk Management.)

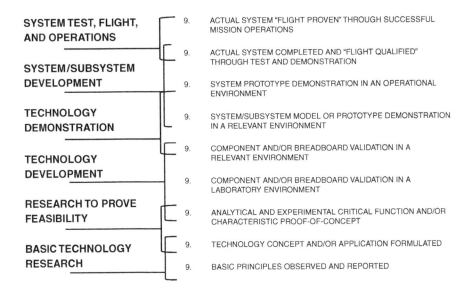

SYSTEM TEST, FLIGHT, AND OPERATIONS
9. ACTUAL SYSTEM "FLIGHT PROVEN" THROUGH SUCCESSFUL MISSION OPERATIONS

SYSTEM/SUBSYSTEM DEVELOPMENT
9. ACTUAL SYSTEM COMPLETED AND "FLIGHT QUALIFIED" THROUGH TEST AND DEMONSTRATION
9. SYSTEM PROTOTYPE DEMONSTRATION IN AN OPERATIONAL ENVIRONMENT

TECHNOLOGY DEMONSTRATION
9. SYSTEM/SUBSYSTEM MODEL OR PROTOTYPE DEMONSTRATION IN A RELEVANT ENVIRONMENT

TECHNOLOGY DEVELOPMENT
9. COMPONENT AND/OR BREADBOARD VALIDATION IN A RELEVANT ENVIRONMENT
9. COMPONENT AND/OR BREADBOARD VALIDATION IN A LABORATORY ENVIRONMENT

RESEARCH TO PROVE FEASIBILITY
9. ANALYTICAL AND EXPERIMENTAL CRITICAL FUNCTION AND/OR CHARACTERISTIC PROOF-OF-CONCEPT

BASIC TECHNOLOGY RESEARCH
9. TECHNOLOGY CONCEPT AND/OR APPLICATION FORMULATED
9. BASIC PRINCIPLES OBSERVED AND REPORTED

Figure 11.5 *Technology readiness level. (Adapted from NASA.)*

necessary technology to satisfy requirements fully or in some acceptable degraded or incrementally improvable form.

Since risk reductions for uncertain technology availability set the stage for planning insertion of backups during development flow, decision points (or gates) can be scheduled. For highly developmental technology, evaluations can be made concerning the use of less developmental, and therefore less risky, replacement, although perhaps on a temporary basis. The timing of this decision should be set to occur by the time that a backup must be initiated to satisfy needed schedules for tests, delivery, or operational capability. At the same time, decisions can be made as to whether and how to continue development of the as-yet unrealized technology.

Barry Boehm, director of the Software Institute at the University of Southern California, has done much in the realm of software risks and extensions to project application. His top 10 software risks are shown in Figure 11.6. These are entirely appropriate for hardware or integrated systems as well, although with software as well as signal sources, timing issues are especially critical. Boehm has integrated risks with actions possible to mitigate these via a management plan applicable to all projects, as shown in Figure 11.7. In particular, the recommendation for standardization facilitates expanding sample sizes as well as a capability to apply mitigation to multiple applications.

Personnel shortfalls are most often related to skill needs. Developing infeasible or incorrect functions with similar properties and interfaces relates to risks that the requirements are not correct or are incomplete, or continually changing. Gold plating, or excessive requirements, are the opposite.

Risk Item	Risk Management Techniques
1. Personal shortfalls	Staffing with top talent; job matching; teambuilding key personnel agreements; training; prescheduling key people
2. Unrealistic schedule and budgets	Detailed multisource cost and schedule estimation; design to cost; incremental development; software reuse requirements scrubbing
3. Developing the wrong software functions	Organizational analysis; mission analysis; operations-concept formulation; user surveys; prototyping; early users' manuals
4. Developing the wrong user interface	Prototyping: scenarios; task analysis; user characterization (functionability, style, workload)
5. Gold plating	Requirements scrubbing; prototyping cost–benefit design to cost
6. Continuing stream of requirements changes	High change threshold; information hiding; incremental development (defer changes to later increments)
7. Shortfalls in components furnished externally	Benchmarking inspections; reference checking; compatibility analysis
8. Shortfalls in tasks performed externally	Reference checking; preaward audits; award-fee contracts; competitive design or prototype team building
9. Real-time performance shortfalls	Simulation benchmarking; modeling; prototype instrumentation tuning
10. Straining computer	Technical analysis; cost–benefit analysis

Figure 11.6 *Software risk item top 10 checklist. (From Boehm,* Software Risk Management.*)*

11.3 RISK MITIGATION PRACTICES

What steps can be taken to mitigate risks, especially with the goal of eliminating risk by the time a product or system is fielded? These lie primarily in planning and management. The first refers to the early and progressive identification and evaluation of risks and attendant consequences. Then there are the trades necessary to make judgments regarding mitigation strategies, including incorporating risk-reduction practices in technical and programmatic domains. Technically, of course, fault tolerance design is risk reduction; others include backup technologies, multisourcing suppliers, and defined work-arounds for schedule impacts. Going back to selecting concepts and architectures, with risk as a criterion, the inclusion of carrying multiple developments and even potential outsourcing in critical, normally in-house-responsible areas must be considered. But with every added consideration for a design, there is the persistent need to trade benefits versus cost (Figure 11.8). Trades can also be made among mitigating practices using comparisons between probabilities of occurrence factored with cost as a determinant.

It was noted that the process of system development involves progressive decreases in the risk of failures. Thus, identification and potential mitigation must be considered throughout the life cycle. As one example, when a backup

OBJECTIVES (WHY?)
  • DETERMINE WYSIWYG EDITOR PRODUCT FEATURES
  • CREATE PROJECT-COMPATIBLE WYSIWYG DEVELOPMENT PLAN

DELIVERABLES AND MILESTONES (WHAT, WHEN?)
  • BY WEEK 3:
    1–TECHNICAL EVALUATIN OF EXISTING WYSIWYG PRODUCTS
    2–USER EVALUATION OF EXISTING WYSIWYG PRODUCTS
    3–ASSESSMENT OF REUSABLE COMPONENTS
    4–STRAWMAN PRODUCT FEATURE DESCRIPTION

  • BY WEEK 7:
    5–OPERATING PROTOTYPE WITH KEY USER FEATURES
    6–STRAWMAN DEVELOPMENT PLAN
    7–REPRESENTATIVE USERS TO EXERCISE PROTOTYPE

  • BY WEEK 10:
    8–USER EVALUATION; ITERATION OF PROTOTYPE
    9–REVISED PRODUCT FEATURE DESCRIPTION
    10–REVISED DEVELOPMENT PLAN

RESPONSIBLITIES (WHO, WHERE?)

  • SYSTEM ENGINEER   : TASKS 4, 6, 9, 10
  • MARKETING MANAGER   : TASKS 2, 7, 8a
  • LEAD PROGRAMMER   : TASKS 1, 5, 8b; SUPPORT TASKS 6, 10
  • PROTOTYPE PROGRAMMER : TASKS 3; SUPPORT TASKS 1, 5, 8b

APPROACH (HOW?)

  • DESIGN-TO-SCHEDULE PROTOTYPING EFFORT
  • EMPHASIZE REUSE, STANDARD INTERFACES
  • USE C LANGUAGE, SHELL SCRIPTS WHERE FEASIBLE

RESOURCES (HOW MUCH?)

  • DEDICATED S.E., L.P., P.P., (10 WK) (3 FSP) ($2/FSP–WK)
  • M.M. DEDICATED IN WKS 1-3, 8-9; PROVIDED BY SOFTWARE HOUSE
  • 4 DEDICATED UNIWINDOW WORKSTATIONS: PROVIDED BY U. MICRO
  • 2 DEDICATED, 2 PART-TIME USERS IN WKS 8-9; PROVIDED BY M. MANAGER
  • CONTINGENCIES

Figure 11.7 Software risk management plan example. (From Boehm, Software Risk Management.)

for a high-risk item is desired, there must be a particular point in the development progress at which to make a determination as to when the primary choice would have to be replaced. As a matter of fact, there could be some risk associated with the preferred backup, and it, too, may require a backup defined to include its own timing for decision.

Figure 11.9 shows the risk planning for an element of the F-22 fighter, the most advanced aircraft of its type in the 1990s. The design called for the use of low-cost thermoplastics, but as the program progressed it became clear that the yield for this material might never equal that required for the vehicle schedule. A second-choice composite material was therefore identified for insertion in the plan at the time of coupon testing of the thermoplastic, and if there were any questions about the success of the second choice, the decision to go for a "last ditch" backup of conventional

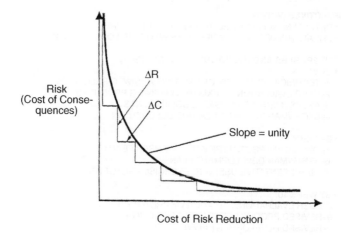

Figure 11.8 *Risk-reduction cost-effectiveness. (From Row,* An Anatomy of Risk.*)*

metals was set for when its lead time would be a schedule driver. Now, if there is still a possibility that the original material, with further design and production research, might be available at a later date, continuing that activity if funds permit is a useful model and could permit insertion in a downstream block of product or system. Clearly, if there are only a few end products to be delivered, that approach is not cost beneficial.

The checklist for software developed by Boehm is, as noted, almost totally applicable to hardware and the integration of these. One salient item is benchmarking, an evaluation of what others have done and what their risk abatement experience has been—either within the organization doing the development or in other

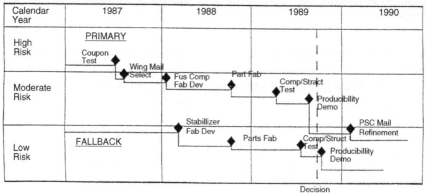

Figure 11.9 *Risk-reduction profile example for the F-22 program. (Courtesy of C. Justice, Lockheed Martin Corp.)*

- Technology delays
  - Backup technology
  - Incremental growth
- Schedule delays
  - Accelerated work
  - Work-arounds
  - Diminished performance
- Cost/finance "failure"
  - Diminished performance
  - Renegotiation
  - Reduced quantities
- Certification and government approvals
  - Safety approvals for medical devices
  - FDA approvals for new drugs
  - EPA approvals of environmental impact statements

Figure 11.10   *Commonly recurring programmatic risks. (Adapted from ISO 14971.)*

companies or organizations. Prototyping and simulations are other means of determining and gaming risks. The former provides a means to test performance and opportunities to demonstrate or find cause and consequence. The latter, with and without hardware in the loop, gives much understanding of interfaces—either to foster standardization or by reducing uncertainty. In addition, programmatics cannot be forgotten, since there are risks intrinsic to funding and schedules as well as management as shown in Figure 11.10. Comments by Sam Savage (a Stanford consulting professor) on dealing with investments that provide insights in many domains, although the terms might have to be altered to fit the circumstance, are featured in Figure 11.11.

Add to these the overall risk of not meeting requirements due to the character of the contract for a given project. Firm fixed price or funding has the highest risk for a developer since it presumes that no funds beyond the fixed price established will be available. For development programs this is clearly not a comfortable approach for the developer or the customer. The problems for the latter may lie with the inevitable changes that induce meticulous cost recovery attempts. If not, a developer out of funds, particularly for an outsourced item, may even drop a project rather than lose heavily or even go into bankruptcy. There have been cases in some major programs where to save a subsystem or equipment development, it has been necessary to send support engineers and process personnel to rescue the project, or, in some cases, even the company. Figure 11.12 shows the progression of financial risk from cost reimbursable to a firm fixed price, with incentive and cost sharing in between.

- Flaw of averages: Make sure that you understand the distribution of data that creates an average as well as the probabilities of the extremes.

- Diversification: Multiple paths reduce risk; choices among options may be apparent just by considering payoff versus risk of individual choices; related to redundancy considerations.

- Portfolio management: Selection by simulation of risk/outcome—an optimization process.

- Uncertainty: Visualization and basis for assessment critical; interdependencies are the real drivers; think of the dependent probability issue.

- Recognize that you never have zero risk or 100% certainty.

Figure 11.11 Principles of programmatic investment. (Courtesy of Sam Savage, Stanford University.)

Factor to be considered	CPFF	CPIF	FPI	FFP
Complexity of item being procured	New or complex item	Complex item	Complex item	Standard commercial or modified
Specification, requirements definition	Soft: changes expected	Adequate for start but some changes expected	Firm but some changes expected	Firm and stable
Desired baseline maturity	Not yet established	Adequate for start but changes expected	Firm but some changes expected	Firm and stable
Cost baseline of item being procured	Uncertain	Reasonable forecast but uncertain	Reasonable to firm	Firm estimate
Desired seller's risk	Minimum	Minimum	Moderate	Maximum
Subcontractor's motivation to control cost	Minimum	Moderate to high	Moderate to high	Maximum

Figure 11.12 Contract risk characteristics. (Adapted from T. Kendrick, Defense Management College, and others.)

Some tools are available to aid this problem of risk management. These fall into the categories of schedule building and uncertainty analysis, such as critical path methods and program evaluation and review, both of which are discussed in Chapter 15. There are also cost-estimating tools such as constructive cost modeling that deal with personnel and schedule estimating, along with a bevy of other cost-estimating methods (also discussed later). There are, in addition, numerous decision support techniques, some of which we discussed in Chapter 8 along with contract and subcontract analyses.

RESOURCES AND NOTES

Reliability Engineering and System Safety, M. Cowing, M. Pate-Cornell, and P. Glynn, HTML, 2004.

This work deals with modeling of trade-offs among safety, reliability, and productivity.

Probabilistic Risk Assessment of Engineering Systems, M. Stewart, and R. Melchers, Chapman & Hall, London, 1997.

This book ranges from identification of risks and modeling of failure modes to assessment of probabilities associated with each of the above. Broadly based coverage, including fault trees and Bayesian approaches.

Identifying and Managing Project Risk, T. Kendrick, AMACOM Books, New York, 2009.

This is an American Management Association publication dealing with the programmatic risks of schedule, economics/funding, and technical issues in major projects.

Some Web-based or software tools: see Chapter 10 plus probability trees.

REVIEW CHECKLIST

- ☐ Are risk/reward ratios consistent with the enterprise as well as with the customer's philosophy?
- ☐ Are controllable risks addressed with mitigation strategies?
- ☐ Are uncontrollable risks identified to the customers as well as the enterprise or organization?
- ☐ Is the limitation to the capability to precisely identify risk probability understood by all stakeholders?
- ☐ Where backups to technical or operational scenarios are defined, are the backups themselves secure or do they need secondary backups themselves?
- ☐ Where risks to funding and schedule are possible, what planning is in place?

12

Integration, Verification, and Validation

Once an architecture identifies the basis for design development and facilitates an understanding of failure modes and risks, there must be assurance that the baseline has been implemented with verifiable quality and that all interfaces are intact. The role of the hierarchical architecture is to define entity relationships so that integration and the satisfying of interfaces are understandable. Adding to this in a system of systems, account must be taken of both inter- and intrasystem interfaces. In every case, integration requires the successive combination and verification of system assemblies, software components, and modules and operator tasks to progressively prove the performance, quality, and compatibility of all elements.

12.1 DEFINITIONS

The process flow for development, the *value stream*, identifies what and when to produce and integrate all the elements of a product or system, once defined. The term *verification* connotes awareness of quality and integrity, or proof of compliance with all definitions of the product or system. *Validation* is the action that proves that stakeholder values have been satisfied with end items and performance. The latter two related terms for ensuring value are often referred to as V&V.

Two other elements of verification and validation, qualification and certification, are accomplished through performance and demonstration. *Qualification* provides proof that the product will survive with margins in the intended performance

Product and Systems Development: A Value Approach, First Edition. Stanley I. Weiss.
© 2013 John Wiley & Sons, Inc. Published 2013 by John Wiley & Sons, Inc.

Predelivery and Shortcuts

The predelivery environment, particularly in test cycles, can also be significant in causing failures. Here the issues lie with handling, overload from power sources, failure of warning systems, excessive temperatures or pressure swings, or human missteps. One study found that approximately 20% of all fixable failures came within test cycles, excluding those induced by quality issues in product design and manufacture.

Short cuts, to save either money or time, have also taken their toll. One of the most egregious was the failure to do a critical test to save money in a cost-overrun program for the Hubble Space Telescope. This failure to screen out aberrations in the optics eventually caused the entire satellite to be retrieved through a Space Shuttle mission and then reorbited, all at a cost of over $1 billion and two years of delay. Others involve fixes for problems arising during operations or in the field. One incorporated wiring around a sensor safety system without feeding this back to the design team. Absent this knowledge, when change kits were incorporated, units with the "fix" became totally disabled.

environment; *certification* is the stamp of approval, usually through a signed certificate, that the product and its performance meet a legally established standard such as those established by the Federal Aviation Administration and the Pure Food and Drug Administration of the Department of Agriculture, the latter basing their premarket approaches on certification by safety agencies such as the Underwriters' Laboratory.

Integration and test planning must be part of the requirements development in a systems engineering and development process. This activity emphasizes the need for designs to take into account how they are going to be verified. Fundamental are considerations of many interfaces and design-influenced processes: access for testing and inspection and tooling for assemblies, supplier involvement in both, as well as interface compatibilities for hardware and software. Relationships among these can also be understood using QFD or N^2 matrices. In sum, design and planning for integration must also facilitate V&V (Figure 12.1).

- Functional flows of the assembly, integration, and tests are critical to optimization.

- Interface analysis includes tools and test equipment as well as hardware and software.

- The test plans at all levels influence system or integrated testing.

- Testing at various levels of componentry through a system involve trade-offs.

- Resources, including personnel and facilities, are part of the trading process.

- Architectural definition of modularity is critical to the manufacturing plan.

- Design reviews must include all the considerations noted above.

Figure 12.1 *Integration and test planning is a systems engineering process.*

12.2 PLANNING ISSUES

In assessing hardware and software issues, it is not unusual to find that customer requirements are often skewed toward hardware (and the allocation between hardware and software treated superficially). Unfortunately, communications between hardware and software developers can be weak links. For that reason, system-executable models or simulations of hardware and software interactions are extremely valuable, and these relationships should be emphasized during design reviews.

Test planning will also govern system and element verification testing at every level of the architecture, from integrated systems through componentry, all often involving trade-offs of level and environments in which to test. Those trades must also include personnel and facilities resources, together with schedules. This can be benefited by considerations of modularity in all aspects of design. As a reminder for the planning phase, methods of V&V as a recipe for reviews and tests are shown in Figure 12.2, with their inclusion incorporated in the overall value stream of development activities.

12.3 DESIGN VERIFICATION AND VALIDATION

How can there be certainty that what is required by customers and stakeholders, let alone the design developers, will be realized? To this end, design verification during the development cycle may be accomplished in many ways. Examples include experimentation at the bench level for new technology at the part and subsystem levels. These serve, in effect, as technical feasibility models or demonstrations, or assembly and test physical fit models, each employed in conjunction with mock-ups or three-dimensional simulation. All methods may be used to solve critical design issues and to substantiate baselines for top and lower system levels. Production or process proofing can also be valuable, with particular attention directed to outsourced elements of the product or system. In some cases, interim acceptance from

- Requirements reviews
  - System requirements review
- Design reviews
  - Concept design
  - Preliminary design
  - Detail design/check
  - Critical design
- Software
  - Requirements
  - Architecture
  - Code
- Testing
  - Development
  - Qualification
  - Acceptance
- Hardware/software simulation
- Process/tool proofing
- Inspection
- Operations/performance

Figure 12.2 *Verification and validation.*

- Requirements conformance
- Design realization evaluation
- Technical availability assessment
- Interface integrity
- Analysis validity
- Simulation integrity
- Software logic/algorithm consistency
- CONOPS linkage
- Element integration: outsourced and supplied

Figure 12.3   *Design verification.*

customers might be valuable. Such a list serves as a sample of the cataloging amplified in Figure 12.3.

The first design verification issue lies with requirement flaws, contained either in ambiguities, conflicts, or excessive demands. Then there considered flows in the design details to be at all levels: unworkable tolerancing, interface mismatching, and in this world of standardization of measurement units, mixed use within an integrated design and, particularly, with a variety of international suppliers. In addition, issues of producibility and testability are concerns. Included in this category is the inability to achieve objectives or requirements with specified technology, use of off-the-shelf or prior-use software and hardware, or simply having an excessively costly solution.

There are also some specific means that may be used for progress measurement. Some, such as design reviews, should be part of the project and value stream schedules. Most should include key stakeholder and supplier involvement. Other specific criteria will be part of the acceptance process, either on delivery by the customer or at interim points for acceptance of subelements, including those furnished by the customer, from suppliers, or with associated entities, external or cooperating, to ensure meeting performance objectives.

12.4   QUALITY ASSURANCE

Inspection and verification are generally referred to as *quality assurance*, which is, in fact, the job of reducing defects and the need for rework in any phase of the development process. One emphasis, process improvement, has progressed from detailed manual inspection of every part, subassembly, and system rigorously, including appropriate tests, to sophisticated computerized sensor-based multi-million-dollar equipment, such as that used in semiconductor inspection, as illustrated in Figure 12.4. It has also changed largely from performing these practices for every entity to using sampling and design-of-experiment techniques to limit the number of parts and test points that it is necessary to examine. This Taguchi method is covered in the Roberts reference.

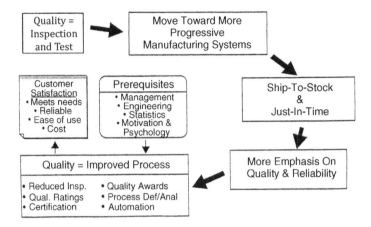

Figure 12.4 *Quality assurance trends. (Courtesy of the Lean Advancement Initiative.)*

There are two factors in the progressive manufacturing realm that permit less inspection at the part and subassembly levels. The first is building into the production "tools" self-checking techniques, providing feedback in automated systems. The second is ownership by the producer or technician of the manufacturing and checking in order to have "first part" perfection. Figure 12.5 shows the progression, in terms of quality practice recognition. In the United States, the Malcolm Baldrige award signals an extremely high order of performance by a company. Recipients include Motorola, John Deere, and Lockheed Martin.

An interrelationship in integration and testing, (Figure 12.6) was viewed earlier to emphasize the impact of interfaces on the value stream. It serves as a reminder that the processes involved in integration, together with V&V, are interwoven. It can also serve as a concept diagram for this phase of the development life cycle and as a basis for users to examine their activities to ensure the inclusion of all players and their roles.

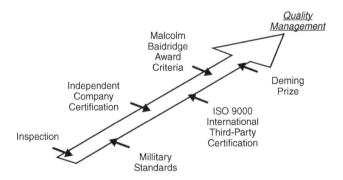

Figure 12.5 *Quality system model continuum. (Adapted from Craig,* No Nonsense Guide to Achieving ISO 9000 Registration.*)*

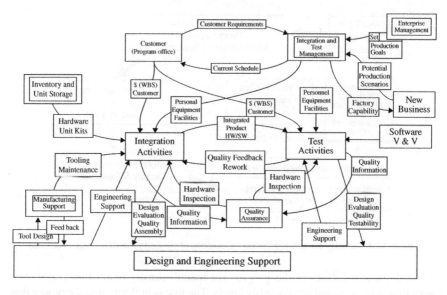

Figure 12.6   Complex interrelationships in integration and testing. (Adapted from multiple flow diagrams.)

During the life cycle, the progression over time applied to validation and verification is shown in Figure 12.7. Analysis is a factor throughout design and is used heavily in its assurance. Inspection, using appropriate methods, carries through from parts, to outsourced materials and elements supplied, to final integration, delivery, and subsequent maintenance during operations. Demonstration and various tests provide the expectation of meeting all functional requirements at every level, especially noting that many test designations extend over the entire period and have numerous overlaps. This also suggests that in tool and equipment planning there should be consideration of multiapplication use.

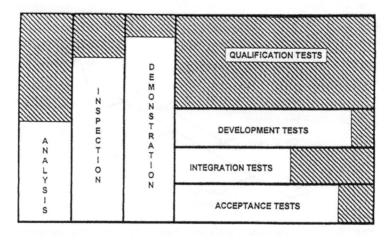

Figure 12.7   Validation and verification progression. (Courtesy of S. I. Weiss and C. Boppe.)

- Customer requirements are often unbalanced on the hardware side.

- Allocation of functions to hardware and software is often treated superficially.

- Hardware and software developers have the weakest communication links.

- From a co-design perspective, software engineers the must late-start
  after hardware and software engineers complete the initial design and specifications.
  In addition, project closure is often delayed until software flexibility is implemented
  to make up for hardware functionality shortfalls.

- System-level executable models of the hardware and software system design
  are often not implemented, and the actual performance of the system is not
  known until all of the hardware and software configuration items are assembled
  and operated. Then change cycles are used to get performance up to specifications.

- Large-block system integration tasks are typically infrequent
  and placed late in the project schedule.

Figure 12.8 *Software and hardware integration concerns and problems.*

It has been emphasized that V&V applies to all levels of the architecture and in all phases of development, from requirements development through demonstrations and qualification. It carries through acceptance at all decision points or gates as part of the integration process and then into operations and maintenance. For hardware, these are at the component, subsystem, and system levels; for software, it applies to the logic design and coding. The methods include analysis, evaluation by similarity, inspection, demonstration, testing and hardware/software in the loop simulation. Thus, each activity must be reflected in the development value stream. In addition, some special issues pertaining to software should be noted. Most are pinpointed in Figure 12.8, paying significant attention to elements that plague hardware and software as integrated wholes: lack of documentation for procedures as well as inadequate record keeping and configuration management. Each of the items shown can foster other fallout but can be mitigated by careful planning and monitoring along the path toward completion.

12.5 TEST CONSIDERATIONS

Planning and adherence to plan, except with careful change control, cannot be overemphasized. Test planning can take the form of the outline in Figure 12.9, with those elements not applicable to the product or system deleted only after careful consideration. In addition, qualification has some special critical issues to be resolved if results are to be validated. Some of these are concerned with a true understanding of operating requirements. There have been too many highly publicized cases of inadequate understanding of loads, whether structural, mechanical, or electrical. Unfortunately, qualification is often expensive, so one can be led to shortcuts by rationalizing similarity to other designs or even to partial simulations or extrapolations of testable environments.

There is a unique regimen that must be considered when only a one-of-a-kind item is available, without the use of a separate qualification unit to permit margins beyond

- Object of test
- Description of unit(s) to be tested
- Test schedule(s)
- Test team
- Evaluations
- Unit tests
  - a. Function
  - b. Performance
  - c. Stress items a and b
  - d. Sample-size selection if appropriate
- System tests
  - a. Functions
  - b. Performance
  - c. Stress items a and b
  - d. Simple-size selection
- Environmental tests
  - a. Temperature/humidity/altitude
  - b. Vibration
  - c. Shock
  - d. Acoustics
  - e. Hostile environment (gaseous, particulate)
  - f. Electromagnetic
- Serviceability
  - a. Diagnostic aids
  - b. Special tools and instruments
- Human factors
  - a. Controls
  - b. Indicators and displays
  - c. Anthropometric dimensions
  - d. Product organization
  - e. Input formats and procedures
  - f. Output formats and display message/screen design

Figure 12.9   Example of a test plan outline. (Adapted from Boehm, Software Risk Management.)

operating loads to be applied with confidence. One must also take into account the accumulation of energy from multiple tests induced by acceptance, demonstration, and qualification. A valid answer in this case is to produce a single unit with built-in margins or safety factors higher than normal, often in the range 25 to 50%. Many very large construction projects, such as bridges and complex buildings, fit this approach, as do NASA's one-of-a-kind space systems.

There is, however, a rational basis for levels of testing applied progressively through the chain of events leading to delivery. Essentially, this test funnel concept

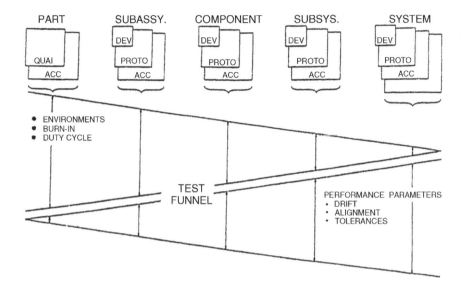

Figure 12.10 *Test funnel concept minimizes system-level test downtime. (Adapted from Forsberg et al.,* Visualizing Project Management.*)*

(Figure 12.10) states that the strongest environmental test levels may be applied at the lowest levels of product architecture and assembly, progressively narrowing the funnel with high assurance in the elements that make up the assembled system to ensure minimizing problems in integrated testing.

RESOURCES AND NOTES

CAPP: From Design to Production, J. Tulkoff, Editor, Society of Manufacturing Engineers, Dearborn, MI, 1988.

This is a major work, with many contributors, covering everything from small parts to assemblies with the benefits of computer-aided manufacture.

Space Mission Analysis and Design, 3rd ed., J. Wertz and W. Larson, Editors, Microcosm Press, Kluwer Academic, Norwell, MA, 1999.

Although this is a system engineering–focused book, it does contain one of the only thorough discussions on testing for verification and validation, including critical environments.

Quality Assurance in Research and Development, G. Roberts, Industrial Engineering Series, Marcel Decker, New York, 1983.

This book describes a relatively early approach citing the elements of quality assurance and means of verifying quality in R&D, where it is often neglected.

REVIEW CHECKLIST

☐ Does integration follow a value stream approach? Does it follow the architecture? If not, should one or the other be revisited?

☐ Are interfaces critically reviewed for tolerancing with hardware, electrical compatibilities, and timing issues with software?

☐ Has provision been made for delivery and incorporation of outsourced elements?

☐ Are interface control documents in place?

☐ Is verification planning governed by requirements documentation as well as drawings?

☐ Has the potential of test equipment to cause failure of equipment being tested been considered?

☐ Are all environments to be encountered incorporated in the test program or adequate simulation provided?

☐ Are there provisions for recording of all inspection and testing results?

☐ Have the levels and sequence been planned so that testing can be done most efficiently and cost-effectively?

13

Integrated Product and Process Development

It is now time to think about how to generate the best outcomes in the development processes discussed so far. Noted many times are the difficulties in trying to arrive at complete stakeholder sets and development of priorities that lead to requirements. In addition, it has hopefully become clear that decision processes involving individual judgments may inflict bias or limited knowledge on the outcomes. But often cited has been a need for the involvement of others who have expertise and experience in all of these efforts; this is the use of teams and teamwork. In addition, the involvement of critical stakeholders in many of these activities can ensure that their inputs are considered where vital, as well as fostering the negotiations and compromises that will yield outcomes meeting the expectations of customers and operators as well as other interested parties.

13.1 DEFINITIONS

The term *integrated product and process development* (IPPD) involves doing the job in a multidiscipline fashion involving key individuals and groups as a team. Applying this approach in development should involve team establishment as early as possible, particularly starting with any phase involving multiple disciplinary contributions, such as requirements development. It is also a technique used in addressing critical activities such as the evaluation of failures and accidents. Thus,

Product and Systems Development: A Value Approach, First Edition. Stanley I. Weiss.
© 2013 John Wiley & Sons, Inc. Published 2013 by John Wiley & Sons, Inc.

IPPD definitions carry the elements of multiple disciplines and teamwork in their expression:

- A process that utilizes the expertise of functional disciplines to integrate and act concurrently to develop and produce a product that meets customer and user needs.
- A methodology that uses a systematic approach to incorporate all facets of the life cycle of a product or system through concurrent application of disciplines involved in every phase.
- A modification of concurrent engineering that treats all product and process aspects of the life cycle, with the expectation that one can get the best performance and cost with the minimum possible need for rework (Figure 13.1).

Complex development almost always requires parallel activities, so *concurrency* and *IPPD* are complementary terms. Regardless of the extent of parallelism, integration is necessary throughout development so that interdisciplinary and related information flow in continuum. The same is true for supplier activities and the involvement, or at least knowledge, of customers and critical stakeholders. These considerations certainly drive organization design, much as was possible by the teams described at Toyota and Honda.

This approach is also a means of optimizing the character and utility of architectures and the deployment of their elements. Many elements of process and design development require integration of all disciplines. In small projects, the participants usually operate intuitively in team fashion. In very complex projects, there are simply too many disciplines and stakeholders to have all the implementers in a single unit where everyone knows and does everything. Thus, the creation of teams representing elements defined by the product or system architecture becomes the means of incorporating all disciplines in what we call *integrated product teams* (IPTs).

- Complex developments require many parallel activities.

- Integration among system elements is necessary during their development.

- Interdisciplinary information flow leads design and organization decisions.

- Nonconcurrent effort requires "stakeholder" concurrent knowledge.

- IPPD involves stakeholders from full product development and operations cycle.

- Product elements making up a system product require integration.

- Integrated product teams must therefore themselves be integrated.

Figure 13.1 *Concurrency and IPPD.*

13.2 INTEGRATED PROJECT TEAMS

It is interesting to note that Toyota and Honda were innovators of the IPT approach. Their model is shown in Figure 13.2. While in some measure they were extending the "skunkworks" model of the U.S. aircraft industry, they were in fact used as role models in a number of nonaerospace firms in the United States, such as General Motors' initial Saturn plant in Tennessee. One precept was that personnel assigned to a team served as representatives of key stakeholders and as a liaison to all disciplinary areas involved in production of the product. Another precept emphasized continuity of personnel, so that knowledge remained connected throughout the development and initial production phases of the life cycle. In addition, each team member was empowered to stop activity if there were defects or aberrations and to have the team address causes and corrective action. The silo world of post–World War II America was the antithesis of the IPT concept, although this approach is now a focus of reform in current industry practice. The Toyota–Honda approach first focused on production issues, and IPTs were often established to solve factory problems in Kaizen or red team events. This approach, adopted initially by U.S. auto firms for manufacturing, in recent years has migrated to engineering and development. Other applications of this lean practice are described in Chapter 15.

The virtues of the practice include establishing more alternative solutions to problem decision making, together with early and continuing design review, all necessitating common tools and databases for every activity. The inclusion of early supplier involvement is another valuable asset. Key outcomes are the occurrence of fewer changes and rework as a result of common understandings, and rapid interchange of information as well as more rapid closure in dealing with problems—thus yielding reduced errors and data transfer time. Since this approach must be invoked at the front end, some see it as front-end loading of costs and schedule, which it usually is, but the end result is a shortening of the total cycle time and

- Tightly knit teams
  - Use of matrix with functional experts from all affected and affecting disciplines assigned to teams
  - Market assessment
  - Product planning
  - Styling
  - Detail engineering
  - Production engineering
  - Factory operations

- Continuity
- Personnel on teams retained continuity through vehicle development and into production

Figure 13.2   *Honda Accord model cases. (For cars of comparable performance and capacity, Honda used about 485 engineers to about 900 for Chrysler.) (From Womack et al.,* The Machine that Changed the World.*)*

- Average makeup for complex products: 45% engineering, 15% manufacturing,

  13% management/material, 7% operations

- Membership: 10 to 40; full-time core, part-time specialists

- Supplier and customer involvement are benefits

- Organization: generally follows product architecture

- Applications: new products, upgrades, new processes and technologies, failure analysis

Figure 13.3 *Integrated product team characteristics. (Penn State University Industrial and Manufacturing Engineering, from D.A. Nembhard, Cross training research for Lean Advancement Initiative.)*

leveraging of these early costs. There are many case studies from a variety of industries and postdelivery activities such as maintenance and repair facilities. Included are the aerospace industry, automakers, farm machinery and pharmaceuticals manufacturers, defense maintenance and supply depots, and an increasing number of more retail-oriented companies.

The characteristics of integrated product teams reflect principally the involvement of engineering, manufacturing, material, and operations segments, with supplier and customer involvement an added advantage. A representative personnel breakdown for complex products might be 50% engineering, 25% manufacturing and quality assurance, 13% project management and materiel, 7% operations, with the remainder made up of customer and/or suppliers. Membership of 10 to 40 full-time core and part-time specialists represents approximately the minimum to maximum levels. Figure 13.3 presents a summary of the makeup of an IPT.

Except for small tightly knit projects, say one incorporating an engineering shop, the description above does not at all suggest inclusion of an entire projects organization in a single IPT, as one company vice-president proudly proclaimed for his 1200-person program. These are also just reference guidelines, since all projects have a different makeup of stakeholder and producer involvement. The use of the team will vary depending on its employment in design development or for such efforts as failure analysis and corrective actions. For example, in medical device development, it is critical to included quality assurance, legal and regulatory affairs, compliance, and often, source and maintenance representation.

One notable example was the use by the then McDonnell Douglas firm (now Boeing St. Louis) for the F-18 E&F fighter, with the teams defined as in Figure 13.4. Emphasis is on the fact that concurrent consideration of all requirements necessitates the existence of a multidisciplinary team. At this point the only participant lacking was the customer. In a later project by the same contractor, a customer representative was on site and a member of the IPT from the very beginning. His ability to respond to issues, including the approval of changes, was significant in beating both cost and schedule targets. It is worth noting that the General Motors' practices that made them a liability to their shareholders and the buying public have, coincidentally, been changed with the management strategies that rescued them from bankruptcy.

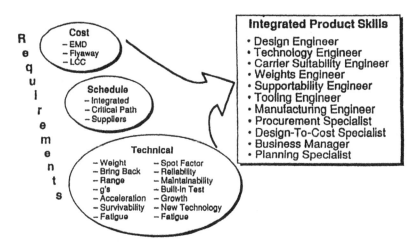

Figure 13.4 *Boeing (formerly McDonnell Douglas) approach to F-18 E&F aircraft. (Courtesy of Boeing for the Lean Advancement Initiative.)*

In particular, the introduction of lean practices, including IPPD, has had a beneficial effect. In terms of IPTs, the powertrain division has incorporated a number of teams, corresponding to the powertrain architecture. The assignments shown in Figure 13.5 identify these teams with their intersections for communication and transfer of data and the possibilities for common use of specialists in overlapping areas.

Another question lies in how teams can be assembled and integrated. An extensive study conducted by Pennsylvania State University's Industrial Engineering Department identified technologies, processes, and interactions (Figure 13.6). The first recognizes communication of information and management decision making. The need for strong and supportive project management, with key disciplines reporting directly, is critical, as are the environments in which the tasks are carried out, in

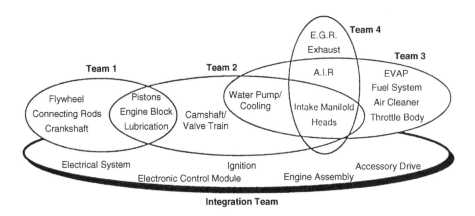

Figure 13.5 *Product-to-system team assignments. (Courtesy of General Motors Research.)*

- Information technology
- Communication technology
- Management hierarchy
- Heavyweight project manager
- Conflict-resolution engineers
- System engineering
- Task forces
- Town meetings, interteam communications
- Technically independent teams
- Engineering liaisons

Figure 13.6 *Mechanisms for integrating teams.*

addition to systems engineering practices, technically independent self-supporting teams, and the organizational facilitation.

Participants must, of course, be flexible, experienced people, to ensure their ability to deal rapidly with new products, upgrades, new processes and technologies, and failure analyses using corrective action. Figure 13.7 is a Venn diagram showing

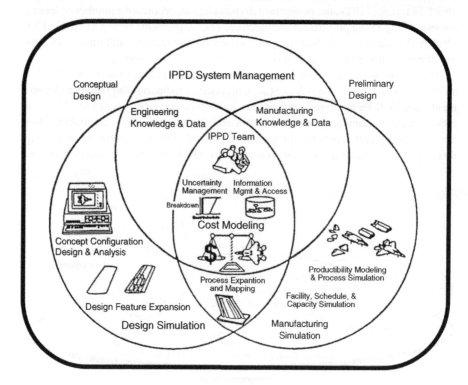

Figure 13.7 *Advanced design IPPD environment. (From D. Schrage, Georgia Institute of Technology and AIAA course instructor.)*

Other IPT Applications

It is common to pull together teams to solve quality, schedule, or operational problems. These usually involve experts in the problem area to apply their knowledge collectively The difference between these and conventional IPTs is that the latter are multidisciplinary groups generally applying their expertise in multiple areas toward development or other process-oriented issues. There has been a growing recognition, however, that a multi-disciplinary approach to the solution of special problems has many advantages. Thus, the shuttle failure investigations included experts from specific technical domains, such as physics, rocketry, failure analysis, and psychology, as well as in the normally suspected realms for failure. Another example existed in solving the cause for failures in tests of a major U.S. Department of Energy development. A team or true IPT involving people from fields ranging from materials to probability with the addition of systems engineers was established, with resulting identification of the cause as well as the direction toward solutions in less than two weeks versus the months-long lack of problem resolution by standard design and functional support personnel. The interaction of perceptive, if unrelated participants can often unearth unexpected solutions.

the intersection of IPPD with other aspects of the design phase. Integrated product and process teams (IPTs), with membership established for significant elements of the work breakdown structure, must themselves be integrated at the top of the product or system architecture.

13.3 IPPD BENEFITS

So how do we measure the benefits of IPPD? Are there real metrics? Many are quantifiable by making comparisons with previous ways of doing a job. They may include such reductions as drawing and specification release times; even more significant is reduction in design changes and, most important, customer response, especially to the degree of cost/price/return on investment achievement. Figure 13.8 shows the impact on change traffic with IPTs on a "partnered" or customer-inclusion basis versus those experienced previously. Other results, shown in Figure 13.9, indicate the variety of industries that have benefited. Another benefit identified at Cal Tech's Jet Propulsion Laboratory and studied at Stanford's Center for Integrated Facility Engineering is the reduced latency in reaching design or problem-solving solutions. Consequently, where normal practices in serial-based activity may have standard spans, the use of teams has been shown to reduce schedules by factors of 5 to 10. This also facilitates the iteration of solutions with much less schedule impact.

What, then, can we call key lessons learned using IPPD? First, the team must consist of true believers in the method. Second, it must be multifunctional, with personnel co-located either physically or virtually. Third, there must be linkages with ready response capability for all functional activities. Fourth, the customer should be "on board" either in person or at least virtually and interactively. Fifth, this must also apply to suppliers. Sixth and finally, all involved, including supporting upper

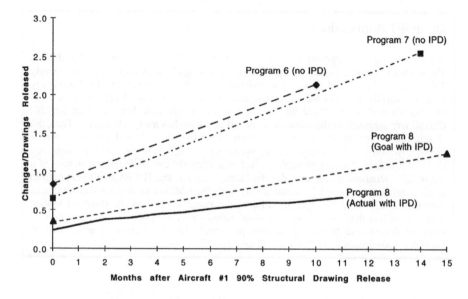

Figure 13.8 Industry example of design changes made over time during a "partnered" project. (Courtesy of the Lean Advancement Initiative.)

management, must remain focused on the task. Thus, starting with a clear statement of purpose and objectives, tracking of progress and action items requires frequent status meetings as well as rapid detection and resolution of problems and bottle-necks, both technical and programmatic.

Company	Cost	Schedule	Quality
McDonnell Douglas Missile Systems	60% savings on bid for reactor and missile projects	18 month savings on TAV-8B design	Scrap reduced 58% rework cost reduced 29% and non-conformances reduced 38%
Boeing Ballistic Systems Division	30% below bid	Parts and materials lead-time reduced 30%	99% defect-free operations
AT&T	Cost of repair for new circuit pack production cut at least 40%	Process time reduced 46%	Defects reduced by 30% to 70%
Deere & Company	30% actual savings in development cost for construction equipment	60% savings in development time	Number of inspectors reduced by two-thirds
Hewlett-Packard Instrument Division	Manufacturing costs reduced by 42%	Reduced development cycle time by 35%	Product field failure rate reduced 60%; scrap and rework reduced 75%
IDA Report R-338	**30-40% improvement**	**40-60% improvement**	**50-75% improvement**

G4146-7B

Figure 13.9 Some published results. (From Womack, Roos et al., The Machine that Changed the World, and the Lean Advancement Initiative.)

RESOURCES AND NOTES

Agile Competitors and Virtual Organizations, S.L. Goldman, R.N. Nagel, and K. Press, Van Nostrand Reinhold, New York, 1995.

> Although interaction through computer networks has advanced in the past decade, this description of how interdisciplinary teams can enhance performance in many environments and can use technology to solve the need to integrate experts from remote sites provides a basis for further use of technology in emphasizing the benefits of teamwork.

Planning, Performing, and Controlling Projects, 3rd ed., R. Angus, N. Gundersen, and T. Cullinane, Prentice Hall, Upper Saddle River, NJ, 2002.

> This dense book discusses team activities in the life-cycle phases of projects from design through development and implementation.

Concurrent Engineering Approach to Materials Processing, S. Dwivedi, A. Paul, and F. Dax, Editors, The Minerals, Metals and Materials Society, Warrendale, PA, 1992.

> This 20+-year-old tome is recommended for its many descriptions of concurrent interdisciplinary engineering and the inclusion of suppliers, the latter only recently accepted as good practice, and a derivative of the Toyota manufacturing system.

Nearly all current books on design and manufacturing practices emphasize the importance of teams. Many confine this to engineering phases, but increasingly these teams are carried through the development life cycle. The concept is also a key to texts focusing on lean, agile, and six sigma approaches. Notably, they include product design and development, visualizing project management, development performance, lean enterprise value, and lean enablers for systems engineering. These have appeared earlier or are identified more specifically in later chapters.

REVIEW CHECKLIST

- ☐ Have participants in IPTs included all multidisciplinary contributors?
- ☐ Are they sufficiently expert in the domains represented?
- ☐ If dealing with supplied or outsourced elements, are suppliers included as part of the team?
- ☐ Are team leaders trained?
- ☐ Are IPTs constrained to no more than 40 or fewer than eight in number? If not, why is this appropriate?
- ☐ Are common IT, databases, and communications being used by all?
- ☐ If there are multiple teams within a project, is the means for integrating them in place?

14

Design for X

Another facet of interdisciplinary team play is the enhanced capability to support designing for multiple purposes. The involvement of all stakeholders in the IPPD process facilitates the practice commonly known as *design for X* (DFX), X representing many necessary postdesign activities, the best known being design for manufacturing and assembly and design for or to cost. But a host of "design-for's" are possible. Some of these, such as design for testing and inspection, are to ensure provisions for access for equipment and personnel, with the same considerations as in designing for maintenance and repair as well as for downstream upgrading or incorporation of technologies. Clearly, having a design team that includes personnel directly responsible in these areas is a major contribution. One other X, considered too infrequently, is designing for outsourcing, with careful consideration of interfaces, delivery schedule needs, technology development, and other integration issues. In a sense, the Xs reflect an identification of all facets implied by the full body of requirements. Figure 14.1 shows this linkage in designing for cost, performance, and availability.

As noted above, designing for cost is a common target, but many elements affect cost and cycle time. This list of factors (Figure 14.2) indicates the complexity of the issues that must be addressed. Another set of considerations applies to designing for manufacturing and assembly. Simplicity is a key mantra. One such example is the use of laser alignments for large structures rather than expensive complex tools and fixtures.

Similarly, designing for serviceability emphasizes access and simplicity of interfaces with obstructive or sensitive equipment. The same considerations apply in designing for upgrading and technology insertion. Finally, designing for outsourcing goes back to the architectural configuration that defines work packages.

Product and Systems Development: A Value Approach, First Edition. Stanley I. Weiss.
© 2013 John Wiley & Sons, Inc. Published 2013 by John Wiley & Sons, Inc.

What?		
Cost	Performance	Availibility

How?

Simplicity	Reliability
Quality	Safety
Technology insertion	Change
Manufacturing. assembly	Test
Inspection	Maintainability
Operations	Sustainment
Procuremnt	

Figure 14.1   *Design for "What" and "How".*

- Size of the program buy
- A priori cost estimates
- Requirements stability
- Technology risk
- Perceived industry capability
- Number of contractors
- Head count
- Number of review steps
- Quality of system design

- Production rate
- Profitability
- Funding stability
- Skill mix
- Actual capability
- Experience
- Productivity
- Communications
- System management

Figure 14.2   *Factors affecting cost and cycle time.*

This consideration can be tabulated as in Figure 14.3. But, of course, this has touched on only some of the X's that prove significant. All of the so-called "-ilities," such as reliability, testability, adaptability, environmental suitability, as well as technology insertion anticipated, are considerations for true system thinking in design development. It is also interesting to note the guidance the Defense Systems Management College provides in its program for project management. It contains many of the terms and "design for" recommendations as have been described earlier in this chapter.

- Establish architecture with work packages in mind.

- Establish elements with common process needs and capabilities.

- Modularize wherever possible.

- Ensure that interfaces with in-house and other outsourced elements are defined.

- Assure communication among outsourced elements wherever possible.

- Use integration sequences as a means of defining outsourced elements.

Figure 14.3   *Design for outsourcing.*

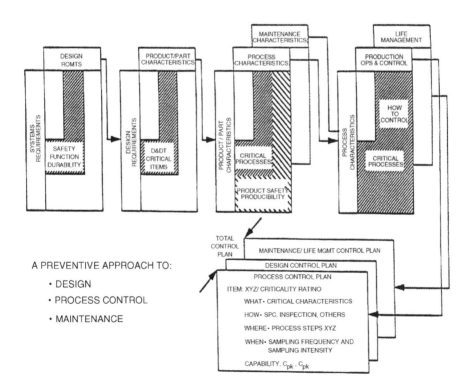

Figure 14.4   *Design for outsourcing.*

RESOURCES AND NOTES

Product Design and Development, 2nd ed., R. Egpert, High Peak Press, Meridian, ID, 2010.

Like its predecessor by Ulrich and Eppinger, the need to include in designs the capability to manufacture and assemble is stressed in this work. Also noted are considerations of designing-in provisions for reliability and maintenance and the benefits of interdisciplinary teams to make this possible. However, no reference specifically addresses the need to design-in provisions to facilitate outsourcing or subcontracting.

Product Design: Techniques in Reverse Engineering and New Product Development, K. Otto and K. Wood, Prentice Hall, Upper Saddle River, NJ, 2000.

Some of the limitations of the source above apply; however, this book does stress modularity and platform approaches that lend themselves more readily to outsourcing, for both manufacturing and engineering design.

These methods are often seen as outgrowths of integrated product development, with the multidisciplinary team character making the broader design impacts possible. Reference to the need for such teams appears in most modern books on design and as cited in the references in Chapter 13.

A DFX Tool: Springer Link.

REVIEW CHECKLIST

- ☐ Are representatives of the "design for" activities represented as part of the design team?
- ☐ When designing for outsourcing, are the potential suppliers involved with most contributive timing?
- ☐ When designing for manufacturing and assembly, are the tools or fixtures considered?
- ☐ Are the suppliers of such equipment and controls part of the design team?
- ☐ Has designing for acceptance of all types of changes been included?

15

Development Management

Since the entire product development process is implicitly a management process, programmatic issues such as schedules, costs, organization, and application of skills that can affect the success of a project must be established and controlled. Successful performance in these areas may be a deciding factor in ensuring continued support for a project, within a larger corporation as well as with the customer. Any management plan must therefore define these so that all players understand the goals and ground rules and how they will be achieved. Clearly, communication using common language and databases are important requirements for success.

15.1 KEY INTEGRATIONS

One way of looking at the development management process is shown in Figure 15.1 a diagram linking key practices and their organizational relationships. The emphasis on planning includes the flow of value-creating activities; budgeting both performance and programmatic targets for the groups responsible for these actions; and setting the bases for monitoring and, if necessary, adjusting metrics and goals. The ensuing performance against these targets falls in the category of project control, with periodic reviews of progress against expectations, resolution of issues in achievement and provision for the negotiation of any changes induced or introduced. Regardless of successes or failures, there are always lessons to be learned that require analyses and documentation that hopefully will benefit subsequent activities or projects. Delivering value also requires maintaining status and issues with customers, key stakeholders, and internal management facilitating rapid resolution of problems.

Product and Systems Development: A Value Approach, First Edition. Stanley I. Weiss.
© 2013 John Wiley & Sons, Inc. Published 2013 by John Wiley & Sons, Inc.

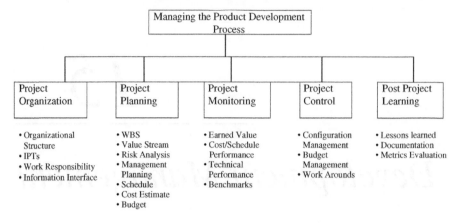

Figure 15.1 *Developing management architecture.*

The considerable time spent in creating a functioning architecture for a product or system has as one leading payoff the defining of a product or work breakdown structure. From a management standpoint, the architecture shown in Figure 15.1 is an expression of where and how these tasks are planned, executed, monitored, and controlled and where key integrations must take place, at all levels. This definition of interfaces is critical not only in work assignments, but also as an element of working effectively with supplier and outsourced increments of the integrated whole.

15.2   STRATEGIC APPROACHES

A number of strategies can drive development approaches. One is to get to market rapidly to preempt competition, incorporating new technology as rapidly as possible. Another is to incorporate technological improvements after initiating a product with limited but useful early capabilities. There are strategies that derive from specific development goals and delivery definitions.

As shown in Figure 15.2, the term *unified development* most often matches our concept of products: delivery of an item usable by a customer as is. *Incremental development*, on the other hand, is a modular delivery concept, with elements delivered over time, either to enhance utility or, in some cases, to provide elements to the user for familiarization and training prior to full deployment. Similarly, *linear development* refers to development along a linear value stream for a completely integrated system, as opposed to a planned evolutionary approach akin to the modular definition above. One consideration often overlooked by ardent developers is the influence of delivering one- or few-of-a-kind systems versus systems delivering multiple quantities. The latter must have facilitated, in the design itself, those processes that can be repetitive for all participants contributing to the value stream. The former has its own issues of limits to testing and handling and the need for an emphasis on simulations.

- *Unified development*: development as a single entity: a lump

- *Incremental development*: development of modules for later integration: may be performed over time to add capability in stages

- *Linear development*: development in a single pass without experimentation

- *Evolutionary development*: development of successive versions to benefit from the experience of previous versions or to respond to new requirements performed over time to add capability in stages

- *Single delivery*: one planned delivery

- *Multiple Deliveries*: planned or unplanned delivery of successive increments or versions of increments

Figure 15.2 *Development and delivery definitions. (Based on material in Forsberg, Mooz & Cotterman,* Visualizing Project Management.*)*

15.3 MEASURING PROGRESS

The importance of considering the entire life cycles of products or systems cannot be overstated. Implicit is the expectation that there will be steps along the value stream to provide events or gates that will govern continuing without waste or needed recoveries. These decision gates reflect significant completion of process intervals or the necessity of introducing changes in the flow. This evidence of progress drives the approval to proceed as well as the use of allocated resources. The flow can be linked to several delivery approaches. The following charts identify steps or processes in the value stream to delivery. The first, Figure 15.3, is a reminder of the role that initial values play and identifies the many elements introduced by the development culture

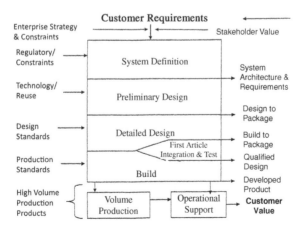

Figure 15.3 *Process to realize customer value.*

Even research can be managed to the
logic of a project cycle

Portions of this cycle may precede a
development project cycle

Basic Research			Applied Research			Optimized Research		
Establish Objectives	Prepare the approach	Conduct Research	Establish Objectives	Prepare the Approach	Conduct Research	Establish Objectives	Prepare the Approach	Conduct Research
1	2	3	4	5	6	7	8	9	10

Decision Gates

Figure 15.4   *Research project cycle. (From Forsberg et al.,* Visualizing Project Management.)

of an organization. The next two reflect on the phasing of activities and specific decision gates. Figure 15.4 shows that even in a research-based project, an approach that incorporates decision steps can be valuable; another example of interest is the Six Flags amusement park project (Figure 15.5), with the decision points noted for critical funding steps.

At any rate, when a project has many elements of complexity, particularly when there are numerous stakeholders, sponsors, and partners, the necessity for order and

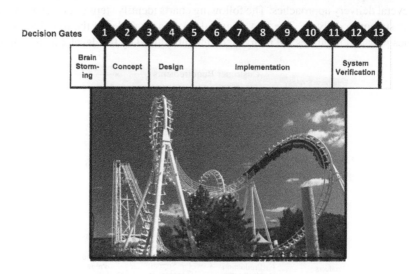

Decision Gates												
1	2	3	4	5	6	7	8	9	10	11	12	13

Brain Storm- ing	Concept	Design	Implementation	System Verification

Figure 15.5   *Amusement park developer project cycle. (From Forsberg et al.,* Visualizing Project Management.)

- GE Aircraft Engines has put into place a chief engineer's office which serves as an integrating function in an organization that is otherwise fragmented into product development teams. It uses documented design practices, design boards (which function like in-house professional societies), and design reviews, and provides a consulting function by senior members of the engineering staff.

- The separate identifiable planning function has been in and out of favor in GE over the years. Strategic planning was once a GE signature activity. Planning is now the responsibility of all individual managers, and identifiable planning activities are hard to find in the organization.

- Management, as a distinct professional activity, was once very much favored at the corporate level and looked on disdainfully by GE Aircraft Engines, which was the maverick organization that was run by engineers. Although the word *manager* is in disfavor (the word *leader* is preferred), the professional manager is now very much the norm. The last head of GE Aircraft Engines was a lawyer with a background in the satellite business. The current head of GE Aircraft Engines comes to it from the light bulb business.

- The implication is that a professional manager can manage any type of business without significant experience in that business.

Figure 15.6 *General observations on the characteristics of General Electric Aircraft Engines. (From GE Avondale input to the Lean Advancement Initiative.)*

structure becomes mandatory. Particularly in research and highly developmental projects, there is a pitfall for those scientists who believe that they are the exclusive base of knowledge and innovation. Often, while their technical genius and contribution are undeniable, the budgetary and schedule aspects may well be left wanting or even ignored, with consequences inimical to the project and the scientist. In view of that, organization is clearly a factor to be considered. Most successful product or system developments rely on dedicated project management organizations in which the critical functions report to the *project manager* [a term that may vary depending on the culture; for example, GE (Figure 15.6) uses the term *chief engineer*, Proctor & Gamble, the designation *product manager*]. Unfortunately, to have all functional aspects reporting directly may limit the flexible use of personnel in other critical applications and inhibit cross-project knowledge. Thus, the most common arrangement is the *matrix approach* (Figure 15.7), in which key functional personnel and functions come from and are assigned by a parent organization. This is particularly the case with engineering, with its many disciplines necessary for complex projects.

Aside from organizations designed specifically for one type of development, such as pharmaceuticals, differing development tactics may be employed. Perhaps most common is the *waterfall* or "goes into" tactic, which deals with a linear progression of steps or subelement developments that feed progressively toward the integrated end item (Figure 15.8). It is also a basis for scheduling and monitoring the progress of

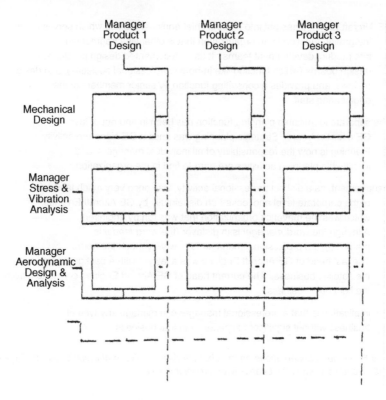

Figure 15.7 *Matrix organization for product design.*

- Two-dimensional model originally for software development model

  System Requirements

- Sequential phases that may overlap

  Software Requirements

- Emphasizes orderly development

  Preliminary Design

  - Requirements before design

    Detailed Design

  - Design before coding

    Code and Device

- Emphasizes requirements flowdown

  Test and Pre-Operations

Promotes orderly development

Operations and Mantinance

Figure 15.8 *Waterfall design scheme.*

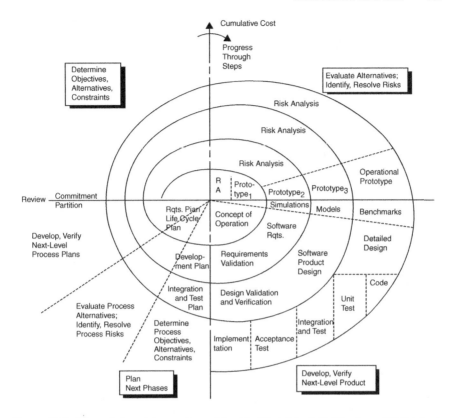

Figure 15.9 *The spiral model promotes solving identified risks first. (Courtesy of B. Boehm.)*

each element and was memorialized for software by Win Royce of TRW and Lockheed. Yet another, the *spiral model* (Figure 15.9), applied to software by Barry Boehm, provides for scheduled development iterations that lead repeatedly to evolving technical capability. Its evolutionary approach is used for developments that necessitate continuing technological innovation and testing before integration. It may be seen as an incremental but smoothly defined process. Another model looks at a V-shaped group of activities, evidencing in one leg the creative development activities following the descending path progressively until there is a basis for validating and verifying all aspects of the product, as shown on the ascending leg. However, although progress along a leg appears linear, the process anticipates crossing to the other leg whenever interim verification and validation are appropriate (Figure 15.10).

The next consideration is how to schedule so as to monitor and measure progress. Closest to the waterfall approach is the *Gantt chart* (Figure 15.11), effectively a bar chart of the scheduled progress of each element and the phasing of each element as it integrates with others. It is an assembly sequence chart, a work progress chart, a budget allocation chart, and the method most widely used in industry and government because it fits the most common, linear thinking practice.

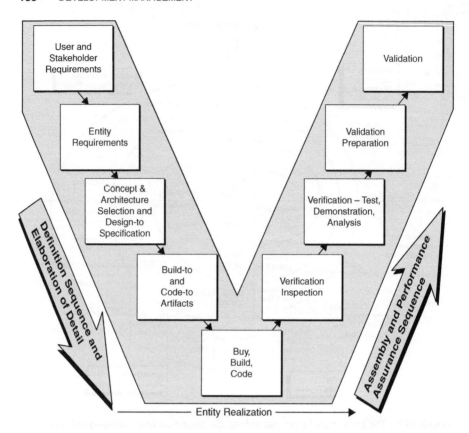

Figure 15.10   *Project cycle V+ model diagram. (Derived from "Entity Vee Model," Forsberg, Mooz, and Cotterman,* Visualizing Project Management.*)*

PERT (performance evaluation and tracking, Figure 15.12) is a method of scheduling that links each activity to those interfacing with it and with times and cost or resources for each so as to provide a means of judging progress as well as cost incurred while providing diagrammatic means of incorporating changes. The nodes are established to reflect gates employed for decisions on performance and schedule. It is a complement to earned-value assessment. *CPM* (critical path mapping) merges earned value assessment of progress by linking work accomplished in terms of value added against predicted cost incurred, thus making judgments of expected conformance to schedules and budgets (Figure 15.13).

Another management consideration is prioritizing the sequencing of activities. One means of deriving the best order of activities is a *precedence* or *affinity matrix* (Figure 15.14), which establishes relationships among the activities and organizes those with the highest affinity and least waste. Also called a *design structure matrix* (Figure 15.15), there are now computer programs for this that evaluate the clustering of efforts around a diagonal and thereby establish a preferred sequence. For various reasons, including the peculiarity of organizations, facilities, or suppliers, these

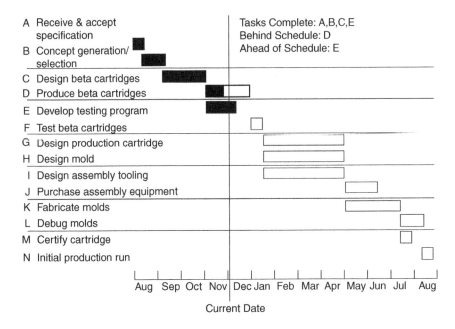

Figure 15.11 *Managing project development projects: Gantt bar chart for the Cheetah tape cartridge. (Courtesy of Epsom Computers.)*

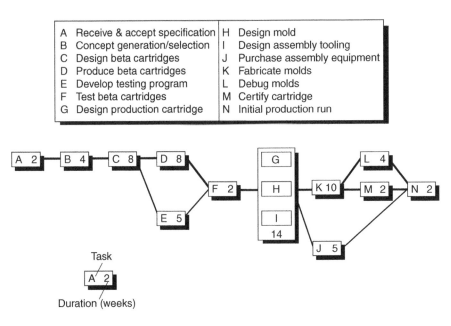

Figure 15.12 *PERT chart for Cheetah project. The critical path is designated by the lines. (Courtesy of Epsom Computers.)*

- CPM charts are similar to PERT charts and are sometimes known as PERT/CPM. In a CPM chart, the critical path is indicated. A critical path consists of that set of dependent tasks (each dependent on the preceding one) which together take the longest time to complete. Although it is not normally done, a CPM chart can define multiple equally critical paths. Tasks that fall on the critical path should be noted in some way so that they may be given special attention. One way is to draw critical path tasks with a double line instead of a single line.

- Tasks that fall on the critical path should receive special attention by both the project manager and the personnel assigned to them. The critical path for any given method may shift as the project progresses. This can happen when tasks are completed either behind or ahead of schedule, causing other tasks that may still be on schedule to fall on the new critical path.

Figure 15.13 *Critical path method description.*

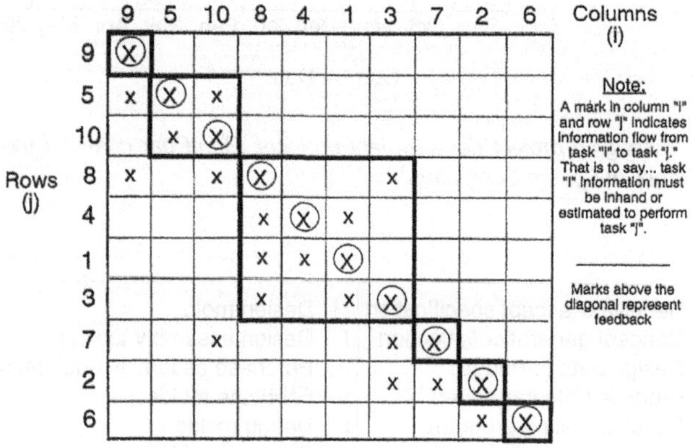

Figure 15.14 *Refined process precedence matrix. (Adapted from: Steward,* Systems Analysis and Management.)

orders are often modified, although the DSM provides a useful starting point. It is covered in more detail in Appendix I.

In summary, looking at what might be considered the most prevalent and critical problems of development management, surveys and case studies make it clear that the leading issue is communication, keeping everyone informed and "on the same page" in a timely fashion. Beyond communication problems, one can list other impediments that make up a catalog of "do nots":

· Poor or inadequate planning up front
· Poor or inadequate direction
· Incomplete analyses of stakeholders and values

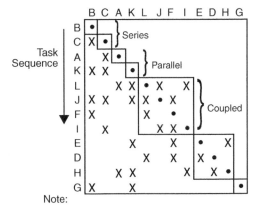

Note:

Coupled tasks can be identified uniquely.

The display of the matrix can be manipulated to emphasize certain features of the process flow.

Figure 15.15 *Design structure matrix. (S. Eppinger & T. Browning,* Design Structure Matrices.*)*

- Lack of clearly understood requirements
- Critical work slippage without functioning work-arounds
- Getting work to or from sources outside the immediate project control
- Biased selection of designs and processes
- Precluded judgment of best performance, cost, schedule, and customer and user satisfaction
- Failure to consider risk at all points along the value stream
- Lack of common or directly relatable databases
- Misleading budgets or schedules
- Lack of root-cause analysis of all technical and programmatic problems

RESOURCES AND NOTES

Visualizing Project Management, K. Forsberg, H. Mooz, and H. Cotterman, Wiley, Hoboken, NJ, 2005.

This book is aimed at large program management, incorporating and augmenting many of the topics discussed in this chapter. More attention is paid to the V-shaped approach and to the various delivery strategies, so the text provides expansion on these concepts.

Design Structure Matrix Methods and Applications, S. Eppinger and T. Browning, MIT Press, Cambridge, MA, 2012.

The use of DSMs to schedule and optimize organizations and processes is described in detail. The book both augments this chapter's text and provides details, with many examples, to take a reader beyond the appendix on the subject in this book (Appendix I).

Lean Enablers for Systems Engineering, B. Oppenheim, Wiley, Hoboken, NJ, 2011.

Although "systems engineering" is in the title, the material is basically applicable to project management and is being translated for that purpose into a Project Management Institute publication. It also appears as an adjunct to Chapter 17 through the appendix.

Some Web-based or software tools: work breakdown structures, Gantt, CPM, and PERT charting, affinity diagrams, design structure matrices.

REVIEW CHECKLIST

- ☐ Have realistic schedules and financial budgets been established?
- ☐ Do all participants have access to, understand, and agree to abide by them?
- ☐ Has a monitoring system been established?
- ☐ Are there provisions for work-arounds in schedule and contingency planning for finance and cash flow?
- ☐ Have you used techniques such as PERT or design structure matrices for prioritizing activities?
- ☐ In schedules and costing for delivery, are there provisions for packaging, handling, and shipping?
- ☐ Does the organizational arrangement preserve ultimate responsibility with one person, and is it recognized throughout?
- ☐ If there is a matrix organization, do both project manager (or equivalent) and functional manager have joint evaluative responsibility for personnel?
- ☐ Where multiple projects exist in an organization, is a balance or mobility of talent available?
- ☐ Much as with IPTs, are there common or related IT and databases across all elements of the performing organization and suppliers?

16

Cost Estimating

Whereas designing for performance and the "-ilities" is very understandable, there is real difficulty is designing for cost, especially in a developmental project. How can cost be set? How is it possible to determine what will affect costs over the development cycle? Of course, there is a possibility of using similar or competitive products in setting a target. In many large projects it is practical to use comparable architectures to establish a top-down basis for cost. Using such architectures, one can allocate an interim budget and then negotiate to reach a desired target with the contributing groups (defined by the decomposed elements) to reallocate. On the other hand, it is possible to ask questions of all contributing functional activities or disciplines first, totaling their estimates, and then negotiating toward a target. Considering that a competitive cost gives a target that may well require changes in design, each functional element can be challenged to identify what changes would be necessary to reach an achievable target. All of the discussion above presumes that an architecture is the starting base (Figure 16.1).

16.1 STAKEHOLDER INVOLVEMENT

One too common problem is that of hiding costs from a customer, seller, or management until there are problems. Thus, the importance of having these stake-holders involved early is to ensure that any changes to modify costs will be accomplished quickly and logically. It is extremely important to understand the status of the design and all the influences, such as cost, schedule, quality, and performance margins. Of course, most cost-related items are interdependent; one change affects many elements. And this is always the case, particularly for those that

Product and Systems Development: A Value Approach, First Edition. Stanley I. Weiss.
© 2013 John Wiley & Sons, Inc. Published 2013 by John Wiley & Sons, Inc.

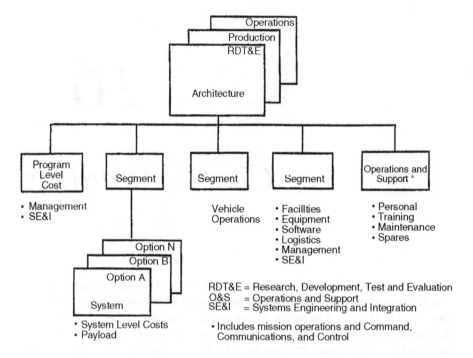

Figure 16.1 *Introduction to cost analysis. The cost breakdown structure is an important tool for organizing cost information and ensuring consistency in comparing alternatives. (Adapted from P. Belobaba lectures at MIT.)*

are furnished externally from customers or suppliers. If cost in one element in the architecture is modified, many others are usually affected.

16.2 COSTING FACTORS

Many factors affect cost and cycle time; these are summarized in Figure 16.2. Some will inevitably affect the criteria for requirements review, concept assessment, risks, and other factors. Changes in any of these will have impacts that must be evaluated and outcomes allocated regardless of whether the factors are governed by management or are influenced externally. The *Tool and Manufacturing Engineers Handbook* describes many elements that apply largely to hardware projects (Figure 16.3). But the elements in this domain have relationships to software as well, especially where overhead costs are involved. The definitions listed are largely self-explanatory and will be addressed further in analyzing cost estimation details.

16.3 ESTIMATING METHODS

Cost modeling in early development phases is sometimes called "guesstimating" because for innovative projects the references are limited and the unknowns are

- Size of the program buy
- A priori cost estimates
- Requirements stability
- Technology risk
- Perceived industry capability
- Number of contractors
- Head count
- Number of review steps
- Quality of system design

- Production rate
- Profitability
- Funding stability
- Skill mix
- Actual capability
- Experience
- Productivity
- Communications
- System management

Figure 16.2 *Factors affecting cost and cycle time.*

unlimited. For example, there was a time when parametric estimating, attributed to consistent or referenced relationships of parameters from a previous project, was a reasonable first estimate upon which funding decisions might be based. Thus, a weight versus cost relationship with a conventional design and the addition of a factor of complexity could provide reasonable approximations. For years this equation held with aircraft until electronics and software, relatively minimal weight additions, became a very large part of the total cost. Some other common parameters are size, geometries for structures, electrical and acoustic power, and number of lines of code for software.

Another method of estimating involves analogous translations of similar projects or products or at least some of their elements. This obviously requires a valid database, which may be generated historically by the performing organization or obtained through benchmarking other organizations' projects. Sometimes, such

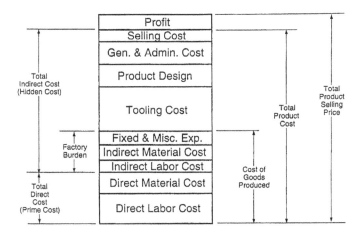

Figure 16.3 *Cost structure characteristics. (From Bakerjian,* Tool and Manufacturing Engineers Handbook.*)*

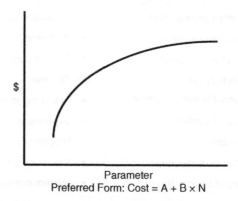

Parameter
Preferred Form: Cost = A + B × N

Figure 16.4 *Cost-estimating relationship, an equation that expresses cost as a function of a design sizing (or performance) parameter.*

information can be obtained through consulting firms. Then, as one proceeds downstream with more and more definition and understanding of design and process, as well as reduced uncertainties, one can get closer to using the bottom-up approach or direct estimating techniques based on a decomposed architecture.

All of the above require a cost-information database. When reuse is involved or where fixed price bids and off-the-shelf elements are considered valid, these come closest to verifiable cost data. Similarly, costs are also governed by time, including forecasts of technology readiness as well as inflation. In addition, when life-cycle costs are included, there are added considerations of logistics, setups and maintenance, training, and the historic utilization of a similar product in the field.

For methods of cost estimation that relate parameters such as weight and size, the cost-estimating relationships involved may be shown as $cost = A + B \times N$ (Figure 16.4). This can be expressed as $ \times$ (or monetary value multiplied by), for example, N the number of conductors, connections, or square footage (as in house construction), for fixed requirements. This may not be too far off the mark if there is no change in requirements or complexity, or if there is a generally applicable standard deviation identified for contingency.

To understand these relationships, regression analysis of the data available is necessary to provide the curves that will define the coefficients. In addition, variance analysis based on the accuracy of previous estimates is a requirement to justify parametrically or analogy-based estimates. Figure 16.5 shows where these types of cost estimation are most appropriate. The recognition of risk in estimating is also critical. Figure 16.6 indicates many factors affecting risk, and although these will vary with organization, the standard deviations cited give an idea of limitations on accuracy.

Looking at the incurring of cost with time, it becomes clear that the smallest amount spent on a substantial project is in the research and development (R&D) phase, with that early investment having multiplier effects downstream. Time is also a major influence on cost. Thus, as a generality, the longer the time for development,

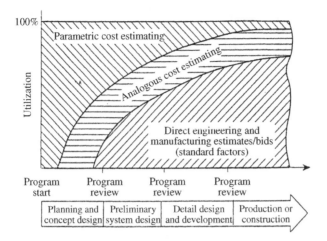

Figure 16.5 *Estimating methods versus project phase. (From Fabrycky and Blanchard,* Life-Cycle Cost and Economics Analysis.*)*

the higher the cost. The implications related to phasing of resources suggest that imposing deadlines may be worthwhile. If technology availability is inhibiting, or if it clearly will be, capability and funding should be provided for progressive insertion. The cost breakdown structure is tied directly to the architecture or work breakdown structure, recognizing certain cost drivers, including utilization practices. But for the life cycle of development there are the R&D costs themselves, sometimes classified

Technology Readiness Level	Definition	Relative Risk Level	Standard Deviation About MLE (%)
1	Basic principles observed	High	>25
2	Conceptual design formulated	High	>25
3	Conceptual design tested analytically or experimentally	Moderate	20–25
4	Critical function or characteristic demonstrated	Moderate	15–20
5	Component or breadboard tested in relevant environment	Moderate	10–15
6	Prototype or engineering model tested in relevant environment	Low	<10
7	Engineering model tested in space	Low	<10
8	Full operational capability	Low	<10

Figure 16.6 *Technology classification and relative cost risk. (Courtesy of NASA.)*

as research, development, testing, and evaluation (RDT&E), and when multiple quantities of end items are involved, the influence of learning curves based on first-unit costs. There are also overhead or administrative impositions to be applied to all cost elements.

16.4 LEARNING CURVES

As suggested above, the number of units to be produced after development is a major factor in average or break-even costs. The use of learning curves is therefore the means to make these estimates of costs per unit a function of the number produced. As an axiom, the more labor intensive a product is to produce, the greater the opportunity for learning, therefore gaining reductions in unit cost with quantity and time. The more highly automated the process, the less the benefit of repetition. For example, a structural or mechanical product requiring many labor hours to produce might have a learning curve of 75 to 80% or a cost realized for each unit or block of that amount contingent on a first-unit baseline value. A highly automated process might yield only a 95% learning curve, with substantially less benefit with quantity. (This suggests a necessity for very careful consideration in changing a high-percentage learning process to robotic manufacturing.)

Figure 16.7 shows the derivation of learning curves based on total first-unit cost and the anticipated number of units to be produced. Figure 16.8 provides some examples of the direct effect of different percentage learning. Thus, one-of-a-kind or a few-of-a-kind may realize very little, if any, learning. One example of this recognition was with the making of fuses, now assembled largely by trained but relatively unskilled labor. Since the marginal difference between cost and selling price was critical, it was determined that automation would eliminate the labor content by 80%. The result was predictable repetition and tough negligible learning. Most important, the types of repetitive actions by the former workers had

- Cost reduction per unit with an increasing number of units
  - Fixed manufacturing setup costs
  - Economies of scale
  - Human learning and efficiency
- Total production cost for N units:

$$P = \text{TFU} \times L$$

where $L = N^B$

$$B = 1 - \frac{\ln(100\%/S)}{\ln 2}$$

L = learning curve factor
S = slope, or percent reduction in average cost per unit when units are doubled

- Wertz and Larson recommend $S = 95\%$ for fewer than 10 units, $S = 90\%$ for 10 to 50 units.

Figure 16.7   Derivation of learning curves. (From Wertz and Larson, Space Mission Analysis and Design.)

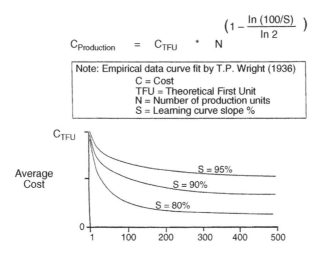

$$C_{Production} \quad = \quad C_{TFU} \quad * \quad N^{\left(1 - \frac{\ln(100/S)}{\ln 2}\right)}$$

> Note: Empirical data curve fit by T.P. Wright (1936)
> C = Cost
> TFU = Theoretical First Unit
> N = Number of production units
> S = Learning curve slope %

Figure 16.8 Learning curve: cost reduction due to human learning, economics of scale, and setup time. (Concept of T.P. Wright in 1936, adapted by P. Belobaba.)

incorporated so much learning by technicians that their production efficiencies outweighed automation benefits. The workers were rehired and much of the automation was scrapped after an expensive lesson.

The understanding of realistic learning curves is also critical. For example, the Lockheed L1011 aircraft never achieved cost forecasts, and the early losses per unit in cost versus sales price were never recovered, although the application of traditional learning curves suggested break-even costs much earlier than was true in reality. In fact, expectations for break-even quantities were continually revised upward until it was realized that each article would never be delivered at a profit; thus, a fine aircraft was terminated.

16.5 COST-ESTIMATING PROBLEMS

NASA, largely a buyer of one or a few of a kind, conducted a survey of the causes of cost growth, and in their language, underestimation of costs was a consistent problem. Others of significance were overly optimistic assumptions as to technical complexity, inheritance savings, management innovation, supplier productivity, and quality improvements. Additional contributors were changes in scope or require-ments as well as funding and schedule modifications. There are parallels in nearly all complex government projects as well as in many commercial developments, particularly in the pharmaceutical and construction industries.

What about those hidden costs that often do not become apparent until their occurrence or visibility makes them an issue? They can lie in unforeseen factors such as changes in personnel mandated by management to benefit other projects, layoff situations with union seniority, or retirements causing changes in key personnel,

Characteristics	Potential Problems	Can Create These Types of Indirect Expenses
Variability	Difficult to control processes; SPC required	Inspect, test, rework, scrap
Precision	Tolerances at limits of capacity	Equipment, tooling, maintenance, scrap
Multistep	Many steps needed to complete process; failure of one defeats all	Excessive handling, long cycle time
Sensitivity	Packaging, rework, field service	Part easily flawed during factory or post-factory stages
Immaturity	Use of unproven processing	Learning curve expense validation time
Environmental impact	Process monitored by governmental agencies	Employee protection, disposal, liability, documentation
Skill-intensive	High degree of training required, number of capable employees limited	Inspection, training, supervision
Nonstandard	Modification of standard processes, use on nonstandard parts	Part number proliferation
Complex architecture	Inside/outside processing	Material handling, tracking, scheduling

Figure 16.9 *Hidden costs. (Courtesy of NASA.)*

equipment limitations, packaging needs, oversight intensity, regulatory changes, and so on. Many are cited in Figure 16.9.

Another very difficult realm for cost estimating is software. Unless there is direct application of programs used previously, the certainty of exact reuse is critical. Witness the failure of the Ariane 5 use of A-4 guidance software, disregarding what proved fatal out-of-nominal performance differences. The cost-savings motivation was as ill-founded as the deletion of tests on the Hubble Space Telescope's mirror. Note in Figure 16.10 the Bell Labs charting of where error sources lay and the costs to correct these. Of greatest importance is the need to pay strict attention to the early phases of development and the tremendous impact on costs of making corrections or changes downstream.

Overall, costing is an extremely difficult and critical part of the development process in the drive to have new competitive products or systems. In addition, as time and complexity increase, so do issues in cost estimating. Thus, evaluating actual and forecasted costs throughout the life cycle of development must be a continuing process.

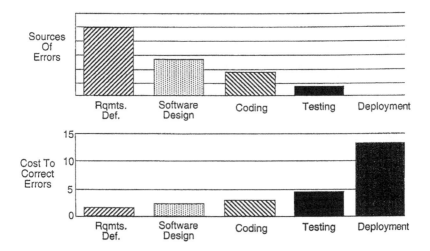

Figure 16.10 *Software error sources and cost to correct. (Courtesy of AT&T Bell Labs/Committee of the ACM.)*

RESOURCES AND NOTES

Few books outside the building construction industry address cost estimating for development, with its many variables and unknowns. Three that provide differing guidance are cited.

Visualizing Project Management, K. Forsberg, H. Mooz, and H. Cotterman, Wiley, Hoboken, NJ, 2005.

A short section describes processes that include projection of labor costs and bills of materials to establish budgets and pricing.

Space Mission Analysis and Design, 3rd ed., J. Wertz and W. Larson, Editors, Microcosm Press, Kluwer Academic, Norwell, MA, 1999.

Although this book is dedicated to space, it has a very complete discussion on cost estimating and adds good insights to estimating variables applicable to any product or system.

Value Driven Product Planning and Systems Engineering, H. Cook and L. Wissman, Springer-Verlag, New York, 2007.

The authors provide useful insights into the means and benefits of added value in products to consumers and stakeholders. There are numerous case studies addressing relative value benefits of differing investments in product attributes.

REVIEW CHECKLIST

☐ Given the cost accumulation for a project or product, what is the probability of achieving any cost estimate?

☐ If you have used bottom-up costs from each function, have you compared these in decomposed fashion with analogous product or system elements?

☐ When incorporating benefits of automation, have you made certain that the benefits of high learning curves for manual operation do not outweigh the costs and time requirements of automation?

☐ Have you done continuous or frequent cost analysis during a project's development and considered appropriate methodology changes as work progresses and realistic time and material apply?

17

Lean Principles and Practices

The term *lean* does not mean, as some critics contend, eliminating people from an organization; it does mean using an understanding of all processes that are part of a product or service life cycle to eliminate waste. The lean concept originated in defining productivity in the automobile industry based on the Toyota production system, so its emphasis at first was on manufacturing. The book *The Machine That Changed the World* compared the Toyota and Honda implementers of this practice to U.S. and European suppliers. It identified the major contributions to productivity by the two Japanese firms and the lack of the same and waste-generating practices of others. This first identification of lean practices, in fact, fathered by W. Edwards Deming, a U.S. industrial engineer, migrated in 1992 to the aerospace industry and since then to many diverse businesses, with significant emphasis in the electronics and health care fields, particularly in hospital operations and medical equipment development. In sum, *lean* refers to the minimization of resources and time leading to the elimination of waste, the smooth adaptability to change, and the flow of information and product elements toward the delivery of value. It was not long before Toyota, as well as others who adopted the practices, extended the concepts to all parts of the life cycle, with new emphasis on development. The lean philosophy is summarized in Figure 17.1.

Product and Systems Development: A Value Approach, First Edition. Stanley I. Weiss.
© 2013 John Wiley & Sons, Inc. Published 2013 by John Wiley & Sons, Inc.

1. The customer defines the *value*.

2. Map the *value stream*: Plan all end-to-end linked actions and append processes required to realize value, streamlined, after eliminating waste.

3. Make value *flow* continuously; without stopping, rework, or backflow (valid iterations OK).

4. Let customers *pull* value: Customer's "pull/need" defines all tasks and their timing.

5. Pursue *perfection*: All imperfections become visible, which is motivating to the continuous process of improvement.

6. Respect *people*.

Figure 17.1 *Six lean principles. (Courtesy of the Lean Advancement Initiative and Lean Academy.)*

17.1 THINKING LEAN PRECEPTS

Lean thinking has been described as a dynamic knowledge-driven and customer-focused process in which all participants in a defined enterprise strive for continuous improvement and the elimination of waste. Even more succinctly, lean's mantra is the pursuit of value with minimum waste. This clearly calls for definitions of what adds value, what doesn't, and what we mean by waste. In general, value added is the necessary effort toward delivery of a product or system done correctly the first time without need for rework. This does not mean that a process that is specifically designed to be developed through iteration is wasteful if iteration becomes part of the value stream and does not cause unplanned delays or excessive inventories in an enterprise.

There are, in reality, two types of waste. One may be called *necessary waste*, that which is intrinsic to any activity in an enterprise, not providing value directly, but imposed due to constraints such as facility maintenance and top management or induced by regulations or legal requirements. These, however, still deserve evaluation for change. *Unnecessary waste* is the use of resources that create no value in the eyes of stakeholders internal or external to the development. Figure 17.2 lists definitions of those critical terms just cited. One key to minimizing waste therefore lies in understanding the total process involved in development.

There is no more important contributor to success than the leadership of an enterprise that vigorously supports identifying and insisting on efficient use of resources, excellent and critical supplier relations, open and clear communications, and low transaction costs. In the creation of lean organizations, these are not easily achieved, so it is useful to look at the maturity of applications in various domains. Figure 17.3 presents some key focus areas of 2010, showing the progress that was being made in all categories, especially aggressively in the development of a body of lean enablers through INCOSE (International Council on Systems Engineering) and the publication of Oppenheim's *Lean Enablers for System Engineering*. This has now been extended to project management, emphasizing the synergies.

- **Value added**
  - The external customer is willing to pay for "Value."
  - Transforms information or material.
  - Provides specified performance right the first time.

- **Non–value added: necessary**
  - No value is created, but values cannot be eliminated based on current technology or thinking.
  - All values are required.

- **Non–value added: waste**
  - Consumes resources but creates no value in the eyes of the customer.
  - If you can't get rid of the activity, it is non–value added but necessary.

Figure 17.2 Lean value definitions. (From Lean Enterprise Initiative and Massachusetts Institute of Technology documents.)

We know this:

- Lean applies to any quantity of products: from one-off (like PD) to large volumes (like cars or aircraft)

- Lean applies to all areas of work !

ENTERPRISE AREA	Maturity
Lean Manufacturing	Very mature
Lean Enterprise	Mature
Lean Supply Network	Mature
Lean Office (we all work in an office environment)	Mature
Lean (Final) Engineering	Mature
Lean Product Development	Less Mature, fast growing
Lean Systems Engineering	Least mature, challenge for our INCOSE LSE WG

Figure 17.3 Lean maturity through the product life cycle. (Courtesy of the INCOSE Lean Systems Engineering working group.)

Results from practitioners are often difficult to ascertain, except for specific projects in organizations that have been able to make comparisons with past practice. But Figure 17.4 shows some that have entered the literature, and others, particularly in relatively new applications to health care, that are becoming available. Suffice it to say, when applied with diligence, the results in manufacturing are clearly palpable whereas those in development regimes are spotty but growing. One cause has been confusion in identifying "lean" with other processes labeled as productivity improvers. Thus, "agile," "total quality management," and "six sigma" all represent practices that can contribute to lean.

Company	Cost	Schedule	Quality
McDonnell Douglas Missile Systems	60% saving on bid for reactor and missile projects	18 month savings on TAV-8B design	Scrap reduced by 58% Rework cost reduced by 29% And non-conformances reduced by 38%
Boeing Ballistic Systems Division	30% below bid	Parts and materials lead-time reduced by 30%	99% defect-free operations
AT&T	Cost of repair for new circuit pack production cut by at least 40%	Process time reduced 46%	Defects reduced by 30% to 70%
Deere & Company	30% actual savings on development cost for construction equipment	60% savings in development time	Number of inspectors reduced by two-thirds
Hewlett-Packard Instrument Division	Manufacturing costs reduced by 42%	Reduced development cycle time by 35%	Product field failure rate reduced by 60%; scrap and rework reduced by 75%
IDA Report R-338	**30-40% Improvement**	**40-60% Improvement**	**50-75% Improvement**

Figure 17.4   *Some published success stories of lean design. (From Womack et al., The Machine That Changed the World, and Lean Advancement Initiative research.)*

Six-Sigma Process

Six sigma is a very popular process used to improve productivity.

Step	Tools
Define	Quality functional deployment
Measure	Process flow (material, information)
	Cause–effect (fishbone) diagrams
	Failure mode effects analysis
	Process measurement and capability
	Statistical process control
	Process capability
Analyze	Univariate and multivariate statistical applications
	Screening designs
Improve	Design of experiments
Control	Various variable and attribute statistical process control charts

---

17.2   DEALING WITH WASTE

Taichi Ohno, one of the key figures in establishing lean practices in Japan, had a seven-set categorization of waste. Although these were established basically for manufacturing (see Figure 17.5), they have direct parallels in engineering and

1. Overproduction: creating too much material of information

2. Inventory: having more material of information than
                       you need

3. Transportation: moving material or information

4. Unnecessary   moving people to access or process
   movement: material or information

5. Waiting: waiting for material or information, or
                       material or information waiting to be
                       processed

6. Defective output: errors or mistakes, causing the effort to be
                       redone to correct the problem

7. Overprocessing: processing more than necessary to
                       produce the desired output

Figure 17.5 *Ohno's categorization of waste into seven types.*

development. For example, overproduction can be construed as an excessive definition of product characteristics, or too many drawings or specifications—in general, an excess of data to an excess of recipients. Figure 17.5 shows the parallels in terms of the value streams for manufacturing and product development. Product development effort today still incorporates a great deal of waste. Surveys of 22 auto and aerospace companies by the Lean Advancement Initiative centered at the Massachusetts Institute of Technology indicated that 40% of effort dedicated to product development is pure or "unnecessary" waste, with 30% of the time charged to product development being spent in waiting. The sizable number of tasks "wasting" time is largely from task idle time, an estimate of 62% by members surveyed through Kaizen, brainstorming assessments by workers. Elaborating on Figure 17.5 and recognizing that the product development process consists largely of information and data development, some categories of information waste are shown in Figure 17.6.

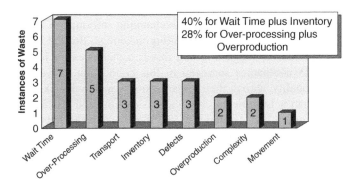

Figure 17.6 *Measurement of information waste for 25 organizations. (Courtesy of INCOSE and the Lean Advancement Initiative.)*

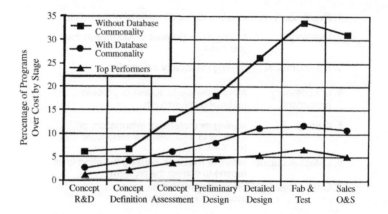

Figure 17.7   *Database commonality. Interoperability and/or commonality of design, cost, manufacturability, and other databases significantly reduces the likelihood of cost and schedule overruns in product development. (Research from Lean Advancement Initiative, MIT.)*

It was stated earlier that the product of research and engineering is information, and Ohno's seven types of wastes have been interpreted in terms related to information critical to development. The first of these has already been cited: waiting, or idle time due to unavailability of information. Another is excess inventory of information: that which is never used for either lack of need or worthlessness. The latter also has its outgrowth in a felt need to generate information, such as overspecifying requirements or demands for information reporting that do not add value. Already addressed is transportation that can be ameliorated by continuity of communication, co-location of people and teams, and along with these, the minimizing of movement by workers to communicate or retrieve tools, Finally, there is that major creator of lost time and resources—defects—in erroneous data, information, reports, procedures, and reporting.

One issue common to all of the above is the lack of database commonality, similar in many ways to problems in interchanging information using different languages, requiring extra effort in translating meanings. But the impact on cost and schedule is intuitive, suggesting that this is a matter easily identifiable and fixable. Of the 25 companies surveyed in this connection, however, only two had such commonality across their organizations, and only six were able to verify that they had it in projects. Implications on cost and schedule are shown in Figures 17.7 and 17.8. Attempts to fix the disconnects have proven very difficult in organizations having multiple projects, especially those involving multiple suppliers. One subcontractor for three different firms cited that he needed to maintain five different computer-aided design systems: CADAM, CATIA, Unigraphics, ProEngineer, and Solid Modeling, with understandably much additional cost in tools and personnel and with the overhead passed on to customers.

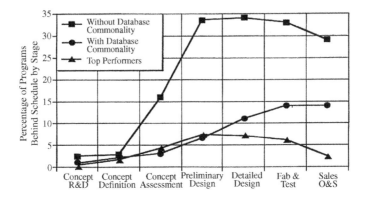

Figure 17.8   Database schedule Impact. (Courtesy of the Lean Advancement Initiative.)

17.3   LEAN MODELS

There have been attempts to provide architectures of lean organization. One that is in wide circulation is the lean enterprise model (Figure 17.9). It consists of a set of principles, "meta-principles," governing enterprise-level metrics. But the heart of the model lies in 12 overarching practices that deal with relationships of flow of material and information, the efficient use of people, the leadership within an organization, and commitment to quality and continuous improvement. This set is underpinned by enabling and supporting practices, determined through dozens of case studies, together with metrics, interactions, and barriers to achievement. This iconic grouping may be viewed as a framework for implementation. The latter, with other

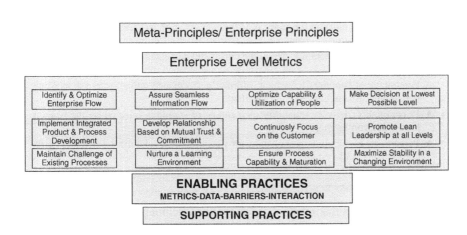

Figure 17.9   Lean enterprise model architecture and overarching meta-principles. (Courtesy of the Lean Advancement Initiative.)

applications, can be found on the website established by the Lean Advancement Initiative (formerly, the Lean Space Iniative), with an elaboration in Appendix II of this book.

Research Supporting Overarching Practices Based on Supplier Relations

1. Proactive design and integration of a supplier network

   Definition I: Optimize the size and structure of the supplier network as a function of minimizing cost, cycle time, and variability while ensuring supplier performance and reliability, minimizing or sharing risk, enhancing technological capability, providing for surge capacity, and creating the best synergy with the firm's core competence.

   Definition II: Proactive design of the size, structure, and governance of the supplier network to optimize competitive advantage through strategic outsourcing driven by "make–buy" criteria rooted in an assessment of core competence.

2. Selection of key direct (first-tier) suppliers at the outset of product development for design and development

3. Supplier performance evaluation (an ongoing process)

4. Supplier selection on the basis of past relationships and proven record of performance; two-supplier policy sector–dependent

5. Selected suppliers responsible for detailed drawings to performance specifications ("black box" parts) for parts, components, and systems

Metrics

- Number of direct-production suppliers (includes contract assembly)
- Cost to spend or place a purchasing dollar; purchasing operating expense as a percentage of total purchasing dollar spent; subcontracting cycle time (from requirements for placement); cost per transaction
- Firm (business unit) performance (cost/price; cycle time/schedule/delivery; quality/ defects); competitive advantage (e.g., market share, firm profitability)
- Percentage of suppliers selected at the outset and delegated design and development responsibility
- Percentage of suppliers for which a formal performance rating system is in place; percentage of suppliers that are certified
- Price, quality, delivery reliability: percentage of suppliers selected on the basis of best-value contracting
- Percentage of suppliers responsible for design and development for major parts, components, and systems

---

It should be noted that many of these practices defining a lean organization or project have been covered in the topics we have explored in the structure of development processes. Although the set of overarching practices of the lean enterprise model is supported by hundreds of enabling practices and case studies,

Program Type	Possible Lean Engineering Approach
Advance R&D for X-vehicle prototype	Small focused co-located team in "protected" environment – aka Skunk works. Rapid desing-build-fly cycles for learning, risk reduction, tool calibration and lifecycle experience.
New product development Major upgrade derivative	Effective capture of customer value expectations. Strong focus on lifecycle value and IPPD with integrated digital and product lifecycle management tools. Utilize "lessons learned" from past programs. Avoid unneeded reinvention, risky technology and unproven tools.
Engineering testing and support Product support Small upgrades	More standardized tasks and lower engineering risk allows direct adoption of many lean practices and tools used in manufacturing. Continuous improvement through value stream mapping and analysis.

Figure 17.10 Tailor lean engineering to fit the program. To use value-added lean engineering, it is necessary to apply lean thinking and to accept the fact that one size does not fit all circumstances. (Courtesy of the Lean Advancement Initiative and Lean Education Network.)

much effort has been directed to defining specific lean enablers to product and systems engineering. These are codified in Oppenheim's book. But although the various lean models and practices can apply to all complex systems and institutions, whether specifically identified or implicit, as in "skunkworks," tailoring to fit the program character or project phase is appropriate. Figure 17.10 provides some clues.

RESOURCES AND NOTES

Lean Product and Process Development, A. Ward, Lean Enterprise Institute, Cambridge, MA, 2007.
This is an excellent book that uses value-driven streams of processes to visualize waste in development, addressed largely to the automobile industry and its components. The foreword by Shook is a concise summary of lean concepts.

Lean Lexicon, 4th ed., Lean Enterprise Institute, Cambridge, MA, 2008.
This work is just what it purports to be: "a graphical glossary for lean thinkers."

Lean Enterprise Value, E. Murman et al., Palgrave Press, Hampshire, UK, 2002.
Cited previously, and not a "how to" book, it contains much history and many interesting examples of lean practices and outcomes.

Lean Enablers for Systems Engineering, B. Oppenheim, Wiley, Hoboken, NJ, 2011.

The full compendium of enablers described in the appendix by the same author.

Some Web-based or software tools: LEM (Lean Enterprise Model), Strategos.

REVIEW CHECKLIST

☐ Have you reviewed your value stream or development plan against the seven wastes?

☐ How have you committed your organization to continuous improvement?

☐ How have you provided for unplanned changes during development?

☐ Is systems thinking and approach incorporated?

☐ Is there continual assessment of processes?

☐ Is there open communication among all elements of the contributing organizations, including suppliers and customers/users if appropriate?

☐ Are IPPD, DFX, systems engineering, and maximum use of off-the-shelf tools intrinsic to your practices?

☐ Is information transfer open and seamless?

☐ If a PERT network has been established, has it been examined for waste and revised?

18

Value Stream Mapping

Rephrasing the definition of Chapter 1, value stream mapping consists of establishing the flow of any process with the goal of incorporating only those activities that deliver value. The value stream is the flow of activities that produces value throughout a development life cycle. The flow may or may not include waste, but the goal of mapping is to reduce non-value-adding activities to a minimum and optimize the flow. This overview of the methodology (Figure 18.1) includes incorporating all activities and processes in the life cycle and using the accumulated set of key stakeholder values to separate value added from waste.

18.1 STREAMLINING THE PROCESS

Eliminating unnecessary tasks, synchronizing the flow with scheduled reviews or handoffs, and minimizing the latter to shorten cycle times and rework can separate value from waste. It is important that each party within the flow understands that their efforts often include waste, so it is necessary that the mapping be conducted with the participation of key players and stakeholders in an atmosphere of mutual respect, with expectations that negotiation will yield results beneficial to the enterprise (Figure 18.2).

It also means that there is an established schedule for planned iterations downstream. Clearly, understanding the process is critical (Figure 18.3). Figure 18.4 shows an image of a process as it existed and the potential simplicity of the process flow after the analyses described above. Not only does it have the goal of eliminating wasteful processes and transfers between development steps, but the effort itself also generates many benefits. First, it helps to visualize the interactions and process

Product and Systems Development: A Value Approach, First Edition. Stanley I. Weiss.
© 2013 John Wiley & Sons, Inc. Published 2013 by John Wiley & Sons, Inc.

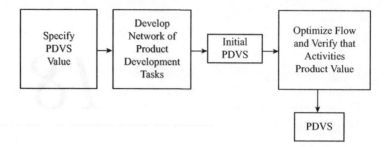

Figure 18.1 Developing the product development value stream. (From McManus, Product Development Value Stream Mapping.)

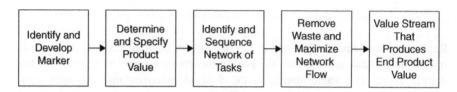

Figure 18.2 Product value stream development.

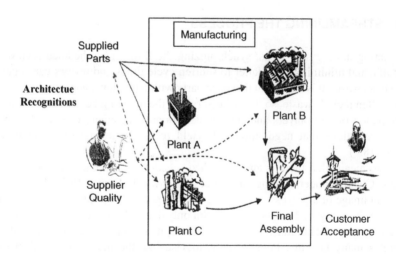

Figure 18.3 Process understanding for value stream mapping. Only processes that are understood can be improved. Understanding is easier when a process can be visualized. (Courtesy of the Lean Academy, MIT.)

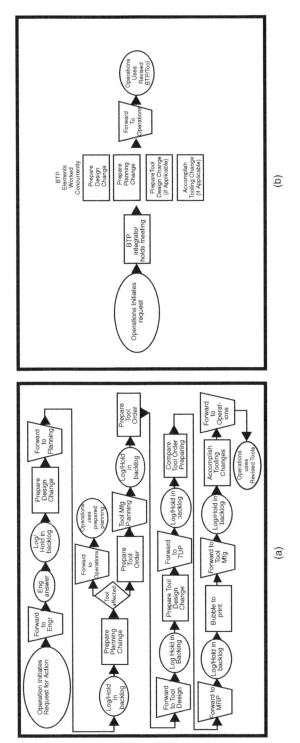

Figure 18.4 *Generating information versus generating knowledge (a) before and (b) after the adoption of lean techniques. (H. McManus for Lean Advancement Initiative, MIT.)*

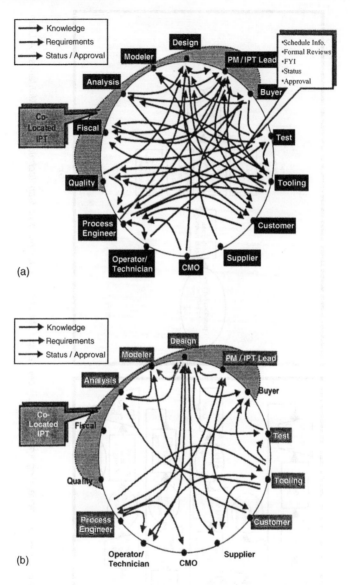

Figure 18.5 *(a) Information versus knowledge; (b) knowledge (value) flow. (Courtesy of Loral Corporation.)*

continuities and shows the linkages between information and material flows. It provides a common language for making judgments as to where wasteful activity takes place and thus can form the basis of an implementation plan. Value stream mapping serves as an excellent learning tool for participants, demanding a thorough understanding of processes and organization.

Scope: *Class II, ECP supplemental
production improvements, and
make-it-work changes initiated by
production requests*
Target improvement: *Reduce
average cycle-time by 50%*
Operational: *1999*
Future applications: *Pursuing
concept installation in other areas*

849 BTP packages from 07/7/99 to 01/17/00

Category	% Reduction
Cycle-Time	75%
Process Steps	40%
Number of Handoffs	75%
Travel Distance	90%

Figure 18.6 *Lean build-to-package support center PDVSM results. (Courtesy of Lockheed Martin Corporation.)*

A striking example of action producing such beneficial changes took place at the Aerojet General Corporation, where excessive hand-offs and sign-offs were associated with the development and delivery of an insulated rocket case. A group of people representing all participating organizations was convened to thoroughly map existing practices, running from engineering to final acceptance. The result, after two energetic days at the blackboard, yielded the cobweb diagram of Figure 18.5a, identifying the flow of paper and electronic transfer. Then, after evaluating the actual knowledge transfer required and value added needed, the information flow shown in Figure 18.5b was the dramatically simple outcome. This experience internally and the publishing of it external to the company has been a major instigator of value stream analysis in many other process flows. In another example, a company evaluated historic design release practices with the goal of streamlining the process. The comparison of flows was photographed and posted on the floor so that everyone involved could see and understand the new practice proposed (Figure 18.6).

18.2 ADAPTING TO NEW DEVELOPMENTS

It is extremely important to recognize that value stream mapping is a systematic process applicable to more than just a modification of existing processes. For new developments, a review of all preceding development projects can signal a revised map to emphasize a flow of value contributions with a consciousness of waste avoidance. The previous lean discussion identified some lists of value-added and non-value-added activity. These are worth reviewing to serve as a framework or checklist in the process of value stream analysis. Remember, the essence of value added is work that shapes or transforms information and material toward the creation of value in the entity delivered and operable. Although there are usually some constraints that retain non-value-added activity due to regulations, policies, or even physical and personnel resources, true controllable waste is that which consumes resources but creates no value to any of the stakeholders.

Even using these criteria, elimination of waste steps may sometimes not be possible, although restaging of activities can eliminate flow blockages. One such action lies in reworking the value stream to accommodate delivery changes from outsourced or externally supplied information or material delivery in a nondisruptive fashion. An example of this approach existed at the Hughes Space Systems Company, where continuously delayed deliveries of an antenna held up assembly and testing. A value stream mapping exercise led to a replanning of sequences that saved 15 days in the flow.

Look again at the non-value-added items that impede the smooth flow of a value stream. Figure 18.7 may seem repetitious, but it represents recurrent themes in examining organization after organization, independent of industry. This collection, in one way or another, has served consultants as a basis for proving their value by exposing and mapping process flows to organizations seeking to improve or to work their way out of problems. It should be no surprise that including attention to quality, reducing defects and resulting rework, does add value in every phase of the life cycle—in fact, eliminating substantial waste in their processes. In addition, attention to information accuracy and management can reduce delays and waiting time. What is really desired is for each successive step in a development cycle to be in "pull" status. When information is needed by one activity, if that information is available just when necessary, or is "pulled" by the using organization, the smoothest flow is obtained. This is also consistent with the flow of materials in a manufacturing or testing activity and represents the "just in time" principle.

This may seem to imply that activity must follow activity without looking back. But practically, the more complex a product or system, the greater the need for iteration loops. This recognition of checkpoints must be built into the value stream as well as in the schedule. However, these iterations themselves can be facilitated by

- **Defective products**
- **Repeated work**
- **Untimely information that causes delays**
- **Excessive information that causes delays**
- **Excessive information**
- **Redundancies**
- **Unnecessary approvals**
- **Delays and wait time**

Figure 18.7   *Non-value-added activities.*

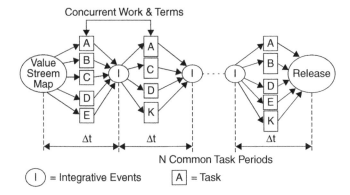

Concurrent Work & Terms

(I) = Integrative Events   [A] = Task

- Use customer-defined value to seprate value added from waste.
- Eliminate unnecessary tasks and streamline remaining tasks.
- Synchronize flow with integration events (stand-up meetings, virtual reality reviews, design reviews, etc.)
- Minimize handoffs to shorten cycle time and avoid rework.
- Maximize horizontal flow and, minimize vertical flow.
- Iterate early to minimize "downstream" iterations.

Figure 18.8 *Optimizing process flow. (Courtesy of the Lean Advancement Initiative.)*

adherence to those practices noted for the ideal "pull" value stream. For example, at check points or gates, are checklists available as a basis of review? Are all the right stakeholders, and only those stakeholders, present? If corrective actions are necessary, is there a mechanism in place to effect rescheduling and work-arounds?

Figure 18.8 represents a flow of activities associated with solving an engineering design problem, the goal being to achieve smooth single-piece flow while incorporating concurrent work through the use of integrated teams. These IPTs are the generators of this flow as well as establishing those activities that can be implemented in parallel without damaging the intended linearity of the total flow. This fosters elimination of excessive iteration and rework.

Although the emphasis has been on reduction of cycle time and therefore cost by use of value stream mapping, there is also a marketing application, in that depiction of the full knowledge of processes and waste elimination to generate a development can be persuasive to management and customers. This battery control unit flow (Figure 18.9) was established to convince stakeholders of the value in going ahead with a new product design development. It became useful through several generations of marketing the concept. Value stream mapping thus becomes a vital practice in establishing a truly lean activity throughout the development life cycle. The summary steps that follow in Figure 18.10 can serve as a template for the use of value stream mapping in pursuing value-added activities in either an existing or a new development cycle.

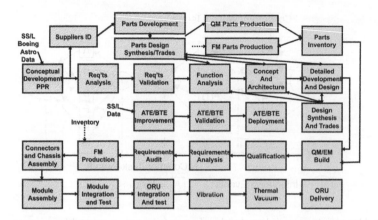

Figure 18.9 *Battery control unit value stream example. (Courtesy of Loral Corporation.)*

1. Define the boundaries.
2. Define the value.
3. "Walk" the process.
   - Identify tasks and flows of material and information between them.
4. Gather data.
   - Identify resources for task and flow.
5. Create a "current state" map.
6. Analyze the current conditions.
   - Identify value added and waste.
   - Reconfigure the process to eliminate waste and maximize value.
7. Visualize the "ideal state."
8. Create a "future state" map.
9. Develop and track action plans.
   - Construct models, diagrams, and schematics that depict how a process is working or should work.

Figure 18.10 *Summary: steps to value stream mapping.*

RESOURCES AND NOTES

Value streams are addressed in all the Chapter 16 references. There are, however, some publications dedicated to the methodology, including:

Product Development Value Stream Mapping, H. McManus, Lean Advancement Initiative, Cambridge, MA, 2005.

This work not only provides a rationale and steps for tactics for engineering process improvement, but also discusses interesting approaches to value creation.

Learning to See: Value Stream Mapping to Add Value, J. Shook and M. Rother, Lean Enterprise Institute, Cambridge, MA, 1999.

This book emphasizes the need for teams with wide experience to develop complete process maps and an understanding of where waste exists. Also noted is the need to integrate all processes due to interactive effects. A good primer.

Value Stream Mapping for Healthcare Made Easy, C. Jimmerson, Productivity Press, Taylor & Francis, Boca Raton, FL, 2010.

This work presents some basics of value stream mapping and important case studies ranging from routine admittance procedures to trauma patient flow.

Some Web-based or software tools: SmartDraw, Enna VSM Solutions.

REVIEW CHECKLIST

☐ Are all information transfer paths reviewed and nonessential ones eliminated?

☐ Has a value stream map for the development been established?

☐ Does it include planned iterations and parallel activities?

☐ Does it include backup technology paths?

☐ Is the value stream map used for evaluation of progress? Productivity? Resource management?

☐ Reflecting Chapters 15 and 18, can the design structure matrix be morphed into a value stream?

19

Case Studies

Three very different case studies are presented. One involves a frequently addressed type of product or system in the development of a unique health monitoring system for an unpiloted air vehicle (UAV); the second is a service-utilized product, that of a system-based identification program for the Indian government. The third, the realization of application software, recognizes the influence of stakeholders and codes that reach out to the linkages with many direct and indirect influences in the construction industry. Each, however, follows the value stream illustrated in this book and can help guide the reader through many of the process sequences, although with different vocabularies in some cases. The UAV has been an active Stanford laboratory project sponsored by a current U.S. aerospace firm. The Indian identification project is a proposed improvement to a program up for approval in the Indian parliament. The solar energy installation software is important not only in its application but also in its linkages to existing design tools. The authors of each are or have been Ph.D. students at Stanford University. Each project is a shortened version of the complete report on the project.

CASE STUDY 1: HEALTH MANAGEMENT SYSTEM FOR A NEXT-GENERATION UAV

Danny Lau and Cecilia Larrosa

In this project we use a product development approach to study the implementation of a health management system for next-generation UAVs. It will include:

Product and Systems Development: A Value Approach, First Edition. Stanley I. Weiss.
© 2013 John Wiley & Sons, Inc. Published 2013 by John Wiley & Sons, Inc.

1. An identification of the objectives, stakeholders, values, and design requirements
2. A study of the function and architecture of the system
3. A trade study between concepts
4. An identification of the failure modes and mitigation
5. A proposed project schedule and management

Design Requirements

From Stakeholders to Values Based on the project description and objectives, stakeholders and their values were identified as shown in Table CS1.1. The research investor was the most important stakeholder because this is the source of funding. UAV operators and maintenance teams were also very important stakeholders, as they have direct interaction with the health management system.

TABLE CS1.1 Stakeholders and Corresponding Values

Stakeholders	Values
Research investor	Return on investment, licensing, research duration, system reliability, engineering feasibility
UAV companies	System reliability, licensing, engineering feasibility, manufacturing cost, system performance, system robustness, flight system compatibility, system operation cost, ease of system maintenance, return on investment, research duration, interdisciplinary support, flight safety, ease of operation
Researchers	Research fund reliability, research duration, engineering feasibility, interdisciplinary support, flight system compatibility
FAA	Licensing, flight system compatibility, system reliability
UAV operators	Ease of operation, flight safety, system reliability, system performance, system robustness, ease of system maintenance, system operation cost, interdisciplinary support, engineering feasibility
UAV maintenance teams	Ease of system maintenance, system reliability, flight safety, ease of operation, interdisciplinary support, engineering feasibility
UAV flight computer programmers	System robustness, ease of operation, system reliability, system performance, ease of system maintenance, interdisciplinary support, engineering feasibility, flight safety
UAV mission planners	System reliability, system operation cost, system performance, system robustness, ease of system maintenance, ease of operation, interdisciplinary support, engineering feasibility, flight safety
System manufacturer	Manufacturing cost, engineering feasibility, flight system compatibility, research duration, research funds reliability, return on investment

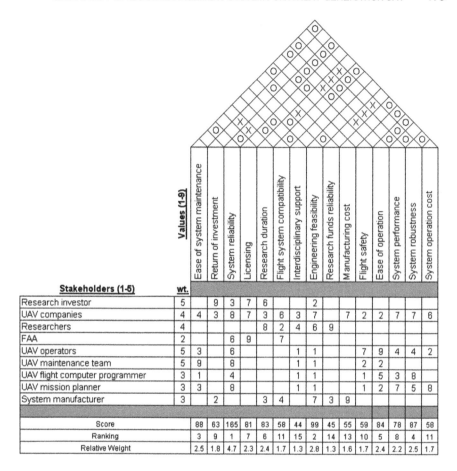

Stakeholders (1-5)	wt.	Ease of system maintenance	Return of investment	System reliability	Licensing	Research duration	Flight system compatibility	Interdisciplinary support	Engineering feasibility	Research funds reliability	Manufacturing cost	Flight safety	Ease of operation	System performance	System robustness	System operation cost
Research investor	5		9	3	7	6			2							
UAV companies	4	4	3	8	7	3	6	3	7		7	2	2	7	7	6
Researchers	4					8	2	4	6	9						
FAA	2			6	9		7									
UAV operators	5	3		6				1	1			7	9	4	4	2
UAV maintenance team	5	9		8				1	1			2	2			
UAV flight computer programmer	3	1		4				1	1			1	5	3	8	
UAV mission planner	3	3		8				1	1			1	2	7	5	8
System manufacturer	3		2				3	4		7	3	9				
Score		88	63	165	81	83	58	44	99	45	55	59	84	78	87	58
Ranking		3	9	1	7	6	11	15	2	14	13	10	5	8	4	11
Relative Weight		2.5	1.8	4.7	2.3	2.4	1.7	1.3	2.8	1.3	1.6	1.7	2.4	2.2	2.5	1.7

Figure CS1.1 *Stakeholders–values QFD.*

From the first QFD (Figure CS1.1), we found that the reliability of the health management system obtained a much higher score than did other values; it is the most critical and shared stakeholders' value. Stakeholders were also very concerned about the feasibility of health management technology and ease of system maintenance.

From Values to Customer Needs   Stakeholders' values were further broken down into customer needs as listed in Table CS1.2. As expected from the project objective and the QFD (Figure CS1.2), the lightweight characteristic for the health management system was significant. Customers also wanted good system redundancy to ensure system reliability, and accurate and multifunctional fault detection to provide support for flight. It is also important to note that although easy and fast deployment did not score high in the second QFD, this customer

TABLE CS1.2 Values and Corresponding Customer Needs

Values	Key Contributing Customer Needs
Ease of system maintenance	Simple or infrequent inspection, replacement parts, good system redundancy
Return on investment	Research costs stay within budget, short research time line
System reliability	Accurate, multifunctional fault detection, good system redundancy, simple or infrequent inspection
Licensing	Compatible with UAV structure, compatible with flight control
Research duration	Short research time line, research costs stay within budget
Flight system compatibility	Compatible with flight control, compatible with UAV structure, lightweight
Interdisciplinary support	Compatible with UAV structure, compatible with flight control
Engineering feasibility	Lightweight, low power consumption
Research fund reliability	Research costs stay within budget, short research time line
Manufacturing cost	Cheap manufacturing materials, simple assembly, replacement parts
Flight safety	Fast response to an abnormal condition, wide range of operational conditions
Ease of operation	Minimal training required, compatible with flight control
System performance	Lightweight, low power consumption
System robustness	Real-time structural prognostics, fast response to an abnormal condition, wide range of operational conditions
System operation cost	Simple or infrequency inspection, lightweight, cheap manufacturing materials

need was, in fact, most commonly shared by the stakeholders' values. Another takeaway from this QFD is that customer needs that ranked between fourth and eighth should not be underestimated because they also had high scores. Some requirements that were omitted from the top tier were those with unresolvable conflicts.

From Customer Needs to Requirements   In the final QFD (Figure CS1.3), the design requirements were derived from customer needs. The analysis showed a very interesting result. Many of the requirements had similar scoring, but those requirements were also complementary to each other. A list of key design requirements is provided in Table CS1.3, and the top three requirements are elaborated further in the following sections.

Another layer of QFD analysis was performed to expand on the technical requirements, yielding the further detail shown in Table CS1.4. For example, intrinsic to light weight is sensor number and layout, the direction of research that followed this preamble.

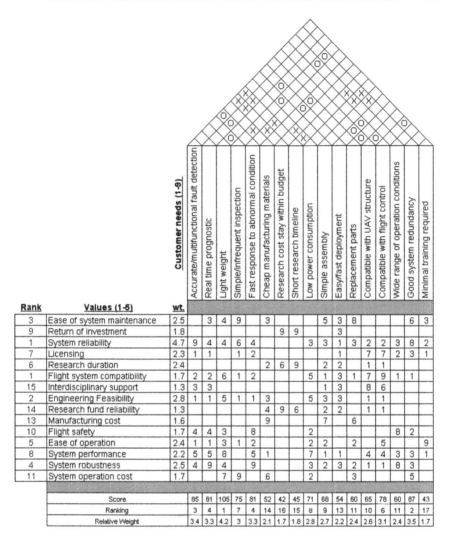

Figure CS1.2 Values–customer needs QFD.

Optimization of Sensor Number and Layout Optimization of the number of sensors and layout on a vehicle is crucial for the successful development of a health management system. The major goal for the optimization will be to minimize the total weight of the sensors, but it is also constrained by the accuracy, efficiency, and redundancy required for the system to perform its function. *Sensor network* refers not only to the sensors but also to the wires that connect the sensors together. For a health management system that covers the entire vehicle, the wire will certainly contribute a significant percentage of weight to the system. As a result, it is critical to

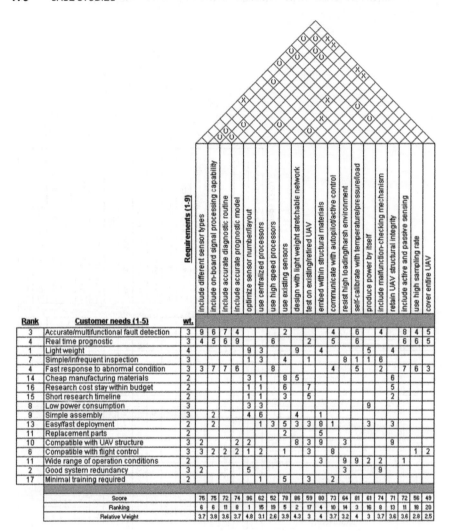

Figure CS1.3   *Needs to requirements.*

Rank	Customer needs (1-5)	wt.	include different sensor types	include on-board signal processing capability	include accurate diagnostic routine	include accurate prognostic model	optimize sensor number/layout	use centralized processors	use high speed processors	use existing sensors	design with light weight stretchable network	test on existing/retired UAV	embed within structural materials	communicate with autopilot/active control	resist high loading/harsh environment	self-calibrate with temperature/pressure/load	produce power by itself	include malfunction-checking mechanism	retain UAV structural integrity	include active and passive sensing	use high sampling rate	cover entire UAV
3	Accurate/multifunctional fault detection	3	9	6	7	4				2				4		6		4		8	4	5
4	Real time prognostic	3	4	5	6	9				6				2		5		6		6	6	5
1	Light weight	4					9	3			9		4						5	4		
7	Simple/infrequent inspection	3					1	3				4		1			8	1	1	6		
4	Fast response to abnormal condition	3	3	7	7	6				8				4		5		2		7	6	3
14	Cheap manufacturing materials	2					3	1		8	5							6				
16	Research cost stay within budget	2					1	1		6		7						5				
15	Short research timeline	2					1	1		3		5						2				
8	Low power consumption	3					3	3									9					
9	Simple assembly	3		2			4	6			4		1									
13	Easy/fast deployment	2		2			1	3		5	3	3	8	1				3	3			
11	Replacement parts	2								2							5					
10	Compatible with UAV structure	3	2			2	2			8	3		9	3					9			
6	Compatible with flight control	3	3	2	2	2	1	2		1			3	8							1	2
11	Wide range of operation conditions	2											3		9	9	2	2		1		
2	Good system redundancy	3	2				5									3			9			
17	Minimal training required	2								1				5		3	2					
	Score		75	75	72	74	96	62	52	78	86	59	80	73	64	81	61	74	71	72	56	49
	Ranking		6	6	11	8	1	15	19	5	2	17	4	10	14	3	16	9	13	11	18	20
	Relative Weight		3.7	3.8	3.6	3.7	4.8	3.1	2.6	3.9	4.3	3	4	3.7	3.2	4	3	3.7	3.6	3.6	2.8	2.5

develop a very lightweight total sensor network. Research is thus directed toward a stretchable network that is very lightweight and can be stretched to cover a large area.

Functional Analysis

The functional flow diagram shown in Figure CS1.4 visualizes the flow of the health management system. There are two ways to activate the system. The first one is by detection of an off-nominal flight condition, which could be, for example, impact, gust, turbulence, and malfunction. The second one is by initiation command by a

TABLE CS1.3   Key Design Requirements

Rank	Key Design Requirements
1	Optimize sensor number and layout
2	Minimize weight for sensor network
3	Self-calibrate with temperature and load
4	Embed sensor network within structure
5	Use existing sensor technologies
6	Include different sensor types or multifunctional sensors
7	Include onboard signal-processing capability
8	Include accurate structural prognostic techniques

flight computer or ground station. Once the health management system is activated, sensors will collect signals by active sensing, passive sensing, or both. Then the signal will be passed on to the processors, and along with the environmental data collected by other passive sensors, the signal will be diagnosed and translated into quantifiable information. The flight condition, which includes aerodynamic information, vehicle stability, and other information, such as chemical exposure, will be sent to the flight computer directly. The structural damage information, on the other hand, will be sent to the structural prognostic program. The life cycle, fatigue, crack

TABLE CS1.4   Customer Needs and Corresponding Requirements

Customer Needs	Key Contributing Requirements
Accurate, multifunction fault detection	Include different sensor types, active and passive sensing, and accurate diagnostic routine
Real-time structural prognostics	Include an accurate diagnostic routine
Light weight	Optimize sensor number and layout
Simple or infrequent inspection	Resist high loading and harsh environment
Fast response to an abnormal condition	Use high-speed processors; include onboard signal-processing capability, accurate diagnostic routine, and active and passive sensing
Cheap manufacturing materials	Use existing sensors
Research costs stay within budget	Test on existing or retired UAV
Short research time line	Test on existing or retired UAV
Low power consumption	Produce power by itself
Simple assembly	Use centralized processors
Easy, fast deployment	Embed within structural materials
Replacement parts	Embed within structural materials
Compatible with UAV structure	Embed within structural materials, retain UAV structural integrity, design with lightweight stretchable network
Compatible with flight control	Communicate with autopilot or active control
Wide range of operational conditions	Resist high loading/harsh environment, self-calibrate with temperature and load
Good system redundancy	Include malfunction-checking technique
Minimal training required	Use existing sensors

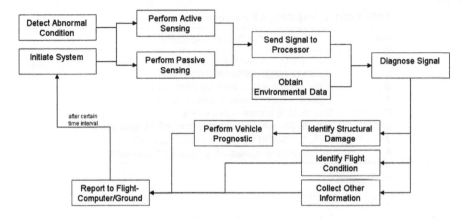

Figure CS1.4 *Functional flow diagram.*

growth, and other parameters will be analyzed and passed on to the flight computer. Finally, the flight computer will be able to trigger the system again after a preset interval. Figure CS1.5 identifies the interaction between system components. There are two main functional blocks, the sensors and the processing units.

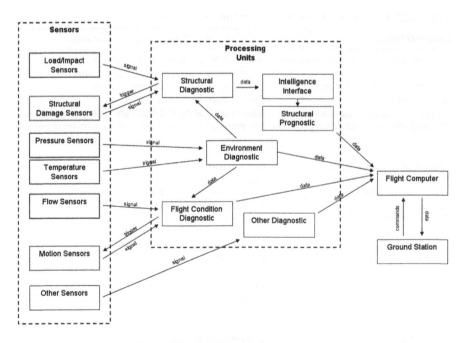

Figure CS1.5 *Functional block diagram.*

SENSORS	DIAGNOSTICS		PROGNOSTICS		SYSTEM OUTPUT
Excitation from environment			Finite Element Model (FEM)	Damage Tolerance Limits/Threshholds	
Sensing devices	wave propagation / electromagnetic signal				
	Interpretation	Damage Location and size	Load history, Probability of detection, environment charact.		
		Initiate Damage	elements of FEM that will be affected		
			Progressive Damage	Residual strength	
			Future Loading, environment charact.	Virtual Environment	Life prediction / Decision

 Inputs   Outputs

Figure CS1.6   *Vehicle health management interfaces.*

Interfaces

Although Figure CS1.5 depicts many interfaces, the N^2 diagram in Figure CS1.6 was very useful in identifying the interface relationships among the components of a health management system. There were three major interfaces: sensors–diagnostics, diagnostics–prognostics, and prognostics–system output.

Concepts Selection and Trades

Two concepts were compared to assess implementation and necessary research areas. The *Intelligent structure* concept is a vision concept which entails technology that is currently in the development stage. The *smart layer* concept is an interim concept which uses the current state of the art on health-monitoring technology.

- *Concept 1: intelligent structure.* The intelligent structure consists of a stretchable network whose nodes can host various types of sensors. This is illustrated in Figure CS1.7.
- *Concept 2: smart layer.* The state of the art in health monitoring is an embedded layer of bulk piezoelectric sensors (Figure CS1.8).

Trade Study   Because of the complexity and interplay of many factors, we decided to approach this problem using the collaborative optimization (CO) technique shown in Figure CS1.9. This approach outputs the most efficient system and can indicate which requirements are being compromised or not met.

Embedded network of sensors (aircraft's skin)

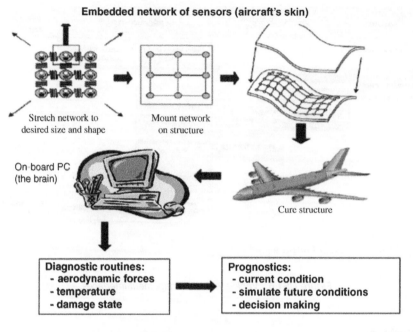

Stretch network to desired size and shape

Mount network on structure

On-board PC (the brain)

Cure structure

Diagnostic routines:
- aerodynamic forces
- temperature
- damage state

Prognostics:
- current condition
- simulate future conditions
- decision making

Figure CS1.7   *Stretchable sensor network.*

"Smart Layer" within structure

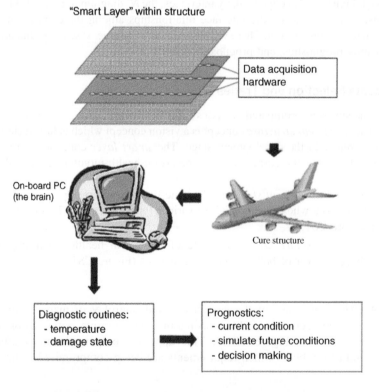

Data acquisition hardware

On-board PC (the brain)

Cure structure

Diagnostic routines:
- temperature
- damage state

Prognostics:
- current condition
- simulate future conditions
- decision making

Figure CS1.8   *Embedded sensors: current state of the art.*

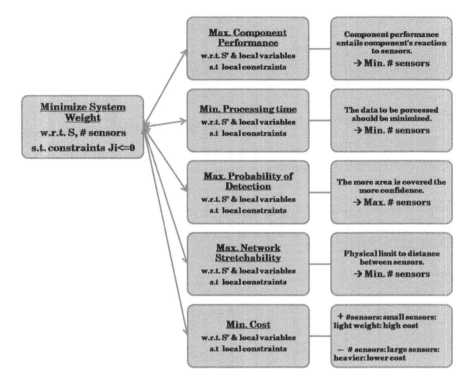

Figure CS1.9   *CO characterizes the logic of weight optimization.*

In Table CS1.5 the trade process is shown in a conventional weighting scheme most related to Kepner–Trego. Using the main constraints from the CO approach, we can evaluate each concept. The weights of the five criteria were set by referring to the results of the QFD analysis. The table shows that concept 1 scored higher than concept 2, so it was selected as more desirable to implement.

System Architecture

The architecture (Figure CS1.10) for the health management system was developed to include a detailed breakdown of components that could not be shown in earlier diagrams. Two major segments were considered: hardware and software.

Failure Analysis and Mitigation

Failure modes for the health management system were categorized into hardware failures and software failures, but most of the failures can be resolved by good system redundancy, as shown in Table CS1.6.

TABLE CS1.5 Trade Weight-and-Rate Approach for Selection

Criteria	wt.	Concept 1		Concept 2	
Component performance	3	Because of its micro dimensions, the structure will not be affected significantly by the presence of the sensor network.	3	Because of their relatively large size compared to a ply's thickness, there are many concerns about structure sensor interaction.	2
Processing time	3	Many sensors which have n neighboring sensors. To process and analyze all these data will be very time consuming.	1	Not as many sensors, which makes processing time not as complex. As of now the technology is still not real-time.	3
Probability of detection	4	Many sensors covering more area will create a more redundant system, which will result in more accurate detection.	3	The small number of sensors and unknown interaction with structures when embedded result in not very accurate detection.	2
Network robustness	3	Because it is designed to be stretchable, it will be easy to transport and introduce into more than one component. It has the potential to act as wireless communication from a microprocessor to the main processor.	3	It is manufactured only to meet the specific component and needs to be placed in such a way that cables to hardware need to be considered when placing. These cables and hardware add weight to the system.	1
Cost	1	Manufacturing techniques require development, nanofabrication equipment, and specific chemicals. Until the process is standardized, the system will be expensive to manufacture.	2	It uses preexisting and commercially available sensors. It is a fairly inexpensive system.	3
Weight	5	This is a very lightweight stretchable network.	3	Large sensors plus cables and hardware result in a fairly heavy system.	1
Score			50		34

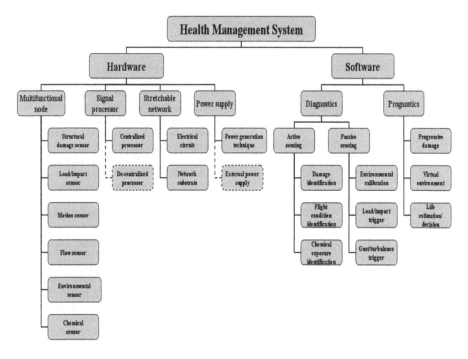

Figure CS1.10 *System architecture.*

Validation and Verification

Hardware   Validation and verification of hardware for the health management system is relatively simple. Laboratory experiments on small panels can be set up to test the signal actuating and receiving capabilities of the sensors and the transmission capability of the wire. Similarly, the connectivity of the processor can be tested by building a test bed with a small number of sensors.

Software   The software validation and verification is more complicated, with iterative functions as shown in Figure CS1.11.

Scheduling and Management

Table CS1.7 presents the needed research areas to be developed and how much time it is expected to take for the different technologies to be ready for implementation. Results show that concept 1 could be ready within six years, and concept 2 could be ready to be implemented within two years.

Proposed Implementation and Management

The approach is to implement concept 2 while concept 1 is being developed. Since diagnostics, interface, and prognostics are being developed and will be ready before

TABLE CS1.6 Failure Modes and Mitigation Plan

Category	Failure Mode	Mitigation Plan
Hardware	Totally failed sensor	Sensors overlap each other.
	Partially failed sensor (can still send and receive a signal, but the signal is wrong)	Same mitigation plan for a totally failed sensor, but in addition, a mechanism such as impedance checking is needed to identify the partially failed sensor because the sensors act normally and the processing software will not know that the signal is wrong.
	Wire disconnection/short circuit	Redundant or alternative circuit paths with a self-calibration algorithm when a disconnection or short circuit is detected.
	Processing unit failure	Include redundant processing power in other processing units and have them share the workload of the failed processor. Pass the signal to the ground station for processing.
	Insufficient power generated	Include emergency power plan that take power from the UAV itself.
Software	Diagnostic/prognostic software crash with flight software	Have a ground pilot standing by and he can take control of the UAV manually and shut down the health management system.
	Program not fast enough or too many signals to process	Use a dynamic sampling rate and prioritize information. For example, when there are gusts, analyzing signals from flow sensors will be more important, and signals from chemical sensors may be omitted.
	Inaccurate diagnostic/ prognostic model due to the lack of data	Implement onboard memory, which is able to store a history of the flight. Diagnostic/prognostic software can use the previous data to interpolate the lacking information.

the stretchable network, it makes sense to implement concept 2 as a first-generation technology. Deploying concept 2 could help mitigate and discover issues that have not been looked at. In the Venn diagram of Figure CS1.12, the darker top circle is highlighted (new sensors, network, node communication, and signal processing) since this is the area of main development that will enable concept 1 to be implemented.

Cost Analysis

It is extremely difficult to estimate the cost of implementation of the health management system because it is in a research stage. In addition, the price for Acellent's system of currently available software for concept 2 is not disclosed and there are no further historical cost data.

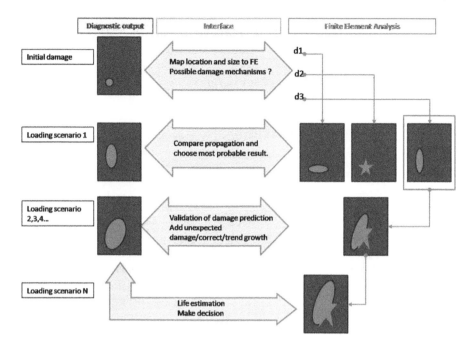

Figure CS1.11 *Prognostic validation and verification.*

TABLE CS1.7 Schedule to Implementation

Concept 1	Concept 2
Sensors	
Stretchable Sensor Network	Acellent's Smart Layer
• Research/developmental stages	• Validated and in use by industry
• Expected completion in 5+years	• Commercially available
Diagnostics	
Physics based; learn how signal changes due to faults, loading, and environment.	Modification of Acellent's diagnostic routines to compensate for loading and environment effects (SACL).
• There are many techniques to be used; the issue to be developed is how to process data from millions of sensors (data mining techniques).	• In-progress: to be completed in 2010.
Intelligent Interface	
A routine that will link diagnostics and prognostics (SACL).	
• Conceptual planning in progress	
• To be completed by 2011	
Prognostics	
Progressive failure analysis based on fracture mechanics and material degradation modeling (Stanford SACL).	
• In progress: to be completed and validated by 2010	

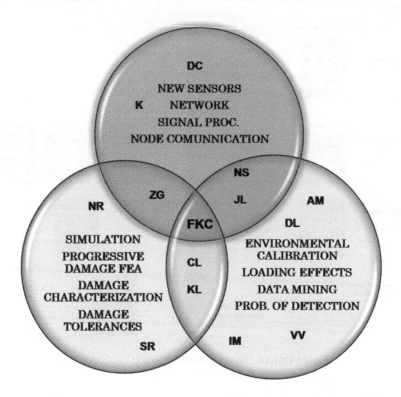

Figure CS1.12 *Proposed management for the implementation of both concepts.*

CASE STUDY 2:   PRODUCT AND SYSTEMS DEVELOPMENT FOR THE UNIQUE IDENTIFICATION AUTHORITY OF INDIA

Adeel Arif and Raghuveer Krishnamurthy

India is home to nearly 20% of humanity and is considered widely as a newly industrialized economy. India today is one of the fastest-growing major economies of the world and is considered to have entered an era of demographic dividend. However, it should be noted that there are several crucial challenges facing the country, especially in terms of corruption, illiteracy, poor health coverage, and widespread poverty. To address some of these issues, in February 2009 the government of India formed the Unique Identification Authority of India (UIDAI), responsible for assigning each resident of India a unique identification number.

Primary Objectives

The primary objectives are to understand the complexities of the UIDAI project and apply the systems-thinking concepts toward analyzing and possibly improving on the project planned by the government. According to the government, the primary goal of the UIDAI is to establish, for all residents of India, the following: identity, residency, and eligibility for welfare benefits. The UID number will track specific information: financial history, health history, welfare benefit payments, driving permits (if any), and inner line permits (required to access certain border areas).

Stakeholders and their Values

Of the 50+ stakeholders identified, we used the top 25 for a detailed analysis using the House of Quality tool. The top five stakeholders and their values are shown in Table CS2.1.

TABLE CS2.1   Top Five Stakeholders and Their Values

Stakeholders	Weight (%)	Key Values
Government of India (ministries)	35	Cost of project
		Cost of maintaining project
		Efficiency and speed of the system
Commercial service providers	16	Ease of data extraction
		Cost to businesses
Law enforcement and judiciary	7	Portability
		Efficiency
UIDAI	7	Accuracy of information
		Transparency
		Price to consumer
Residents of India	6	Privacy of data
		Security of information
		Ease of use
		Reliability

TABLE CS2.2   Converting Values to Needs

Values	Weight (%)	Key Needs
Accuracy	12.3	Secure database
		Accurate collection of data
Reliability	12.2	Good infrastructure
		Multiple large data farms
		Materials: high functional quality
		Materials: high longevity
Security of information	11.9	Restrict database access
		Legislation to enforce penalties for ID theft
		Activity monitoring department
Cost to service providers	9.3	User-friendly interface
		Low latency
Ease of use and maintenance of database	9.2	Personnel training
		Customer support: regional offices
		Customer support: call centers

   As can be seen from the QFD analysis, the leading values that identify the system needs are summarized in Table CS2.2. The transition from the values to needs led to the identification of these top design requirements for the system (Table CS2.3).

Design Requirements

Merely stating system requirements is not a very prudent way to design a system, and we took this process a step further to identify ways in which we could quantify some of the top requirements (Table CS2.4).

Interfaces and Functional Analysis

A primary issue in considering the various stakeholders are their interactions. To highlight these, we established a visual relationship through an N^2 diagram,

TABLE CS2.3   Converting Needs to System Requirements

Needs	Weight (%)	Key System Requirements
Multiple large data farms	9.0	Real estate acquisition
		Technically skilled staff
		Managerial staff
Accurate collection of data	8.7	Linguistically skilled staff
		Retina scan
		Fingerprinting
		Voice recognition
Secure database	8.4	Firewalls
		Network address restriction for server access
Materials: high functional quality	7.8	High-quality materials
Reliable infrastructure	7.8	High-capacity servers
		Captive power generation
		Optical fiber and wireless networks

TABLE CS2.4   Quantifying Requirements

Top Five Requirements	Measures
Optical fiber and wireless networks	$\geq$ 10 gigabit/second national backbone network
High-capacity servers	$\geq$ 12,000 terabits of data storage across multiple data centers Parallel processing with thousands of servers
Human capital management: technical staff	$\geq$ 265 hardware and software developers
Acquisition of real estate	Registration center per 8000 people Central customer care call center
Secure and restricted access to database	Cost for maintenance, patching, or support Time to encrypt or decrypt data Time to identify infractions

Figure CS2.1, which not only gives graphic visibility to these but serves to identify interfaces to be satisfied in functional analysis and concept definition.

Keeping these interfaces in mind, we proceed to identify important functional flows in the system. We begin with the top-level functional flow diagram, presented in Figure CS2.2. The top level of the functional diagram takes you through the complex UIDAI system. To initiate the system, the government of India will table a bill to the parliament detailing how the UIDAI system will work ("1. Enact Legislation"). Simultaneously, the human capital management process will work to recruit, train, and deploy employees ("1. Human Capital Management").

N² Diagram	Legislation	UIDAI	Card Manufacturer	Human Capital Management	Infrastructure developers	Enrollers and registrars	Database Managers	Equipment Manufacturer	Service providers
Legislation	■	✓							
UIDAI	✓	■	✓	✓	✓	✓	✓	✓	✓
Card Manufacturer		✓	■					✓	
Human Capital Management		✓		■	✓				
Infrastructure developers		✓			■				✓
Enrollers and registrars		✓				■			
Database Managers	✓	✓		✓			■	✓	
Equipment Manufacturer	✓	✓	✓				✓	■	✓
Service providers		✓			✓			✓	■

Figure CS2.1   N² diagram.

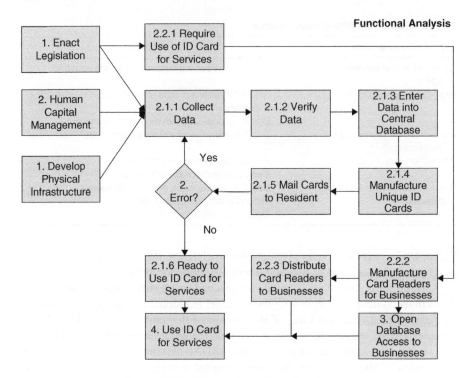

Figure CS2.2 *Top-level functional flow diagram.*

Furthermore, the UIDAI will undertake development of physical infrastructure, such as construction or leasing of office space, captive power generators, optical fiber network and wireless connectivity and data centers and providing facilities for the same ("1. Develop Physical Infrastructure"). While all of the above generate lower-level functional flows, one for the legislative process is shown in Figure CS2.3.

Concept Development and Trades

We have a pretty good idea of what the system looks like with the functional flows in place, and it is a good place to investigate what the concept of the product (i.e., the card) and system will look like. There are some decisions that we assume have been made regarding the conceptual design.

It has been decided that plastic will be used for the physical cards themselves, and magnetic strips will be used to encapsulate data. The information that the card will contain on its face has also been determined. The UID card will have information on its face that resembles information shown on a driving license, such as name, address, blood type, data of birth, and basic biometric information.

Once the material to be embedded in the card was identified, concentration shifted to the most favorable ways to both acquire the data and to implement it. These are illustrated by the six weighted Pugh analyses shown in Figure CS2.4.

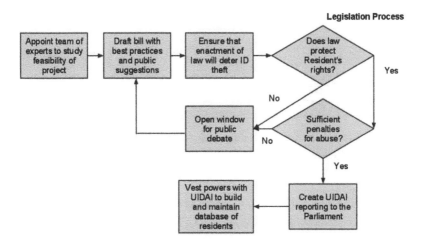

Figure CS2.3 *Functional flow diagram for the legislation process.*

System Architecture

Having made key trades, and having a good idea of the system's functionality, we are ready to develop the system architecture—in this case a system of systems. The architecture is depicted in Figure CS2.5.

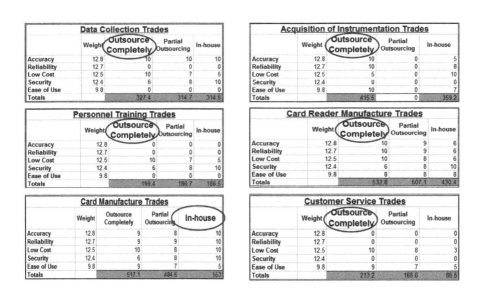

Figure CS2.4 *Concept selection trades.*

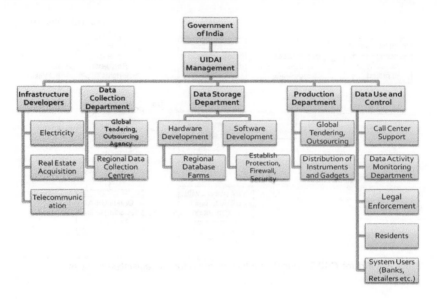

Figure CS2.5 System architecture.

Failure Modes and Mitigation

A system as large and comprehensive as this one is bound to fail at multiple steps, and careful risk assessment needs to be done. Not all possibilities have been enumerated, as expert opinion is required to plug all gaps comprehensively. The important failure modes have been determined to be of two types: product failures and system failures.

Product Failures The most commonly occurring problem that can be foreseen is that of the card not working. This could be due to material damage to the card: for example, the magnetic strip breaks, the card itself gets damaged, or the biometric and other data stored on the card are corrupted. This risk can be mitigated by ensuring strict quality control methods during manufacture with failure rates of materials limited to under 0.1% during the first year of use.

System Failures Some system failures and possible mitigation, including problems that can be addressed bureaucratically, are shown in Table CS2.5.

Project Management: Cost Analysis and Time Frame

The UIDAI has split the process into three initial phases, with the enrollment predicted by the graph shown in Figure CS2.6. We found an estimation of cost and time to enroll over 90% of the population successfully a bit of a challenge.

TABLE CS2.5   System Failures and Their Mitigation

Failure	Mitigation
Database failure	
Hard disk failure	Multiple redundancies
Fire in the storage space	Safety procedures
Complete/partial loss of data	Back-up every day
Breach of data	
Database	Database activity
ID theft	monitoring department
Human error in input of data	Legal enforcement
Connectivity failure	Multiple verification

Cost   We were unable to build a model to generate cost estimates for the project. The costs that we found upon researching and through the UIDAI seem too divergent to be useful. It appears that the government would like to push the project through at any cost.

Cost estimates provided by UID and other sources vary tremendously. By UIDAI estimates, phases I and II will cost the treasury about $3 billion. In fiscal year 2010–2011, UIDAI was allocated $670 million to implement the project. Critics of the program estimate the total cost to be upward of $30 billion. The true cost is more likely to be somewhere in the middle, perhaps between $15 and $20 billion. Even if it is as high as $30 billion, it is our belief that such a system will provide incremental benefits in areas not yet thought of that will far outweigh its incredible cost.

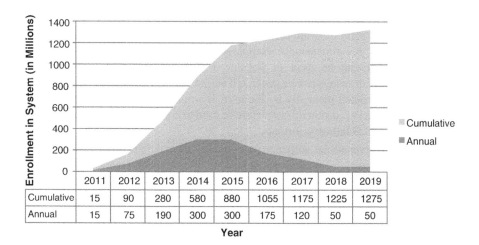

	2011	2012	2013	2014	2015	2016	2017	2018	2019
Cumulative	15	90	280	580	880	1055	1175	1225	1275
Annual	15	75	190	300	300	175	120	50	50

Figure CS2.6   *Target enrollment numbers with time.*

CASE STUDY 3: SOFTWARE DEVELOPMENT FOR A PHOTOVOLTAIC SYSTEM CONSTRUCTION PROJECT

Jumie Yuventi

This somewhat abbreviated case illustrates some common and special considerations for applying the methodology and tools of product and systems development to software design development. It emphasizes front-end systems thinking and tools, with the more standard aspects of writing, coding, and verifying software left to other texts, although some insights were covered in Case 1.

Project Scope and Motivation

This project involves the development of software that automates electrical engineering tasks in the design and engineering phases of photovoltaic system construction projects. In general, this work is an attempt at accelerating the design process to facilitate the rapid exploration of design alternatives and optimization strategies. As a result, the tool should take into consideration the practical constraints of these projects. It should also take into account new design considerations, optimization strategies, and project scopes. The development process is divided into three phases, each with specific goals:

- *Phase I.* Reduce design workflows into software that can autonomously translate project requirements and user preferences into geometric designs. This phase only considers the electrical components of large-scale ground-mounted photovoltaic systems (e.g., modules, fuses, wiring). The geometric design should include the physical location, electrical connections, and the type or manufacturer specifications for each component. The software should also perform certain analyses, such as performance estimation and safety evaluations, either automatically or prompted manually by the user.
- *Phase II.* Expand software functionality to translate the geometric designs into two- and three-dimensional computer-aided design (CAD) drawings and models that can be used in popular design software such as AutoCAD MEP. These drawings can be generated automatically in the autodesign process flow or prompted manually by the user. It would allow system designs to be shared using the current infrastructure or used to create construction permit sets using standard industry formats.
- *Phase III.* Expand the software functionality to make provisions for rooftop-mounted system installations and adjust analyses and optimization strategies to include considerations such as the structural support system, electrical connections to the utility, and charge storage.

Photovoltaic system construction projects are dominated by the electrical system components. Developmental phases I and II focus on large-scale photovoltaic systems primarily because there are fewer physical interfaces to account for, in comparison to rooftop-mounted installations. In addition, fewer engineering and construction parties are involved in the design and installation of these systems, hence limiting the issues that can arise due to the excessively fragmented supply chain typical of the construction industry. This fragmentation has influenced a fierce competitive environment where companies are reluctant to process changes, and innovations are slow to realize and adopt. Additionally, many innovative software solutions geared toward the construction industry have failed, due to a misalignment of the product feature sets to the tasks of the end users. These considerations prompt the need for a value-driven systems engineering approach to development of this software in order to effectively address the needs of all stakeholders, to prioritize development, and to give the product a good chance of being successful in the marketplace. This approach should also assist in the transition between each of the development phases. The lessons learned from developing this tool may be used as a case study for developing other design automation software for other construction projects, such as data centers, industrial facilities, and commercial buildings. A system engineering analysis for phase I of this project is presented here.

Stakeholders and Values

Photovoltaic system designers and engineers are the primary end users of the software. However, the outputs of the tool would also affect other personnel involved in the construction project, including estimating and purchasing teams, construction crews, and other contractors. Since the tool is meant to create realistic designs for construction, it would also need to ensure that designs meet requirements set by governmental ordinances and standards organizations. It must also ensure, for example, that the requests of the ultimate system owner are met. Table CS3.1 lists potential stakeholders in the development and use of the software tool, shown in order of importance to the success of this project. Table CS3.2 lists values that may be common to these stakeholders, also shown in order of importance determined by the QFD shown in Matrix CS3.1, which quantifies the relationships between stakeholders and these values. This analysis takes into consideration the fact that the software tool may be used for practical and research purposes. For simplicity, stakeholders are organized into 10 groups, even though there may be more; the same is done for stakeholder values and later for system requirements. A scale of 0 to 10 is used to rate the importance of elements in the QFDs shown, where 10 indicates the most important. This analysis concludes that system designers are the most important stakeholders and that the quality of the output designs is the most important value.

Requirements and Conflicts

The software tool:

R1. *Should* present analysis results by means of reproducible documents, graphs, and/or spreadsheets.
R2. *Must* generate a representation of a photovoltaic system design based on user input.

TABLE CS3.1   Potential Stakeholders

ID	Name	Description/Comments
S1	System designers	The primary users of the tool: designers and engineers who use the tool in real project workflows, and hobbyists who may use the tool to gain a better understanding of these systems.
S2	Engineering firm	The company that manages the (electrical) system design and engineering for photovoltaic system projects, whose goodwill is associated with the quality of the constructed system and whose bottom line is associated with any time and cost overheads associated with adopting the tool.
S3	Researchers	Anyone in academia or industry who may use this tool for research purposes (e.g., to evaluate optimization strategies) or who may review any research findings developed using the tool.
S4	Government	Representatives of building divisions, fire departments, and so on, who evaluate the system designs to ensure compliance to applicable building codes and industry standards.
S5	Construction crew	Persons responsible for building or installing the designs created by the system designers, based on industry rules and within practical limitations.
S6	System owner	The person, group, or company that will own or maintain the system constructed.
S7	Other contractors	Other construction parties involved in the overall system design or installation that contribute physical components, structures, or logic to the constructed system.
S8	Software developers	Persons involved in programming, verifying, and validating the software; includes any future developers for subsequent versions or developer changes between development phases.
S9	Standard organizations	Agencies, institutes, trade organizations, and so on, which create industry standards that form practical and/or legal limitations for the design and installation of these systems.
S10	Estimating teams	Persons who may use the software to directly aid budget estimations, component purchasing, and work scheduling efforts; may include project management personnel.

R3. *Should* be reliable: have minimum usage errors and create consistent output.

R4. *Should* produce designs that conform to building codes and other regulating standards.

R5. *Must* perform relevant cost and performance analyses based on user preferences.

R6. *Should* define a design so that it is accessible to users and expandable to software developers.

TABLE CS3.2   Potential Stakeholder Values

ID	Name	Description/Comments
V1	Quality of designs	The ability of the tool to create designs and output analyses that meet the requirements set forth by governmental and standards organizations while attempting to maximize or optimize certain design preferences that can benefit groups other than the system designers.
V2	Speed	The ability of the tool to accelerate design and analysis.
V3	Tool expandability	The ability of the tool to be updated, built upon, or used for other purposes.
V4	Robustness	The ability of the tool to minimize faults and errors that can result due, for example, to improper coding, temporary memory glitches, or human error.
V5	Ease of use	The ability of the tool to be installed, set up, and navigated easily.
V6	Scientific accuracy	Beyond the adherence to standards and codes; this includes the incorporation of relevant scientific theories, computational methods, and so on, to increase the granularity of investigations or to increase the preciseness of analysis results for scientific inquiries.
V7	User documentation	The clarity of the information presented to end users on how to use the tool and maximize its capabilities for practical purposes and research endeavors.
V8	Complexity	Maximizing the number of features in the tool.
V9	Commercialization	The potential of the tool to be marketable and propagate rapidly through the industry.
V10	Development time	Minimizing the time required to make a stable, testable, or distributable version of the software.

R7. *Should* have an easily understandable interface.

R8. *Should* be packaged for modularity, not require the use of other commercial software tools (such as AutoCAD MEP), and not take up too many computer resources.

R9. *Must* allow users to be able to generate their own designs or use the tool only for analyses.

R10. *Should* use analysis results to alter dsigns based on user preferences.

The requirements are ordered based on the prioritization determined using the QFD shown in Matrix CS3.2, which relates the stakeholder values to the requirements. The weights shown represent the influence that each requirement has on the corresponding value.

Matrix CS3.3 illustrates the correlations between the stakeholder values that would influence conflict resolution in realizing the requirements or reprioritizing

Matrix CS3.1 Quality Function Deployment Relationships Between Stakeholders and Values

		Values									
Stakeholder	Weight	Quality of designs	Speed	Tool expandability	Robustness	Ease of use	Scientific accuracy	User documentation	Complexity	Commercialization	Development time
System designers	10	8	9	4	9	9	2	7	6	0	0
Engineering firm	9	8	9	5	3	6	0	3	1	3	0
Researchers	8	7	2	7	3	2	10	5	3	1	0
Government	7	9	0	0	1	1	3	1	0	2	0
Construction crew	6	9	0	0	0	0	2	0	0	0	0
System owner	5	9	0	0	0	0	3	0	0	2	0
Other contractors	4	8	7	10	5	0	1	1	7	8	0
Software developers	3	3	3	4	7	3	2	3	8	10	9
Standard organizations	2	10	2	3	1	1	8	1	3	5	0
Estimating teams	1	10	2	5	1	3	0	3	2	0	0
Raw sum		81	34	38	30	25	31	24	30	31	9
Weighted sum		441	230	204	192	181	174	162	153	131	27
Value priority		1	2	3	4	5	6	7	8	9	10
Priority weights		10	9	8	7	6	5	4	3	2	1

Matrix CS3.2   QFD Relationships Between Values and Requirements

Values	Weight	R1	R2	R3	R4	R5	R6	R7	R8	R9	R10
						Requirements					
Quality of designs	10	9	9	0	10	5	1	0	0	0	0
Speed	9	5	6	2	5	5	6	3	1	0	1
Tool expandability	8	3	4	7	1	5	10	0	8	5	3
Robustness	7	0	0	10	1	0	0	8	3	0	3
Ease of use	6	7	0	8	1	1	6	10	4	5	0
Scientific accuracy	5	4	8	8	8	9	1	1	0	3	0
User documentation	4	4	2	0	1	2	2	8	1	0	0
Complexity	3	7	5	1	5	5	6	1	9	8	10
Commercialization	2	7	10	9	8	6	1	9	8	1	1
Development time	1	5	8	5	5	7	3	4	4	4	7
Raw sum		51	52	50	45	45	36	44	38	26	25
Weighted sum		277	267	258	246	228	216	205	169	115	93
Value priority		1	2	3	4	5	6	7	8	9	10
Priority weights		6	8	10	4	3	7	9	1	5	2

Matrix CS3.3 Stakeholder Value Correlations

Priority	Values[a]	1 Quality of designs	2 Speed	3 Tool expandability	4 Robustness	5 Ease of use	6 Scientific accuracy	7 User documentation	8 Complexity	9 Commercialization	10 Development time
1	Quality of designs		↓↓	–	–	–	↑	–	–	↑↑	↓
2	Speed	↓↓		–	–	–	–	–	↓	–	↓
3	Tool Expandability	–	–		↓	–	–	–	↓	↑	↓
4	Robustness	–	–	↓		↑	–	–	↓↓	↑	↓
5	Ease of use	–	–	–	↑		–	↑↑	↓↓	–	–
6	Scientific accuracy	↑	–	–	–	–		–	↑	↑	↓
7	User documentation	–	–	–	–	↑↑	–		↓	↑	–
8	Complexity	–	↓	↓	↓↓	↓↓	↑	↓		↑	↓↓
9	Commercialization	↑↑	–	↑	↑	–	↑	↑	↑		–
10	Development time	↓	↓	↓	↓	–	↓	–	↓↓	–	

[a] ↑, positive correlation; ↑↑, strong positive correlation; ↓, negative correlation; ↓↓, strong negative correlation; –, limited/no correlation e.g., increasing complexity may result in longer development time; therefore, these quantities have strong negative correlations.

those developments. Since the quality of the designs is the most important stake-holder value, it is critical to manage the development of requirements R3, R5, and R6 and how these requirements can affect the speed of operations.

Functional Flow and System Architecture

The proposed tool has to be able to accept user inputs and combine them with engineering logic and supplementary data to generate designs automatically. There-fore, the tool has to have multiple functionalities: that is, an autodesign feature, analysis features, a user interface for entering input parameters and user-defined designs, and a mechanism for communicating results to the users. Figure CS3.3 illustrates the high-level functional flow of the proposed tool, directly addressing requirements R3, R4, R6, R7, R8, and R9. Requirements R2, R4, R5, and R10 are

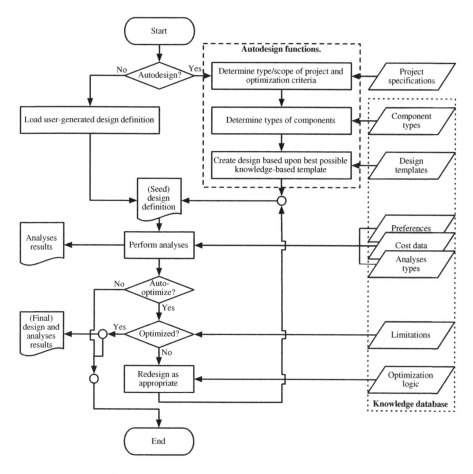

Figure CS3.3 *Preliminary high-level functional flow of the tool proposed.*

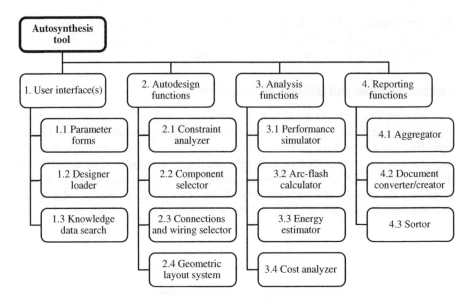

Figure CS3.4 *Preliminary high-level system architecture of the tool proposed.*

addressed in the software system architecture shown in Figure CS3.4. The autono-
mous features and analyses are enabled by the system's knowledge database as
shown in the figure. This database can be a combination of computer code, used to
capture computations and database systems used to store component data and other
information. Optimization limitations can include fundamental and practical limitations or can be based on user preferences. For example, if users want to minimize the
execution time of the tool, they can opt for fewer analysis iterations. This database
can be built further through machine learning, which can be accomplished by
continuously storing output data of prior runs and performing statistical analyses.
These analyses can identify patterns that can be used to improve the functional flow
of the tool and identify logic that can be used to further optimize designs. For
example, these analyses may be able to determine better constraints for creating seed
designs or identify unnecessary iterations in the functional flow.

Mechanisms to Realize (Concepts)

The tool addresses design development issues in real projects. Therefore, it has to
take into account practical constraints such as building codes, realistic performance
models, and verifiable cost data to ensure the quality of the research investigation.
The National Electrical Code (NEC) is the foundation of electrical construction
building codes in the United States. Many local and regional codes are either
condensed versions of the NEC or close derivations of it. Designers use the NEC
handbook constantly throughout the design process to determine commercially
available sizes and types of wires, fuses, conduits, and circuit breakers; the

associated electrical performances of these components; and how these components should be selected and installed to preserve system reliability and the safety of operators. The NEC also provides instructions on how to conduct performance analyses and provides basic calculation models and practical approximations. Although NEC compliance is only mandatory for electrical construction projects within the United States, the rules and standards captured in the NEC handbook are general enough to be applicable to projects in other countries as well. Therefore, the NEC can be used as a starting reference for developing some of the algorithms and component data sets needed in the knowledge database shown in Figure CS3.3. The NFPA70E, a complement to the NEC, can be used to develop logic for safety considerations.

Realistic models for the performance of the photovoltaic modules and performance tracking behavior of the inverters are needed to ensure the accuracy and/or feasibility of the performance analyses. This is in addition to the systems-level calculation models and other performance considerations. The difficulty with developing these models is that the manufacturer specifications do not typically present all the information necessary to completely capture the performance characteristics. Even if this information was provided, the potential differences between manufacturer specifications and actual performance could override any additional accuracy gained from better characterization, especially with regard to the modules. Along the same lines, the knowledge database would need to consist of a collection of photovoltaic modules and inverter descriptions that are either derived directly from real products or a close representation of real products. Information from commercially available components can be used to develop the database for the research tool, but consideration of the legal implications of using this information in a commercial product is required prior to commercialization.

Component prices and labor rates differ based on time and location, and as a result, both will affect the accuracy of construction cost analyses. However, there are excellent references, such as *R.S. Means Facilities Construction Cost Data* and *R.S. Means Electrical Cost Data*, that can be used to construct initial data sets based on the yearly national average costs for standardized construction component, such as the prices for wires or combiner boxes, and labor rates of construction crews within the United States. Estimators typically use these sources to build preliminary estimation models which they then adjust to account for differences in local labor union rates and specific vendor prices. A combination of average prices, vendor quotes, and trend analysis can be used to estimate the material costs of modules and inverters.

Interfaces are required that will allow users to:

- Supply input parameters. The exact parameters are not fully defined at this time, but inputs and outputs would include selecting what type of "optimization" to perform in autosynthesis (e.g., optimize performance or cost).
- Force the tool to consider only a certain set of components for use in autodesign and/or perform only certain types of analyses.

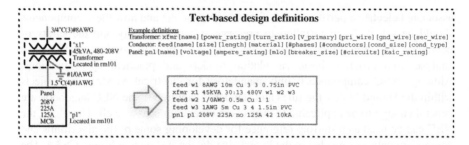

Figure CS3.5 *Example of ASCII-accessible design definitions for electrical connections.*

- Edit certain portions of the knowledge database, such as adding new modules and inverter information and editing cost data.
- Make changes to the design layout, components, and electrical connections.

A GU that would accept inputs using typical textboxes and command buttons can be used as the primary user interface. Results can be stored in structured text files that can be opened in a common spreadsheet program or word processor. ASCII-accessible (text-based) commands can be used to define components, their electrical connections, and their spatial and geometrical properties in the system layout. An example of this is shown in Figure CS3.5 for electrical connections. The tool could use this template to define new designs and conduct analyses. The tool should have an interface that would allow users to alter designs either by direct editing of the text or by graphical manipulation of components (dragging graphical representations of components around on a Cartesian plane, similar to what occurs in typical CAD tools). Alternatively, these commands can be edited using any word processor. This can facilitate the use of scripts to manipulate designs and capture analysis results, further increasing the potential of the future product to decrease design time.

Additional Mechanisms to Productize Additional effort would be needed in developing the knowledge database and refining the user interface for commercialization within the United States. Some of the changes or additions needed would be observed while testing and using the research tool. Other foreseeable developments include:

- Allowing users to add design constraints based on their local building codes and/or company policies. This will ensure the feasibility of the autodesign output.
- Allowing users to add cost considerations based on the market and/or company policies. This is important if designers want to get an even better idea of the construction costs or if the company operates using a concurrent engineering model, in which case the product would be used to replace certain estimating tasks.

- Adding interfaces so that users can read and sort through analysis results within the tool.

- Expanding the component data sets to come prepackaged with many types of modules, inverters, fuses, and so on, based on (or representing) real modules.

- Ensuring that the interfaces are robust and similar to what users are used to (e.g., GUI interfaced or typical Windows software). This will include the ability to digitally manipulate spatial locations and electrical connections, since many electrical contractors may not have much computer programming experience, which may be needed to reap the value of text-based design manipulation.

- Providing additional reporting schemes, such as power-flow diagrams, so that users can have another method for understanding the design performance.

- Ensure that minimum computer resources are needed to use the tool. This includes not having to use any additional software (besides the operating system) and the fact that the programming is resource efficient.

An analysis of the legal implications of using manufacturer specifications and cost data references is needed to ensure that there are no copyright violations. Also, a patent investigation may be needed to ensure that none of the product's functional and aesthetical attributes violate any U.S. patents.

Roadmap for Improvements and Phase II Ways to improve the product further and align this analysis for future phases would be determined during testing. However, possible improvements may include:

- Adding building codes from other countries to facilitate those markets.

- Adding cloud-based features to minimize computation on the user's computers. This can allow the tool to be used on simpler computing devices, such as cell phones and tablets.

- Finding ways to update the knowledge database automatically to reflect new methodologies and cost data based on user preferences, geographical location, and so on.

- Generating AutoCAD MEP drawings directly from the system design. This has to be handled carefully because it absorbs certain responsibilities of CAD drafters. Effort has to be made to demonstrate that the product is not a CAD tool but is a device for designers that may speed up CAD tasks or remove the role of CAD drafters altogether.

Risks and Usage Failures

The goal of the quality function deployment strategy discussed is to minimize risks in each phase or segment of this project. These risks include:

- *Development risks* such as not having enough time or funding for software development and testing; not having the technology, data, or logic needed; and not having the skills needed to carry out this project.

- *Usage risks* such as misunderstandings when it comes to navigating through the tool or using its functions and system malfunctions. Process documentation (and user documentation by correlation) and minimizing software errors were made a high priority in the quality function deployment strategy discussed. Therefore, these risks should be minimized if this system engineering approach is taken. Another concern is to ensure that the design and/or analyses outputs are not incorrect and do not result in faulty installation or unsafe conditions for installers and operators. This concern is also a high priority in this approach, and therefore every effort would be made to prevent faulty situations from occurring.
- *Research risks* such as having improper testing scenarios, misinterpreting the data collected from tests, and poor documentation throughout this project.

REVIEW CHECKLIST

- ☐ For each case study, are all critical stakeholders and their values considered?
- ☐ Are value and requirement conflicts addressed?
- ☐ Can you define a value stream map for each and include an activity that would follow the last practice defined by the case (i.e., preparation for delivery, customer acceptance, postdelivery support)?

20

Process Summary and Tools

We have covered many steps in the process of product and system development toward the goal of delivering value to customers, users, and interested stakeholders. It has been set in a relatively structured process, but it is not intended to be a constraining approach. It does, however, provide a framework that incorporates most of the considerations that should be included for effective and efficient development performance. In this chapter we highlight practices and phases of the process, including repeating some key tools, particularly those available via the Internet, together with reminders of the organizational, personnel, and quality issues.

Planning

There has been a great deal of emphasis on front-end activity, which may seem to be the beginning of a relatively orderly process. But there are many preparatory considerations to ensure that the right product or system will be the development outcome. These must include the corporate goals of the developing organization or the sponsoring customer. They can also include the economic environment and, in many cases, the expectations of customers and competitors. Marketing is often disdained, but good market analysis is essential and can be accomplished by research, field interactions, and benchmarking. The last, while often done by consultants, can be understood and managed by checking www.benchnet.com.

Product and Systems Development: A Value Approach, First Edition. Stanley I. Weiss.
© 2013 John Wiley & Sons, Inc. Published 2013 by John Wiley & Sons, Inc.

Value and the Stakeholder

Recall that we talked first about value and the character of the deliverables that incorporates values for the stakeholders. We cited that value propositions were the basis for agreement on what those values must obtain and the resources required. The flow of activities that addresses these goals can be seen as a value stream that takes us through the development cycle with all related process elements.

There are certainly a large number of steps that may not match every organization and how they do business. Thus, the more than 20 steps attending the development value stream may be modified by virtue of the project size, the character of the practices necessary, and the physical capability to have people, materiel, and information flow in an integrated fashion. One such skunkworks approach reduced the steps by eight, but with all practices, at least implicitly, incorporated in some fashion.

Systems Engineering

Systems engineering was shown to be a key methodology, incorporating most of the planning and validating in every phase of development and deployment. Its elements provide an interdisciplinary structure for translating stakeholder values to delivery of workable products and systems. This outcome of development itself is dependent on the total value chain, including all aspects of supplier networks and sometimes less visible, though critical, contributors to the chain (Haskins, *Systems Engineering Handbook*).

Requirements Development and Management

Like the old saying "Measure twice before cutting," it is critical to get the requirements right before designing or pursuing those activities that will govern design development. Certainly, stakeholder values are the initial guides, and translating these is facilitated using quality function deployment (QFD) tools applied to identifying and prioritizing values and thence requirements and technical drivers. This organizing matrix permits identification of stakeholders and their values and the capability to relate these to design requirements and potentially to process. But the primary use has been in the development of design requirements and technical characteristics with appropriate priorities. Since that use is subject to ranking and weighting of parameters and requirements, the scoring must be done carefully and include the judgments of specialists and stakeholders, together with recognition of sensitivities in the scoring process. Some Websites are: QFD Capture, Qualipak, Pathmaker, QFD online, and DOORS.

Functional Analysis

Another step leading to an understanding of how the product or system will realize the requirements so as to aid in the development of concepts is the use of functional flows and block diagrams. The former are action elements characterized by verbs and flow diagrams, the latter are the interconnected elements performing those functions in what can be called functional schematics, produced by using such drop and draw programs as SmartDraw, Visio, Hobby Projects, and Barrett.

Concept and Architecture Development

Critical steps in product and system development are the conceptual and structural definition of end items. The first is established as a result of satisfying requirements, usually based on functional analysis that incorporates performance activities, their implementers, and their interactions. Multiple concepts satisfying requirements require trades or other optimization techniques to develop a choice that will establish the baseline depiction of the end item. This, in turn, leads to an architecture or organization of elements in products or systems and provides a hierarchical arrangement for evaluating operating capability, work breakdown, supplier involvement, and character of integration of the product or system. This tiered framework should usually be implemented to five subordinate levels of definition and will influence both in-house and externally supplied products and systems. Several different formats exist for architectures, from the traditional one noted, to those used in various information networks, incorporating linear status and ring configurations.

Decisions and trades are involved in making the right choices in both concept and architectural elements. Now the job of the system developer involves decision making at every step. There are a good number of decision processes, ranging from tabular weighting and rating schemes to probabilistic decision trees. But regardless of approach, the most critical process is the establishment of criteria or parameters by which we make judgments. These must be as unbiased, objective, and as quantitative as possible, so as to permit selecting the best possible choices. There are a number of commonly used decision tools, such as decision trees and probability maps, Kepner–Trego and Pugh matrices, and MATE (multiattribute trade space).

Interfaces

Interfaces are, of course, of special concern for defining and understanding interactions of information, material, and personnel. Understanding them and their character is of great influence in developing functional interrelationships and the establishment of concepts and architectures, the description of what will be developed or built. This has special importance not only for design development but also for work and supplier assignments, budget allocations, organization, and the implication of changes. Organizing and managing tools are, respectively, N^2 matrices and interface control documents.

Risk, Reliability, and Fault Tolerance

At the point of having a good definition of a product or system, areas of risk consideration should be evident. Of course, risks are a factor from the very beginning of development, with uncertainties in market evaluation, requirements definition, and finally, customer acceptance and operation. Most often studied are the performance risks associated with product design and use. There are many well-established methods for making these evaluations, but programmatic risks associated with cost containment, funding, critical skills availability, and others, also fall under risks that can affect success and, while less definable, demand visibility and flexibility for response.

Risk is often seen as the opposite of reliability, and the numerical assignment of each is the inverse of the other. Reliability incorporates issues of failure analysis and potential and is characterized by special types of testing and quality assurance and redundancy. The latter is also intrinsic to fault tolerance, the recognition that certain faults may occur but can be compensated for by design or operational alternatives when they do occur. These consist of the use of duplicative or redundant capabilities or the ability to operate in degraded or safe modes. In any case, the compensation for failed functions or even postfailure analysis requires knowledge of fault location and character, known as *coverage*. Then, there can be reasonable expectation that the design of fault tolerance can be based on identification of location and impact as well as the mode of any failure. Again, these are areas where decisions and simulation are important: decision trees, Excel and Monte Carlo simulations, and Palisade software.

Verification and Validation

Along with these considerations is the need for verification and validation. The former ensures that a system or element was completed with quality according to design definitions; the latter is that the system or element meets all the expectations of customers and operators. These attributes apply at any and all points of the life cycle. The means of providing these assurances include inspections and tests verifying performance, with the latter ranging from functional proof-of-concept demonstration to operational acceptance at delivery and in operation. Testing may cover from the smallest component up to the full operational system or integration of systems subject to all interface and environmental demands. The latter is particularly critical in qualifying elements by demonstration of performance with appropriate margins in extreme environments. It should be noted that where there is no capability of testing with interfacing hardware or software due to scheduling or technical difficulties, the use of simulations involving elements may provide the best means for verification.

Product Development Management

In the realm of management we have reviewed costing techniques, organizing methods, program strategies, scheduling and controls, and finally, the lean practices that can yield the most effective means to apply the various assets available for the development cycle. In our discussion of organizing with the use of integrated teams, we indicated that a team approach facilitates incorporating the "-ilities" and the "design for" characteristics to include assembly, testing, and outsourcing as well as another dozen factors of benefit in ensuring value from the design process. The team approach also facilitates cost estimation with those responsible for performance intrinsic to applying the various means of estimation. These, from most speculative top-down estimates derived by comparison with similar programs, progress to increasingly accurate element-by-element figures as fixed-price items and designs approach completion and implementation. In between these extremes are cost-estimation ratios, built on relationships of cost to parameters such as weight, volume, and number of lines of code, as well as the use of analogous relationships with elements of other items factored by a predicted complexity factor. In addition, we considered production quantity as a factor in end-item costs, with learning curves benefiting item value, with increasing quantities from the progressive improvement of process performance by labor. Thus, the more labor-intensive the work, the steeper the increase in learning and decrease in cost. The more automated the processes and thus more consistently repetitive, the less the learning and more consistent the cost per item.

Other management aspects covered strategies behind the product or system development, including the desire to get to market before the competition, producing the lowest-cost functional performance and baselining the development as an initiator of low- or high-volume production and delivery. The various scheduling strategies covered (1) the linear progression of activity serially, with the need for each step to precede or feed into a next step, termed "waterfall" or "goes into"; or (2) evolutionary approaches which deal with progressive development from a basic product capability that can be upgraded periodically to reach maximums in technical or functional performance. All of the above involve architectures; work breakdown structures; Gantt, CPM, and PERT charting; affinity diagrams; and design structure matrices.

Design for X

Among the techniques employed to ensure that a product or system incorporates capabilities for production and operational as well as management needs, designing initially for these, is critical to meeting cost, schedule, and customer and user satisfaction. This can be aided by such methods as design for manufacturing and assembly, testing, or outsourcing as examples and using Internet tools such as SpringerLink.

Lean and Value Stream Mapping

The optimization considerations we have been considering also lead to incorporating lean thinking into the total flow. Lean emphasizes the elimination of waste through understanding of the total value stream development and with application of lean practices as identified by the lean enterprise model and lean enablers, which include hierarchies of lean principles and practices supported by hundreds of research projects on implementation successes and limitations. The creation of a map of

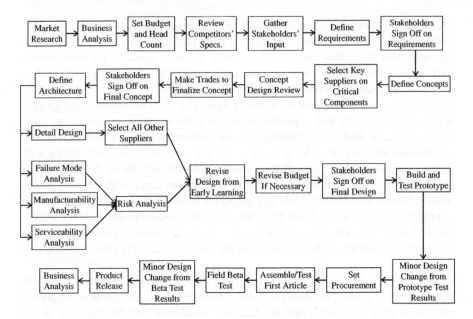

Figure 20.1 *Representative product development value stream. (Courtesy of Steve Jeon, KLA Tencor Corporation.)*

value-delivering activity over the life cycle or value stream (Figure 20.1) should then express a waste-limited state of development, either projected for new projects or as a correction of a current waste-laden process. Flow diagram mapping tools can be useful: Stategos, SmartDraw, Enna VSM Solutions, and the MIT Lean Advantage Initiative (LAI).

Appendix I

Notes on the Design Structure Matrix

Tyson R. Browning

M.J. Neeley School of Business, Texas Christian University

We introduce the design structure matrix (DSM) with a simple example, a process for getting and putting on socks and shoes, represented by the flowchart in Figure I.1 and the DSM in Figure I.2. The matrix shows the activities and their interactions. The shaded cells along the diagonal of the matrix represent the activities, while the off-diagonal cells represent potential interactions among the activities. That is, a mark in one of these off-diagonal cells signifies information transfer or dependency. Marks above the diagonal imply, for example, that *Get Socks* provides a deliverable (*Selected Socks*) to *Put on Socks*, and *Get Shoes* provides a deliverable to *Put on Shoes* and *Inspect Shoes*. The mark below the diagonal in the DSM indicates that once shoes have been inspected, they may be found wanting (e.g., too scuffed up or the wrong color for the clothes), requiring an iteration (rework), *Get Shoes* (again).

More generally, as shown in Figure I.3, a DSM is a square matrix with corresponding rows and columns. The diagonal cells represent activities, which are listed from upper left to lower right in a roughly temporal order. Off-diagonal cells indicate the dependency of one activity on another. Reading down a column shows deliverable sources; reading across a row shows deliverable sinks. For example, row 1 indicates that activity 1 provides information to activities 2, 4, 5, and 6. Column 2 shows that activity 2 depends on information from activities 1 and 6.

J

Product and Systems Development: A Value Approach, First Edition. Stanley I. Weiss.
© 2013 John Wiley & Sons, Inc. Published 2013 by John Wiley & Sons, Inc.

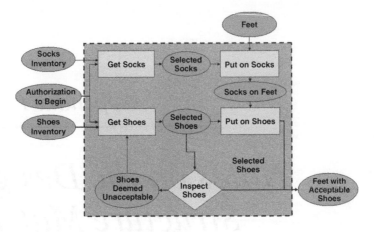

Figure I.1   Process model.

GET SOCKS
GET SHOES
PUT ON SOCKS
PUT ON SHOES
INSPECT SHOES

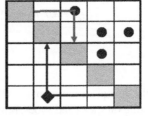

Figure I.2   DSM representation of example process. (Adapted from Denker et al., 2001.)

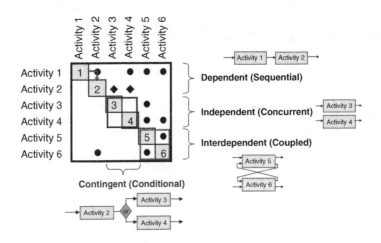

Figure I.3   Activity relationships in DSM. (Adapted from Browning, 2001.)

Figure I.3 also shows how the DSM displays dependent, independent, and interdependent activity relationships. Since activity 2 depends on information from activity 1, these two activities will probably be executed sequentially in the workflow. Activities 3 and 4 do not depend on each other for information, so they may safely proceed in parallel (barring other resource constraints). Activities 5 and 6 both depend on each other's outputs. These activities are said to be interdependent or coupled and are discussed below. Note also that decisions are a kind of activity, one that produces information upon which other activities depend. The sequence of decisions in a process will have a great bearing on its efficiency and effectiveness.

Of particular interest are the cases where marks appear in the lower-triangular region of the DSM. Such marks indicate the dependence of an upstream activity on information created downstream. If project planners decide to execute the activities in the given order, activity 2 will have to make an assumption about the information it needs from activity 6. After activity 6 finishes, activity 2 may have rework if the assumption was incorrect. The DSM conveniently highlights potential iteration and rework (a capability that traditional the project evaluation and review technique and critical path method cannot deliver), especially when it stems from activities working with potentially flawed information.

When we see a mark in the lower-left corner of the DSM, we know that there is a chance of having to return to the beginning of the process, which could have a catastrophic impact on project cost and schedule. The marks in the lower-left corner of the DSM may represent key drivers of cost and schedule risk. Rearranging the activity sequence (by rearranging the rows and columns in the DSM) can bring some subdiagonal marks above or closer to the diagonal, thereby reducing their impact. The goal is to minimize the adverse impacts of iteration and rework. Simple algorithms automate this exercise. Adding quantitative information to the DSM and using simulation can quantify the impacts of activity sequence changes on cost and schedule risk.

For example, in the "getting and putting on socks and shoes" project (Figure I.2), the activities *Get Shoes* and *Inspect Shoes* are interdependent, so there is no way to reorder the rows and columns of the DSM to get all the marks above the diagonal. Failing this, we would like to get the subdiagonal mark as close to the diagonal as possible, to minimize the scope of the iteration. Currently, once we *Get Shoes*, we go ahead and *Put on Socks* and *Put on Shoes* before we *Inspect Shoes*. If, instead, we move the inspection step upstream, as in Figure I.4, we minimize the impact of a need

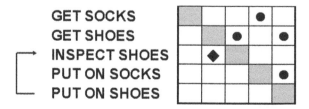

Figure I.4   *Resequenced DSM from Figure I.2. (Adapted from Denker et al., 2001.)*

to *Get Shoes* again. (Essentially, this act of moving activities upstream demonstrates concurrent engineering: We minimize the feedback loop in the process in hopes that we will decrease the variance in total process lead time.) Although in this example we could not eliminate the potential iteration entirely, it is often possible to reduce the number of potential iterations substantially by resequencing rows and columns. Again, algorithms exist to help with this, although simple examples like this one can be done manually.

We can notice some additional things from this example DSM, such as which activities can be accomplished in parallel without causing additional iteration. For example, in Figure I.4, *Get Socks* and *Get Shoes* can be done simultaneously, as can *Inspect Shoes* and *Put on Socks* (if we have enough resources!). Sometimes, planners choose activities to work in parallel without first considering their information dependencies, which can result in *additional* iteration and thus a longer, not a shorter, project duration.

As we saw with the *Get Shoes* and *Inspect Shoes* activities in the previous example, sometimes a subdiagonal mark cannot be brought above the diagonal without pushing another mark below the diagonal. This is a case of interdependent activities, such as activities 5 and 6 in Figure I.3. Each activity depends on the other. They must work together to resolve a "chicken and egg" problem. Or perhaps one must verify or review the work of another. Typically, coupled activities work concurrently, exchanging preliminary information frequently. If a subset of coupled activities must begin before the rest, the more robust (less volatile and/or sensitive) information items should be those appearing below the diagonal in the DSM. If coupled activities are functionally based, an opportunity may exist to fold the activities into a single activity assigned to a cross-functional team.

Integration, testing, and design-review activities typically have marks in their rows to the left of the diagonal. These activities create information (including results of decisions) that may cause changes to (and rework for) activities executed previously. Unfortunately, most process planners "plan to succeed" and their process models fail to account for these possibilities. Fortunately, the DSM provides an easy way to document potential process failure modes and their effects on other activities. The simple marks in the DSM can be replaced by numbers indicating the relative probability and impact (together, risk) of information change, iteration, and so on. This enables an analysis of process failure modes and their effects on cost, schedule, and risk. Process improvement investments can then target mitigation of the greatest risk drivers.

By accounting for contingent activities and feedback loops, the DSM can provide a basis for exploring adaptive processes. Although the DSM itself is a static view of a process, the DSM can be updated over time to reflect a dynamic situation. The remaining activities in such a situation can then be resequenced quickly in an advantageous way, providing rapid project replanning.

As a real-life example, Figure I.5 displays a DSM of the conceptual and preliminary design phases for the preliminary design of an unmanned Boeing combat aerial vehicle fully documented in Browning's 1998 dissertation. The first dozen activities comprise the conceptual design phase. In this phase, design

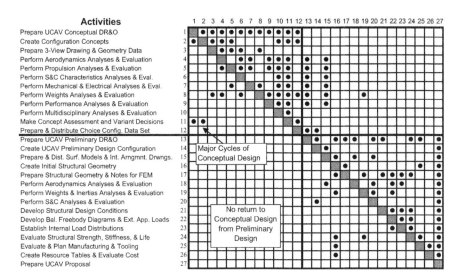

Figure I.5   *DSM of conceptual and preliminary design phases for an unmanned combat aerial vehicle. (Adapted from Browning, 2001.)*

requirements and objectives (DR&Os) are prepared, a configuration concept is proposed, it is analyzed by a variety of discipline perspectives, and then these results are assessed. The assessment may reveal a need to alter the DR&O, to create a new configuration concept, and/or to alter the current configuration concept. This cycle repeats until the design space is sufficiently well understood (or, more likely, until time and money are exhausted). The design process then moves into the preliminary design phase, where the configuration is developed and analyzed in more detail and the objective is to prepare a proposal to acquire funding for additional phases. Figure I.5 shows the process "as is," without any attempt to resequence the process to minimize the feedback marks below the diagonal. This DSM provides a view of part of a richer process model, which served as the basis for process analysis, evaluation, discussion, and improvement. This basic DSM was also augmented with additional regions above and to the right, which represented external inputs and outputs, respectively.

The DSM provides a concise, visual format for representing processes. A process flowchart consuming an entire conference room wall can be reduced to a single-page DSM. After a quick orientation, everyone can see how his or her activity affects a large process. People can see where information comes from and where it goes. They can see why delaying the activities they depend on forces them to make assumptions, which may trigger rework later. It becomes apparent that certain information changes tend to cause rework. Such situation visibility and awareness leads to improved process design and coordination. The DSM can provide a portal to a process knowledge base from which the foundations of process plans and risk assessments can be drawn. Moreover, the DSM is amenable to some simple, yet powerful analyses.

FURTHER RESOURCES

Browning, Tyson R. (1998) *Modeling and Analyzing Cost, Schedule, and Performance in Complex System Product Development*, Ph.D. dissertation, Massachusetts Institute of Technology, Cambridge, MA.

Browning, Tyson R. (1999) Process Modelling with Design Structure Matrices, *INCOSE Insight,* 2(3):15–17.

Browning, Tyson R. (2001) Applying the Design Structure Matrix to System Decomposition and Integration Problems: A Review and New Directions, *IEEE Transactions on Engineering Management,* 48(3):292–306.

Denker, Stephen, Donald, Steward, and Tyson R. Browning (2001) Planning Concurrency and Managing Iteration in Projects, *Project Management Journal,* 32(3):31–38.

Eppinger, Steven D. and Tyson R. Browning (2012) *Design Structure Matrix Methods and Applications*, MIT Press, Cambridge, MA.

Appendix II

Lean Systems Engineering and Lean Enablers for Systems Engineering*

Bohdan W. Oppenheim

Loyola Marymount University

A new body of knowledge called *lean systems engineering* (LSE) and a new product named *lean enablers for systems engineering* (LEfSE) are described. LSE is the application of the wisdom of lean thinking to traditional systems engineering (SE). The LEfSE are a collection of 147 practices and recommendations formulated as "dos" and "don'ts" of SE and containing collective wisdom on how to prepare for, plan, execute, and practice SE and related project and enterprise management using Lean Thinking. The enablers are focused on mission assurance and the satisfaction of stakeholders achieved with minimum waste. The product has been developed by experts from the LSE Working Group (WG) of the International Council on Systems Engineering (INCOSE). LEfSE are organized into six well-known lean principles: value, value stream, flow, pull, perfection, and respect for people. LEfSE are not intended to become a mandatory practice. Instead, they should be used as a checklist of good practices. Several enabler examples are discussed.

*This text has been adapted from references [11] and [13].

Product and Systems Development: A Value Approach, First Edition. Stanley I. Weiss.
© 2013 John Wiley & Sons, Inc. Published 2013 by John Wiley & Sons, Inc.

Introduction

Systems engineering is regarded as an established sound practice but is not always delivered effectively. Sixty-two recent successful space launches indicate that mission assurance can be practiced well. At the same time, recent U.S. Government Accountability Office (GAO) and NASA studies of space systems [1–4] document notorious major budget and schedule overruns, some exceeding 100%. Most programs are burdened with waste, poor coordination, unstable requirements, quality problems, and management frustrations. Recent studies by the MIT-based Lean Advancement Initiative (LAI) researchers [5–8] have identified a mind-boggling amount of waste in government programs, concluding that value is created during only 12% of the program time—and the rest is waste. This waste represents a vast productivity reserve in programs and a major opportunity to improve program efficiency. This applies only to post-milestone B programs: that is, the program segment after the government has issued a contract for the program. Prior to that time, waste is even more significant: The tortuous decision–making process weaving its way through the federal bureaucracy and Pentagon layers for years before it is ready for contracting.

> Waste is abundant in all programs. Failed systems represent the most dramatic manifestation of waste, but even the most technically successful programs are burdened with a significant amount of waste which can be reduced using Lean Thinking.

The new field of LSE is the application of lean thinking to SE and to the related aspects of project and enterprise management. SE is focused on the flawless performance of complex technical systems. Lean thinking is the holistic management paradigm credited for the extraordinary rise of Toyota to being the most profitable and one of the largest auto companies in the world [9]. Toyota is well known for practicing excellent product development and SE (which Toyota refers to as *simultaneous engineering*). For example, the design for the Prius was completed in nine months from the end of styling, a performance level unmatched by any competitor [10]. Lean Thinking has been employed successfully in the defense industry and in the U.S. military itself (e.g., [5], and the Air Force lean initiative, AFSO-21). It has become an established paradigm in manufacturing, aircraft depots, administration, supply chain management, health, and product development, including engineering.

LSE is the area of synergy of lean and SE with the goal to deliver the best life-cycle value for technically complex systems with minimal waste. Emphatically, LSE does not mean *less SE*, or *cutting corners in SE*. It means more and better SE with higher responsibility, authority, and accountability, conducive to better and waste-free workflow and mission assurance. Under the LSE philosophy, mission assurance is nonnegotiable, and any task that is legitimately required for success must be included, but it should be well planned and executed with minimal waste.

Fundamentals of Lean Thinking

Three concepts are fundamental to an understanding of Lean Thinking: value, waste, and the process of creating value without waste (also known as *lean principles*).

Value   The value proposition in engineering programs is often a multiyear complex and expensive acquisition process, involving thousands of stakeholders and resulting in hundreds or even thousands of requirements, which, notoriously, are rarely stable (even at the request for proposal phase). In lean SE, *value* is defined simply as mission assurance (the delivery of a flawless complex system, with flawless technical performance during the product or mission life cycle), satisfying the customer and all other stakeholders, which implies completion with minimal waste, minimal cost, and the shortest possible schedule.

Waste in Product Development   LAI classifies waste into seven categories: (1) overproduction, (2) transportation, (3) waiting, (4) over-processing, (5) inventory, (6) unnecessary movement, and (7) defects. These wastes are discussed in detail in an SE context by Oppenheim [13].

Lean Principles   Womack and Jones [9] captured the process of creating value without waste in the form of six lean principles. The principles are abbreviated as value, value stream, flow, pull, perfection, and respect for people. (The original formulation had five principles; the sixth was added later to emphasize the profound importance of good human relations.)

Beginnings of Lean Systems Engineering

The birth of *lean systems engineering* (LSE) is traced to the first meeting of the LAI Educational Network in March 2003. That year, the LAI consortium invited universities to join the new LAI Educational Network (EdNet). The EdNet mission is to collaborate on the development and dissemination of lean curricula, including incorporation of research findings. Starting with LMU|LA, at the time of this writing the EdNet has grown to 62 universities in the United States, Brazil, China, Europe, and Mexico. The EdNet members soon organized themselves into two small working groups, one devoted to LSE and another to LPD, intending to develop communities of practice in these new fields. The participants shared an understanding that SE is a sound process but is not practiced as well as it could be.

Subsequently, Murman [17] included the LSE topic in two lectures in a graduate course on aircraft systems engineering. The LAI team of Rebentisch et al. [18] laid down some theoretical foundations for LSE. Additional concepts and case studies were contributed by a panel on LSE at the 2004 Annual Symposium of International Council on Systems Engineering (INCOSE) [19].

These early works defined the synergy of lean and systems engineering as follows (paraphrased): "Systems engineering, which grew out of the space industry to help deliver flawless complex systems, is focused on technical performance and risk management. Lean, which grew out of Toyota to help deliver quality products at minimum cost, is focused on waste minimization, short schedules, low cost, flexibility, and quality. *Both* have the common goal to deliver system life-cycle value to the customer. Lean systems engineering is the area of synergy of lean and systems engineering with the goal to deliver the best life-cycle value for technically complex systems with minimum resources." This synergy gave rise to a definition by INCOSE that is included in all LSE literature:

> **Lean systems engineering** is the application of lean principles, practices, and tools to systems engineering in order to enhance the delivery of value to the systems stakeholders.

Lean Systems Engineering Working Group of INCOSE

During 2004–2006, the small LAI EdNet LSE group, consisting primarily of university professors, met several times and enjoyed interesting discussions; however, not much progress was made. To move the LSE project at a faster pace, at the end of 2005 the author made a proposal to INCOSE to form a new lean systems engineering working group (LSEWG), hoping to draw from the collective wisdom of the large and international membership of SE practitioners who belong to that learned society. The proposal was accepted, and the LSEWG became the thirty-ninth INCOSE working group. The first meeting (rather poorly advertised) drew 30 people, which indicates a high level of interest in the idea of applying lean thinking into SE. At the time of this writing (July 2011), the LSEWG has grown to 210 people, all unpaid volunteers, and is currently the largest working group in INCOSE. Most of the members are experienced industrial and governmental SEs, but experience in lean thinking is less common. Those most experienced with lean acted as leaders in the project of developing LEfSE.

The use of term *lean* in the context of SE initially met with concern that this might be an attempt to repackage the Faster – Better – Cheaper initiative, leading to cuts in SE at the time when the profession is struggling to increase the level and funding of SE effort in programs. We categorically disprove these concerns. To restate: *Lean SE* does not mean *less SE* but *more and better SE, leading to subsequent streamlined program execution.*

The LSEWG devoted the first 18 months to conceptual and administrative tasks (creation of website and mailing list, definitions, recommended readings, and formulation of the charter), as well as presentations and panels devoted to various ideas as to how to proceed. The dedicated website contains these results [15]. The working group developed its charter as follows.

Charter of the INCOSE Lean System Engineering Working Group

It is our goal to strengthen the practice of Systems Engineering (SE) by exploring and capturing the synergy between traditional SE and Lean. To do this, we will apply the wisdom of Lean Thinking into SE practices integrating people, processes, and tools for the most effective delivery of value to program stakeholders; formulate A Body of Knowledge of Lean SE; develop amendments to the INCOSE SE Handbook with critical elements of Lean SE; and develop and disseminate training materials and publications on Lean SE within the INCOSE community, industry, government, and academia.

Since October 2007, the main effort of the working group has been devoted to the development of Lean Enablers for Systems Engineering.

Value in Lean Systems Engineering

In traditional SE, value to the customer is formulated using requirements: first the top level or *customer requirements*, then detailed derived requirements allocated for all subsystems at all levels. The value proposition to be captured must involve not only explicit requirements and related documents, but also *unspoken requirements* defining needs, context, operations, interpretations, interoperability and compatibility characteristics, as well as a good understanding of customer culture.

The process of capturing top-level requirements is difficult to perform and is notorious for poor results. Past experience indicates that many programs eager to get under way tend to rush through this phase without a robust process, ending in incomplete, incorrect, or conflicted requirements that burden subsequent programs with waste [12]. Poorly formulated requirements can significantly increase program cost and lead time, and in extreme cases even torpedo entire programs (e.g., the recent presidential helicopter). The long duration of a program tends to introduce additional requirement instability, due to the change in need or threat, which cannot be foreseen at the beginning of the program.

In complex government programs, value formulation is a difficult process not only because of complex technology, but also because of unstable program funding, dissolved management, and policy and politics. The effort may easily take many years and involve thousands of stakeholders, including future system users, the government acquisition bureaucracy, contractors, suppliers, politicians, and lobbyists. Because of competing pressures, value may easily end up suboptimized, benefiting not future users but, rather, a group of stakeholders who exert the strongest pull. For this reason, lean systems engineering strongly promotes program optimization *in the next larger context*. Specifically, in complex national programs, this author believes, the proper context is the good of (the value to) the nation rather than the good of any single contractor, supplier, politician, community, or military unit.

In many technologically complex programs, military customers lack the expertise to describe the needs clearly, and more often than not must be assisted in the task by value creators (the prime contractor), or a proxy SE organization through extensive efforts of interaction, cooperation, and clarification. In Lean Systems Engineering both customers and contractors have a responsibility to formulate requirements as well as the state of the art permits, without blaming one another for inadequate effort while working together as a seamless team of honest, open, trustworthy partners who share the same goal.

Requirement stakeholders often ignore the fact that a requirement is an imperfect and inherently ambiguous way to describe a need. Typically, a requirement is a sentence containing several words. Written in a natural language, especially one as rich as English, where each word in a dictionary has several meanings, it is inherently ambiguous in the linguistic sense. Additional ambiguity arises because of hand-offs: the person writing the requirement has in his or her mind the rich context of the need, whereas the person reading the requirement sees only the requirement text. Because of these structural communicative disjunctions, it is critically important not only to make every effort to make all requirements crystal clear and complete, but also to create means to clarify requirements without causing requirement creep: properly planning effective and efficient channels for clarifications.

In Lean Systems Engineering we continue defining value using requirements. But in view of the difficulties noted above, we place a significantly greater emphasis on the quality of the effort of formulating and clarifying the requirements and make certain that all potential pitfalls are minimized. We also promote development of a robust process for capturing and formulating requirements.

Over the years, the number of top-level requirements in government programs grew at a fast rate, routinely reaching many hundreds and thousands in recent programs. This increasingly drove program bureaucracy and made programs costlier, longer, and usually more frustrating to all stakeholders. By comparison, it is fascinating to recall that the early *Apollo* program, without a doubt the most dramatically successful space program in the entire history of human civilization, started with only three requirements pronounced by President J. F. Kennedy (paraphrasing): to "(1) take a man to the Moon, (2) and back, (3) safely"! Similarly, the highly successful U2 aircraft program started with only a few requirements: defining the flight altitude, speed, endurance, and payload. Perhaps there is a lesson here for Lean Systems Engineering?

In LSE we define value using strong words, to reflect the need for a high level of excellence:

> **Value** in lean systems engineering is defined as a flawless product or mission delivered at minimum cost, in the shortest possible schedule, fully satisfying the customer and other stakeholders during a product or mission life cycle.

These words should be interpreted as a goal rather than as a promise. Clearly, many program aspects besides LSE must be executed well in order to assure the value.

Lean Enablers for SE

LEfSE is a major product recently released in the field of Lean SE. It is a comprehensive checklist of 147 practices and recommendations formulated as the *do's and don'ts* of SE, containing tacit knowledge (collective wisdom) on how to prepare for, plan, execute, and practice SE and related enterprise management using Lean Thinking. Each enabler enhances the program value and reduces some waste. As a set, the enablers are focused on providing more affordable solutions to increasingly complex challenges and on improving response time from the identification of need to release of the system. The enablers deal with mission assurance and promote practices that optimize workflow and reduce waste.

The enablers are formulated as an addendum to traditional SE manuals, such as *The International Council on Systems Engineering [INCOSE] Handbook*, ISO 15288, and similar NASA, Department of Defense, or company manuals, and do not repeat the practices made therein, which are regarded as sound.

The 147 LEfSE practices are organized into the six Lean Principles listed earlier, and 47 topical headings. The practices cover a large spectrum of SE and other relevant enterprise management practices, with a general focus on improving program value and stakeholder satisfaction, and reducing waste, delays, cost overruns, and frustrations. Reference [12] describes all enablers with extensive explanations, suggested implementation, waste and value statements, lagging factors, and recommended reading lists, as well as the measurements of the use of a given enabler in industry, obtained from surveys. The full text of the LEfSE is too long for this appendix; only a brief summary is given herein, followed by a few examples.

- Under the *value principle*, the enablers promote a robust process of establishing the value of the end product or system to the customer with crystal clarity. The process should be customer focused, involving the customer frequently and aligning the enterprise employees accordingly.
- The enablers under the *value stream principle* emphasize waste-preventing measures, solid preparation of the personnel and processes for subsequent efficient workflow, and healthy relationships between stakeholders (customer, contractor, suppliers, and employees), in addition to detailed program planning, frontloading, and use of leading indicators and quality metrics.
- The *flow principle* lists the enablers who promote the uninterrupted flow of robust quality work and first-time right, steady competence instead of hero behavior in crises, excellent communication and coordination, concurrency, frequent clarification of the requirements, and making program progress visible to all.
- The enablers listed under the *pull principle* are a powerful guard against the waste of rework and overproduction. They promote pulling tasks and outputs based on need (and rejecting others as waste) and better coordination between the pairs of employees handling any transaction before their work begins (so that the result can be first-time right).

- The *perfection principle* promotes excellence in the SE and enterprise processes, the use of the wealth of lessons learned from previous programs in the current program, the development of perfect collaboration policy across people and processes, and driving out waste through standardization and continuous improvement. A category of these enablers calls for a more important role of systems engineers, with RAA for the overall technical success of the program.
- Finally, the *respect-for-people principle* contains enablers that promote the enterprise culture of trust, openness, respect, empowerment, cooperation, teamwork, synergy, good communication and coordination, and enabling people for excellence.

LEfSE were developed by 14 experienced practitioners organized into two teams, some recognized leaders in lean and systems engineering from industry, academia, and government (from the United States, United Kingdom, and Israel), with cooperation from the then 100-member strong international LSEWG of INCOSE [11].

Both SE and lean represent challenging areas for research, as they are grounded in industrial and government practice rather than in laboratory work or theory. It is well known that hard data about SE in large programs is difficult to obtain because:

- The programs are classified and proprietary.
- The companies are not willing to release such data even when they exist.
- In many cases, the data are nonexistent, of poor quality, lack normalization, suffer from discontinuities over long program schedules, and are convoluted with other enterprise activities.

As a result, it is difficult to collect the data needed to perform hypothesis testing. Therefore, rather than relying on explicit program data, the enablers were developed from the collective tacit knowledge, wisdom, and experience of the LSEWG members. Such an approach, practiced for ages by numerous institutions, is described by Oppenheim [13].

LEfSE have been formulated for industry SE practitioners, but the development benefited from academic depth, breadth, and rigor, the latter emphasis provided by surveys and benchmarking to published data, as follows. The development of LEfSE included five phases: conceptual, alpha, beta, prototype, and version 1.0. It was evaluated by separate surveys in the beta and prototype phases and by comparisons with the recent programmatic recommendations by GAO and NASA [1–4]. The surveys indicated that LEfSE are regarded as important for program success but are not widely used by industry. The comparisons indicated that LEfSE are consistent with the NASA and GAO recommendations but are significantly more detailed and comprehensive.

Examples of Lean Enablers for SE

ENABLER EXAMPLE 1.   Develop and Execute a Clear Communication Plan That Covers the Entire Value Stream and All Stakeholders   Effective communications are critical for program success, yet surveys indicate that they are poorly practiced. Programs waste significant portions of their budgets and schedules because of inadequate communications. In extreme cases, mission failure may result from bad communications (e.g., the inconsistent units on the failed Mars Climate Orbiter mission). "Poor" can mean both "not enough good ones" and "too many bad ones", as follows.

The best communications involve the widest bandwidth: Person to person is superior to video and phone, which are superior to email, which is superior to automated software tools. Modern trends are to execute programs over a large number of sites with geographically distributed stakeholders. This is not conducive to effective communications. It is difficult to perform good and detailed program planning (mapping both SE and PD value streams) without good knowledge of who is the internal customer for each task, how the task contributes to the overall value, and how to optimize tasks for the best value with minimum waste. As a result, plans tend to be superficial, impersonal, and therefore, ineffective.

Waste also occurs when there is too much bad communications: for example, when emails are abused by excessive dissemination and unneeded attachments. All employees know the phenomenon of receiving unsolicited and unneeded emails from colleagues. Yet, all emails received must be read and sorted to be saved, deleted, or acted upon. Arguably, most of us waste about an hour a day on unsolicited and unneeded email. Assuming that this is the average, it constitutes 12.5% of nominal charged time. (On a $1 billion program, this waste alone costs the program $125,000,000.) The waste can be reduced dramatically with a single instruction from the chief engineer (or equivalent role): Do not cc: unless: (followed by a specific instruction how to disseminate emails).

All together, it is critical to organize from the beginning for frequent, effective, and waste-free communications. A solid plan for communications, with training, can vastly improve the quality of programs.

Suggested Implementation: The chief engineer (or equivalent role) should develop an effective plan for communications among all program stakeholders and make sure that all stakeholders understand the plan. The plan should include instructions for:

- Periodic integrative meetings for addressing issues
- Efficient and effective meetings with a specific purpose, agenda, time, and intent
- Short ad hoc stand-up meetings
- Milestone meetings and programmatic reviews
- Communications between program levels (between different integrated product teams)

- Meeting means (whether in person, by videoconference, computer, phone, etc.)
- Instructions for email (e.g., an instruction to summarize any issue on a standard form and not send other attachments unless requested)
- Promotion of a culture of asking questions immediately rather than sitting on an issue and waiting for the next integrative meeting
- Provision for the means to escalate issues, if needed
- A mandate to identify an internal customer and coordinate task with him or her prior to executing any nonroutine task
- The do's and don'ts of communications with external stakeholders
- Any other applicable aspect of communications

ENABLER EXAMPLE 2.   All Other Things Being Equal, Select the Simplest Solution   Three well-known mantras apply here:

1. "Any fool can make anything complex, but it takes a genius and courage to create a simple solution" – Albert Einstein
2. KISS: keep it simple, stupid—a timeless engineering mantra.
3. "Occam's razor: one should not increase, beyond what is necessary, the number of entities required to explain anything."

Driven by competitive pressures, corporate hunger for large programs, and frequent government demand for *the greatest, latest, and gold plated*, large companies often pursue excessive options, features, and performance envelopes. Often, the majority of these features will never be used. The excessive number of features is also notorious in commercial software. The implementation of too many features results in excessively complex systems, complex software and logistics, long and costly testing, difficult revisions, and complex controls. Such systems can consume budget and schedule before the program is completed. These programs then face the choice to either cut corners on testing or to extend program schedule and budget. Neither solution has objective merits. Altogether, there is great merit in keeping things simple, all else being equal.

Suggested Implementation: Chief engineers (or their equivalents) should emphasize the importance of seeking the simplest solutions, all other things being equal.

ENABLER EXAMPLE 3. Let Information Needs Pull the Necessary Work Activities; and EXAMPLE 4. Promote a Culture in Which Engineers Pull Knowledge as They Need it and Limit the Supply of Information to Genuine Users   Recent complex programs are notorious for including tasks that nobody needs, that perhaps some manager ordered some time ago for a particular reason, the reason long forgotten. Many tasks are included by careless cutting and pasting from earlier programs. All such tasks constitute pure waste. Therefore, rigorous tailoring of tasks and outputs should be done in the planning phase of every program. The cardinal rules should be:

1. Identify the genuine users for each task output and have them pull information as needed, and supply information only to those who need it.
2. If no user can be identified for a given task output, the task is a waste and should be eliminated.

Suggested Implementation: The implementation is quite easy; all it takes is an instruction from the chief SE issued at the beginning of the planning phase to practice these rules, emphasizing the following:

- Do not copy tasks from previous programs to the present program carelessly.
- If you cannot find a user for a task output, delete the task.
- The task is legitimate if it supports value creation.

ENABLER EXAMPLE 5. Ensure That Both Data Deliverers and Receivers Understand the Mutual Needs and Expectations Engineers tend to be proud professionals who like to think they know what they are doing. Frequently, they execute their assigned tasks according to written specifications—only to discover that the next person in the value chain (the receiver, a.k.a. internal customer) rejected the task output because it did not exactly conform to the receiver's needs or expectations. In our complex technological world, few tasks are so routine that written specifications are sufficient and that follow-up verbal clarification and coordination are not needed. When a task output is rejected, it must be redone, causing the program to suffer the waste of rework, consuming resources and delaying progress. This waste is notorious in "stovepipe" organizations, in which engineers receive written task specifications from their managers and send output back up to managers for approval and passing on. Frequently in such organizations, an engineer executing a task (the giver) does not even know who his or her receiver is (internal customer other than his on her own manager).

To avoid this waste, for every nonroutine task, the following is promoted by the enabler: (1) learn who the internal customer (receiver) is for your task (it is rarely your manager, who should, rather, serve as an enabling party and a *traffic cop*); (2) coordinate task nuances (scope, modalities, output format, etc.) with the receiver customer before work on the task begins, reach a clear consensus, and minimize bureaucracy; and (3) stay connected to the receiver to resolve any doubts or questions that may appear during task execution. This will promote correct execution *the first time* and avoid rework waste and delays.

For this transaction to work, both data deliverer and receiver must understand one another's mutual needs and expectations, basing their expectations on professionalism, teamwork, trust, honesty, openness, and respect. In those rare cases of conflict, issues must be resolved by maximizing value to an end customer.

Suggested Implementation

- An instruction from a top manager explaining this enabler and demanding compliance
- General training in a lean culture
- Mentoring and good examples

Intended Use of LEfSE

LEfSE are not intended to become a mandatory tool. Instead, they should be used as a checklist of good holistic practices. Some are intended for top enterprise managers, some for programs, and others for line employees. Some companies are better at, say, requirement development but worse at execution, and vice versa; it is therefore important to select those enablers who resonate the most with the need of a particular enterprise and program. Some enablers are more actionable than others, and some are easier to implement than others. Some enablers may require changes in company policies and culture. However, employee awareness of even those enablers least actionable and most difficult to implement should improve the thinking at work. The creators believe that as many systems (and other) engineers, enterprise managers, and customer representatives as possible should be trained in the LEfSE, as that will lead to better programs.

After release of the enablers, a major effort was begun of offering tutorials and lectures about the LEfSE throughout INCOSE chapters, industry, and academia. At the time of this writing, over 50 lectures and workshops have been offered to about 3000 people in 16 countries on four continents. Lean SE is becoming a household word.

A formal online process of continuous improvement and periodic new releases regarding the LEfSE has been set up as new knowledge and experience becomes, available.

A comprehensive description of the history of LSE, the development process of LEfSE, the full text of enablers, the survey results, and industrial examples may be found in the literature [13].

REFERENCES

1. GAO. Defense Acquisitions: Assessments of Selected Weapon Programs. GAO-07-4065SP. Washington, DC: U.S. Government Accountability Office, Mar. 2008. www.gao.gov/new.items/d08467sp.pdf.
2. GAO. Best Practices: Increased Focus on Requirements and Oversight Needed to Improve DOD's Acquisition Environment and Weapon System Quality. GAO-08-294. Washington, DC: U.S. Government Accountability Office, Feb. 2008. www.gao.gov/new.items/d08294.pdf.
3. GAO. Space Acquisitions: Major Space Programs Still at Risk for Cost and Schedule Increases. GAO-08-552T. Washington, DC: U.S. Government Accountability Office, Mar. 4, 2008. www.gao.gov/new.items/d08552t.pdf.

4. NASA Pilot Benchmarking Initiative: Exploring Design Excellence Leading to Improved Safety and Reliability. Final Report, Oct. 2007.

5. LAI. Phase I. Jan. 1, 2009. http://lean.mit.edu/index.php?/about-lai/history/phase-one.html.

6. McManus, Hugh L. *Product Development Value Stream Mapping Manual.* LAI Release Beta. Cambridge, MA: MIT, Apr. 2004.

7. Slack, Robert A. Application of Lean Principles to the Military Aerospace Product Development Process. Master of Science–Engineering and Management thesis. MIT, Dec. 1998.

8. Oppenheim, Bohdan W. Lean Product Development Flow. *Journal of Systems Engineering*, Vol. 7, No. 4, 2004.

9. Womack, James P., and Daniel T. Jones. *Lean Thinking.* New York: Simon & Schuster, 1996.

10. Morgan, James M., and Jeffrey K. Liker. *The Toyota Product Development System: Integrating People, Process and Technology.* New York: Productivity Press, 2006.

11. Oppenheim, Bohdan W. Leal Enablers for Systems Engineering, CrossTalk. *Journal of Defense Software Engineering*, July–Aug. 2009. www.stsc.hill.af.mil.

12. Oppenheim, Bohdan W., Earll M. Murman, and Deborah Secor. Lean Enablers for Systems Engineering. *Journal of Systems Engineering*, Feb. 2011.

13. Oppenheim, Bohdan W. *Lean for Systems Engineering with Lean Enablers for Systems Engineering.* Hoboken; NJ: Wiley, 2011.

14. Webb, Luke. Knowledge Management for Through Life Support. Doctoral thesis (in progress) via private communication. RMIT University (Australia), 2008.

15. Young, J. Memo to the Secretary of Defense. U.S. Department of Defense, Jan. 30, 2009.

16. [INCOSE LSE WG. Lean Systems Engineering Working Group website, 2011. www.incose.org/practice/techactivities/wg/leansewg/

17. Murman, Earll M. Lean Systems Engineering I, II, Lecture Notes., MIT, Course 16.885J, Fall 2003.

18. Rebentisch, Eric, Donna Rhodes, and Earll Murman. Lean Systems Engineering: Research Initiatives in Support of a New Paradigm. Conference on Systems Engineering Research, University of Southern California, 122, Apr. 2004.

19. Rhodes, Donna, Cihan H. Dagli, Al Haggerty, R. Jain, and Eric Rebentisch. Panel on Lean Systems Engineering. INCOSE 2004, Toulouse, France, June 20–24, 2004.

Appendix III

Introduction to Modeling and Simulation

Heinz Stoewer

President, Space Associates GmbH, Germany*

This appendix provides introductory material on model-based methods for design development. It includes a discussion on model-based engineering (MBE) and model-based systems engineering (MBSE) as summarized in the keynote address by this author at the first NASA Symposium and Workshop on Model-Centric Engineering held at the Jet Propulsion Laboratory in January 2012.

Modern Examples of Complex Systems

- Cruise ships
- CERN particle accelerator
- Automobiles

None of these call their engineering development and integration model-based or systems engineering, but all of them employ extensive modeling and simulation.

* Professor Stoewer is also a Professor Emeritus at the Aerospace Faculty of Delft University of Technology in The Netherlands; former Managing Director of the German Space Agency; and past President of INCOSE.

Product and Systems Development: A Value Approach, First Edition. Stanley I. Weiss.
© 2013 John Wiley & Sons, Inc. Published 2013 by John Wiley & Sons, Inc.

History of Modeling and Simulation

Figure A3-1 summarizes the history of modeling and simulation.

- *Modeling* and *simulation* are often used interchangeably and have application in hardware, software, and hybrid forms.
- We have known modeling and simulation for centuries. Almost all games were developed as simulations, with chess as a prime example

Examples

- Astronomers observe the universe and have modeled relationships of planets, stars, and galaxies and their movements.
- Naval officers modeled and simulated their journeys over the ages to establish repeatable courses, with maps as evidence of such models.
- Architects design artifacts, build physical scale models, and simulate geometry, functions, model behavior, and so on, and today, with computer advances, do simulated walk- or fly-throughs of building and progressive construction.
- Engineers design machinery, build (partial) models, test them and simulate real-life use as well as incorporating hardware and software into simulations in

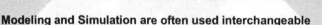

Figure A3-1

the laboratory prior to integrating them for real-world deployment to verify performance, functionality, and other elements.

- Space scientists simulate missions and test them with instruments within simulated environments, looking to validation in the real environment of space.

What Is a Model?

- Models are "representations" of real life.
- Simulations test models to verify performance, functionality, and so on.
- A model can be a small thing, such as an algorithm for a cube, or a big thing, such as models for climate change or the universe.
- In our space world we model hardware components, such as batteries, gyros, or functions of attitude control and guidance, processes, orbit dynamics, and more.
- We create virtual products and attempt to integrate them into higher-level (system) models.
- We successively verify our models against real components and software, or we test them on shakers, vacuum chambers, and so on.

For decades our inventories have contained models and tools, including more recently specific models for Systems Engineering.

MBE and MBSE Have Several Dimensions

1. Bottom-up disciplinary models with limited multidisciplinary capabilities, supported by lots of validated tools in the fields of structures, thermal, AOCS, communication, and so on.
2. Top-down system models, with some integration capabilities, supported by early tool sets in the fields of architecting, requirements management, and others.
3. Life-cycle time and process models for development, testing, manufacturing, and so on.

These add up to a large inventory with lots of ever-growing (partial) capabilities but nonetheless many areas not well covered. *Note*: The current INCOSE tools database lists some 1600 commercial and government off-the-shelf (COTS and GOTS) tools of interest to SE, including, for example, 34 requirements tools.

MBE: A Continuing Revolution in Industry

- MBE has taken decades to develop to the point that it has become common-place; it continues to revolutionize most branches of industry, including space.

- MBE has enormously increased efficiency, product quality, and lowered cost and development and production time.
- MBE has enabled collaborative engineering across continents and fueled the global economy.
- Multidisciplinary cross correlation is progressing and advances toward higher levels of (engineering) integration.

Aspects of Models Across Life-Cycle Milestones

Project milestones progressively increase the scope and maturity of engineering models utilized (see Figure A3-2).

MBSE Status

A summary of MBSE today is shown in Figure A3-3; the comments below recognize future activity.

- There has been much MBSE progress in the past few years! Nonetheless, the discipline is still in its infancy.
- Similar to MBE (CAD), MBSE represents a "cultural" change and will take time to mature (it took less than the 30 years for CAD).

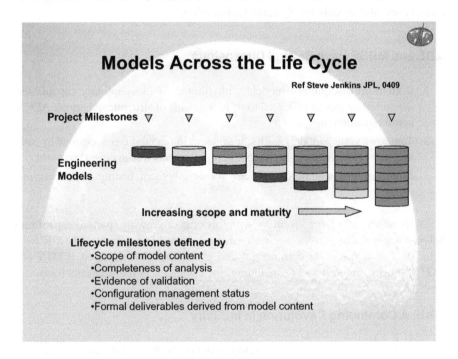

Figure A3-2

MBSE today

- A first set of non interfacing non encompassing tools and some databases

- Mostly driven by software and tools specialist, e.g. SysML, Doors, et al

- Focus upon requirements management, architecture studies, et al, incl. initial interactions with MBE and lot's of visualizations

- Many applications and pilot studies indicate huge prospects

→ Mainstream Project Implementation SE not (yet) onboard - too complicated/tools driven, non proven, not end-to-end; SEs in general are not up to date on developments

MBE & MBSE in Context, NASA Symposium on Model-Centric Engineering, Prof. Dipl.-Ing. Heinz Stoewer, M.Sc., JPL 02 2012

Figure A3-3

- Continue the path of step-by-step advancement along with demonstrations of practical examples to the broader SE and engineering communities.
- PM databases and methods and SE equivalents should grow together and be closely linked.
- Attention to "soft disciplines" and decision making is imperative.
- Attractive visualizations are considered indispensable in today's multimedia world; for example, SysML presentations are "bland," so the MBSE community should embrace up-to-date visualization means available from the game, movie, and other industries.

Appendix IV

Introduction to Multidisciplinary Analysis and Optimization

Juan J. Alonso

Stanford University

A structured *systems engineering* process can enable the development of complex products that "add value" to a carefully-chosen set of stakeholders. In traditional systems-engineering processes, however, a number of key choices are typically supported by subjective measures of value, performance, risk, and cost that are often based on the opinions of the various stakeholders involved. Because of significant increases in computational power and the ability to develop physics-based models of the various components of a system, we have the opportunity to embed quantitative system-level analyses in our decision-making processes. The inclusion of such ideas would only serve to enhance the effectiveness of the well-established systems engineering process described in this book.

So you have determined your stakeholders, values, requirements, and conflicts. You might even have created a number of concepts that potentially satisfy the driving performance requirements. Now what? The process of concept development, evaluation, and trade-off is indeed where the "rubber meets the road." Should you base your decisions regarding the suitability of different concepts on opinion? Would you instead rely on a group of ad-hoc analyses that are not necessarily well coordinated or well integrated? Or would you prefer to depend on

Product and Systems Development: A Value Approach, First Edition. Stanley I. Weiss.
© 2013 John Wiley & Sons, Inc. Published 2013 by John Wiley & Sons, Inc.

a well-structured analysis and optimization capability that can guide your design efforts to a successful product?

The field of MDAO (multidisciplinary analysis and optimization) has been developed to provide an analysis-based, synergistic capability to assess and improve various characteristics of a system that can include many different disciplines and modules. In some circles, it is also referred to as multidisciplinary system design optimization (MSDO), and sometimes even simply as multidisciplinary optimization (MDO). Although, based on the name, the emphasis appears to be placed on the optimization/design aspects of the problem, the field also attempts to tackle the ability to analyze (for performance, cost, risk, reliability, etc.) complex multidisciplinary interactions that are usually present in the design of complex system. MDAO provides a rich toolbox for multidisciplinary systems that can be embedded into the systems-engineering process.

What can these modern computational capabilities and formal mathematical techniques help you with? Among others, MDAO techniques can aid in:

- Creating new concepts
- Determining which is the "best" concept (with a specific definition of "best")
- Dealing, quantitatively, with realistic problems during concept selection
- Resolving multiple conflicting objectives
- Accounting for uncertainties and risk
- Ensuring a clear understanding of the impact of requirements on the overall characteristics of a concept.

An analogy can be drawn with the notion of "design thinking" proposed by some leading members of the product design community. In this context, "design thinking" involves the *process* for structuring creativity that results in added value to a customer, where various *methods* (brainstorming, understanding customer requirements, etc.) are employed to ensure success. In a similar fashion, systems engineering is the *process* that can be followed to generate complex systems/products, while MDAO is the toolbox of *methods* that can be used to ensure that the outcome of systems engineering processes can be traced back to the original values and objectives of the major stakeholders.

If we attempted to define the concept of MDAO, it would be possible to say that MDAO is an area of engineering and physics that proposes the use of integrated analysis and design methods, based on analytical and numerical predictions of the behavior of the system, to assess the performance, cost, and risk of a potential concept instantiation of a given system. It must be recognized that there is a key difference that is sometimes lost in discussions that involve systems engineering and MDAO. It is one thing to create a concept from scratch (with its major defining parameters, topology, and architecture) and another to optimize a system starting from a feasible baseline. MDAO techniques are reasonably good at the latter, but notoriously bad (or at least the research is ongoing at present and the techniques are not fully mature) at the former.

However, the capability of analyzing and optimizing afforded by MDAO techniques can lead to the following benefits in the systems engineering process:

- Help sort out the promise of several different candidate concepts,
- Provide feedback to the value/requirement selection process regarding feasibility and needed compromises so that requirements can be revised until the design loop "closes,"
- Add quantitative information to a mostly-qualitative methodology that is often opinion-based.

Research in MDAO methods has been cognizant of the fact that, in order to be successful, it must conform to the organizational structures already present in industry. Although a disruptive methodology that requires re-organization of the various elements inside a design group might lead to more efficient system design processes, historically such approaches have failed. Instead, modern MDAO architectures attempt to decompose the analysis and design problem in a way that (a) maps easily onto existing organizational structures in industry, and (b) adds value to the existing processes by guaranteeing better quality answers, by ensuring that optimal designs can be achieved, and by forcing thinking about the information transfers across portions of the organization so that many of the tedious-but-essential processes can be automated appropriately. In such approaches (including collaborative optimization, bi-level integrated system synthesis, analytical target cascading, etc.) a large-scale design problem is decomposed in a way that lends itself to reasonably-straightforward mapping to an existing organization.

ANALYSIS AND OPTIMIZATION AS A NONLINEAR PROGRAM

The early development of MDAO techniques drew heavily from the theory of optimization and the nonlinear program (NLP):

Minimize $f(\mathbf{x})$ such that
$\mathbf{x}$ in R^N $\mathbf{x}_l < \mathbf{x} < \mathbf{x}_u$
                 $g_i(\mathbf{x}) <= 0, i = 1, \ldots, M,$

where boldface denotes a vector quantity. In other words, we seek to find the values of the many design parameters in the vector $\mathbf{x}$, which define our system, so that we maximize a cost function of interest $f(\mathbf{x})$ that defines the "goodness" of our system, while satisfying bound constraints in the components of $\mathbf{x}$, and satisfying a possibly large number M of nonlinear constraints $g_i(\mathbf{x})$ that represent elements of the design that must be satisfied.

This legacy of influence from the optimization community left its mark in early MDAO tools. Soon, however, it was recognized that the NLP was not able to capture all of the problems that engineers wanted to treat: sometimes designs were sought that traded the values of different objective functions (multi-objective optimization) and, at other times, it was necessary to deal with problems that require both real and integer values of the design parameter vector **x**. Furthermore, the methodologies that can be used to efficiently solve the NLP, namely gradient-based optimization algorithms, could run into trouble when the analyses were noisy, when gradients were not readily available, or when the design spaces were discontinuous. Regardless of the difficulties of the system design problem at hand, over the years a number of different MDAO optimization techniques have emerged that are the cornerstone of the field and are worth describing in a concise fashion. All of these techniques represent approaches to improve the performance (measured in any way desired by the user) of a system from a baseline definition or concept. The process uses an iterative evolution of the design represented by changes in the design variable vector, **x**.

1. **Intuition** is often used by seasoned designers in all industries who, using knowledge of the performance of a particular system, can guess at what changes in **x** might be needed in order to improve performance while satisfying all constraints. Unfortunately, the value of intuition decreases rapidly as the dimensionality of the design space increases. In addition, intuition can only be used with a human in the loop and in situations where a large experience database already exists that enables the evolution of the design to one that is near optimum.

2. **Grid and random searches** are a brute-force technique where each of the elements of the design variable vector, **x**, are discretized into a number of intervals and all of the design possibilities implied by this discretization are evaluated at great computational cost. Given the resulting analyses, one can easily choose the best among all the options considered. The cost of this procedure increases rapidly (actually, exponentially) with the number of variables being considered, and is impracticable for anything but the smallest (two- or three-dimensional) design problems.

3. **Gradient-based methods** utilize not just the analyses of the system, but also the gradients of the cost and constraint functions to greatly speed up the convergence of the optimization process and to enable very large numbers of design parameters and constraints. Of course, gradients need to be provided to these algorithms and these can be very costly to compute (or even impossible). Other pitfalls include the fact that some disciplinary analyses can be noisy and/ or discontinuous, and the fact that the only guarantee is that of convergence to the nearest local minimum (and the more interesting global minimum may be missed). Regardless, this class of algorithms has proven to be, without a doubt, the most widely-used optimization algorithm in MDAO and the most efficient at solving realistic problems.

4. **Non-gradient-based methods** such as genetic algorithms, SIMPLEX methods, etc., have added the possibility of dealing with multiple objective/cost functions, noisy and/or discontinuous design spaces, and mixtures of discrete and continuous design variables, but they do so at great computational cost that effectively limits the magnitude of the design problem that can be treated. Advances in

parallel computing and analysis concurrency have enabled us to increase the size of the problems treated, but extreme computational cost is still present.

5. **Response surface formulations and adaptivity** have been pursued as an alternative. In these methods, a response surface (a fit or approximation of the cost and constraint functions as functions of **x** is constructed. This typically requires the evaluation of the design at multiple values of the deisgn vector **x**, sprinkled around the design space (typically using some kind of sampling technique such as Latin Hypercube Sampling). The response surface is then constructed using the information from these analyses. Many response surface types have been pursued, from those that are purely polynomial, to others based on neural nets and Gaussian Process Regression. In some cases, only function value information is used, while in others gradients can be included. Such response surfaces can be global in nature and, through adaptive procedures whereby additional analyses are conducted in areas of the design space that have been observed to have interesting characteristics.

HISTORY OF MDAO

The roots of MDAO can be traced back to early efforts in structural optimization (finite-element based), where the initial objective was to reduce the weight of a structure by thinning the major structural components while ensuring that a number of pre-specified load cases did not lead to structural failure. These early efforts influenced the evolution of the field.

The first set of MDAO tools were often single-discipline focused, were relatively simple in terms of the problems tackled, combined simulation/analyses directly with optimization tools, and almost exclusively devoted all efforts to improving the efficiency of the optimization techniques that drove the MDAO process. This first generation of MDAO tools existed towards the late 1980s and early 1990s and resulted in significant accomplishments in structural design, aerodynamic shape optimization, and other airflow-related problems mainly in the automotive industry, where the technology was also beginning to take hold.

As initial MDAO tools (of the first generation) began to show promise, the need to add more disciplines to the representation of the system became clear. However, as additional disciplines were included, the number of interdisciplinary interactions to be modeled and accounted for began to grow significantly. If all disciplines in a system interact or exchange information with all others, this presented an N^2 problem (where N is the number of individual disciplines being modeled and N^2 is the number of interactions). In addition, the way in which the disciplines interacted with each other, often included iterative loops (as is the case in aero-structural optimization of an aircraft) that needed to be converged before other elements/disciplines in the system were analyzed. For these reasons, the complexity of MDAO calculations began to grow significantly and the *second generation of MDAO* (pursued during the 1990s and the early 2000s) began to focus on the management of the execution of complex, inter-linked models, the resolution of implied (whether necessary or not) iterative loops, the possibility of distributing the analyses over a number of separate computers so as to speed up the overall process, and various alternatives to manage the interdisciplinary communication process.

Over the past 5–10 years (since the mid 2000s) the focus has been on taking MDAO tools one step beyond into what we could call the *third generation of MDAO* tools. These, more recent, efforts have focused on decomposing not just the analysis problem but also the optimization itself so that each of the disciplines can have the autonomy to make decisions regarding the design variables in the problem that are specific to that discipline. This decomposition approach also has the advantage that it can be tailored to existing industrial organizations and infrastructures so that MDAO does not impose wholesale change when adopted. Moreover, key elements that have been introduced during this current generation of MDAO tools are:

- The ability to represent each of the participating disciplines with different analysis modules that lead to different accuracy at different computational cost. These multi-fidelity approaches are becoming a major topic of research.
- The inclusion of uncertainties (both of an aleatoric and epistemic nature) so that concepts of robust design and reliability-based design can be included in the MDAO techniques.
- Better problem decomposition approaches with distributed design (not simply analysis).

As the capabilities of these various generations of MDAO continue to improve, further adoption of MDAO techniques within industrial design processes is taking place. Today, the use of first-generation MDAO techniques in industry is common-place. Second-generation tools are making their way into specific areas of the aerospace industry and will continue to penetrate other areas as the techniques mature. Third-generation MDAO tools are still very much being investigated in academic settings and will require further refinement before they can be used routinely in large-scale projects in an industrial setting.

REFERENCES

Haftka, R. T., Optimization of flexible wing structures subject to strength and induced drag constraints, *AIAA Journal*, **14**(8):1106–1977, 1977.

Joaquim R. R. A. Martins, Juan J. Alonso, and James J. Reuther. High-fidelity aerostructural design optimization of a supersonic business jet. *Journal of Aircraft*, **41**(3):523–530, 2004. doi: 10.2514/1.11478.

P. E. Gill, W. Murray, and M. H. Wright, *Practical Optimization*, Academic Press, 1982.

J. Nocedal, S. J. Wright, *Numerical Optimization*, Springer Verlag, 2006.

J. E. Dennis and Virginia J. Torczon. Derivative-free pattern search methods for multi-disciplinary design problems. AIAA Paper 94–4349, 1994.

Ian P Sobieski and Ilan M Kroo. Collaborative optimization using response surface estimation. *AIAA Journal*, **38**(10):1931–1938, 2000. doi: 10.2514/2.847.

Bibliography

Angus, R., Gundersen, N. and Cullinane, T., *Planning, Performing, and Controlling Projects*, 3rd ed., Prentice Hall, Upper Saddle River, NJ, 2002.

Bakerjian, R., *Tool and Manufacturing Engineers Handbook*, 4th ed., Society of Manufacturing Engineers, Dearborn, Ml, 1992.

Bedford, T., *Probabilistic Risk Analysis: Foundations and Methods*, Cambridge University Press, New York, 2001.

Blanchard, B., and Fabrycky, W., *Systems Engineering and Analysis*, 5th ed., Prentice Hall, Upper Saddle River, NJ, 2010.

Blache, K., Editor, *Success Factors for Implementing Change*, Society of Manufacturing Engineers, Dearborn, MI, 1988.

Boehm, B. W., *Software Risk Management*, IEEE Computer Society Press, Los Alamitos, CA, 1989.

Boeing Proprietary, *Vehicle Synthesis Environment, Review of IPT Development*, MIT Lean Aerospace Initiative, 1996.

Clark, K., and Fujimoto, T., *Development Performance*, Harvard University Press, Cambridge, MA, 1990.

Clausing, D., *Total Quality Development: A Step-by-Step Guide to World Class Concurrent Engineering*, ASME Press, New York, 1998.

Considine, D., Editor in Chief, *Energy Technology Handbook*, McGraw-Hill, New York, 1977.

Cook, H., and Wissman, L., *Value Driven Product Planning and Systems Engineering*, Springer-Verlag, New York, 2007.

Product and Systems Development: A Value Approach, First Edition. Stanley I. Weiss.
© 2013 John Wiley & Sons, Inc. Published 2013 by John Wiley & Sons, Inc.

Cowing, M., Pate-Cornell, M., and Glynn, P., *Reliability Engineering and System Safety*, e version, Elsevier, 2004.

Craig, R. J., *No Nonsense Guide to Achieving ISO 9000 Registration*, ASME Press, New York, 1994.

Dawson, V., *Engines and Innovation*, NASA Scientific and Technical Information Division, Hanover, MD, 1991.

DeNeufville, R., and Stafford, J., *Systems Analysis for Engineers and Managers*, McGraw-Hill, New York, 1971.

Duncan, W., *Just-in-Time (JIT) in American Manufacturing*, Society of Manufacturing Engineers, Dearborn, MI, 1988.

Dwivedi, S., Paul, A., and Dax, F., Editors, *Concurrent Engineering Approach to Materials Processing*, The Minerals, Metals and Materials Society, Warrendale, PA, 1992.

Egpert, R., *Product Design and Development*, 2nd ed., High Peak Press, Meridian, ID, 2010.

Eppinger, S., and Browning, T., *Design Structure Matrix Methods and Applications*, MIT Press, Cambridge, MA, 2012.

Ertas, A., and Jones, J., *The Engineering Design Process*, Wiley, New York, 1996.

Fabrycky, W. J., and Blanchard, B. S., *Life-Cycle Cost and Economic Analysis*, Prentice Hall, Englewood Cliffs, NJ, 1991.

Fairbairn, A., *Systems Engineering Sharing the Future*, INCOSE UK, Ilminster, UK, 1999.

Forsberg, K., Mooz, H., and Cotterman, H., *Visualizing Project Management*, Wiley, Hoboken, NJ, 2005.

Gershwin, S. B., *Manufacturing Systems Engineering*, Prentice Hall, Upper Saddle River, NJ, 1994.

Goldman, S. L., Nagel, R. N., and Press, K., *Agile Competitors and Virtual Organizations*, Van Nostrand Reinhold, New York, 1995.

Haskins, C., Editor, *Systems Engineering Handbook, INCOSE TP-2003-002-03*, International Council on Systems Engineering, San Diego, CA, 2006.

Held, G., *Understanding Data Communications*, Wiley, New York, 1997.

Horenstein, M., *Design Concepts for Engineers*, 2nd ed., Prentice Hall, Upper Saddle River, NJ, 2002.

Howard, R., and Albas, A., *Foundations of Decision Analysis*, Prentice Hall, Upper Saddle River, NJ, 2009.

Jimmerson, C., *Value Stream Mapping for Healthcare Made Easy*, Productivity Press, Taylor & Francis, Boca Raton, FL, 2010.

Jones, J., *The Engineering Design Process*, Wiley, Hoboken, NJ, 1996.

Kendrick, T., *Identifying and Managing Project Risk*, AMACOM Books, New York, 2009.

Khisty, C., and Mohammadi, S., *Fundamentals of Systems Engineering*, Prentice Hall, Upper Saddle River, NJ, 2001.

Kockler, F., Withers, T., Poodiack, J., and German, M., *Systems Engineering Management Guide*, Defense Systems Management College, Fort Belvoir, VA, 1990.

Lattanze, A., *Architecting Software Intensive Systems*, CRC Press, Boca Raton, FL, 2009.

Lean Enterprise Institute, *Lean Lexicon*, 4th ed., LEI, Cambridge, MA, 2008.

Leveson, N., *Safeware: System Safety and Computers*, Addison-Wesley, Reading, MA, 1995.

Lody, C., Little, P., and Dawson, V., *Engineering Design*, NASA SP-4306, 1991, Wiley, Hoboken, NJ, 2000.

McManus, H., *Product Development Value Stream Mapping*, Lean Advancement Initiative, Cambridge, MA, 2005.

Moody, P., *Strategic Manufacturing: Dynamic New Directions*, Dow Jones-Irwin, Homewood, IL, 1990.

Murman, E., et al., *Lean Enterprise Value*, Palgrave Press, Hampshire, UK, 2002.

Oppenheim, B., *Lean Enablers for Systems Engineering*, Wiley, Hoboken, NJ, 2011.

Otto, K., and Wood, K., *Product Design: Techniques in Reverse Engineering and New Product Development*, Prentice Hall, Upper Saddle River, NJ, 2001.

Ramo, S., and St. Clair, R., *The Systems Approach*, KNI, Inc., Anaheim, CA, 1998.

Ranfti, R., *R & D Productivity*, Hughes Aircraft Company, Culver City, CA, 1978.

Rechtin, E., and Maier, M., *The Art of Systems Architecting*, 2nd ed., CRC Press, Boca Raton, FL, 2000.

Reinertsen, D., *Principles of Product Development Flow*, Celeritas Publishing, Redondo Beach, CA, 2009.

Roberts, G., *Quality Assurance in Research and Development*, Industrial Engineering Series, Marcel Dekker, New York, 1983.

Rosenkrantz, W., *Introduction to Probability and Statistics*, McGraw-Hill, New York, 1997.

Row, W. D., *An Anatomy of Risk*, Wiley, New York, 1977.

Sage, A. P., *Systems Engineering*, Wiley, New York, 1992.

Sage, A., and Rouse W., Editors, *Handbook of Systems Engineering and Management*, Wiley-Interscience, New York, 1999.

Shook, J., and Rother, M., *Learning to See: Value Stream Mapping to Add Value*, Lean Enterprise Institute, Cambridge, MA, 1999.

Smith, J., *Mathematical Modeling and Simulation for Engineers and Scientists*, Wiley, New York, 1987.

Stamatis, D., *Failure Mode and Effect Analysis: FMEA from Theory to Execution*, 2nd ed., ASQ Quality Press, Milwaukee, WI, 2003.

Steward, D. V., *Systems Analysis and Management*, Petrocelli Books, Princeton, NJ, 1981.

Stewart, M., and Melchers, R., *Probabilistic Risk Assessment of Engineering Systems*, Chapman & Hall, London, 1997.

Thurman, A., and Mehta, D., *Handbook of Energy Engineering*, CRC Press, Boca Raton, FL, 2008.

Tulkoff, J., Editor, *CAPP: From Design to Production*, Society of Manufacturing Engineers, Dearborn, MI, 1988.

Ullman, D., *The Mechanical Design Process*, 2nd ed., McGraw-Hill, New York, 1997.

Ulrich, K., and Eppinger, S., *Product Design and Development*, 5th ed., High Peak Press, Meridian, ID, 2010.

U.S. Congress, Office of Technology Assessment, *Advanced Materials by Design, OTA-E351*, Superintendent of Documents, Washington, DC, 1988.

Ward, A., *Lean Product and Process Development*, Lean Enterprise Institute, Cambridge, MA, 2007.

Wellman, J., Hogan, P., and Jeffries, H., *Leading the Lean Healthcare Journey*, Productivity Press, Taylor & Francis Group, Boca Raton, FL, 2012.

Wertz, J., and Larson, W., Editors, *Space Mission Analysis and Design*, 3rd ed., Microcosm Press, Kluwer Academic, Norwell, MA, 1999.

Westinghouse Defense and Space Center, *Integrated Electronics Systems*, Prentice-Hall, Englewood Cliffs, NJ, 1970.

Womack, J., and Jones, D., *Lean Thinking*, 2nd ed., Simon and Schuster, New York, 2003.

Womack, J., Jones, T., and Roos, D., *The Machine That Changed the World*, Rawson Associated, Macmillan, New York, 1990.

Index

Product and Systems Development: A Value Approach, First Edition. Stanley I. Weiss.
© 2013 John Wiley & Sons, Inc. Published 2013 by John Wiley & Sons, Inc.

Printed and bound by CPI Group (UK) Ltd, Croydon, CR0 4YY

23/04/2025

14660907-0003